CLARK MCGINN was born in Ayr and sta... hardly stopped since. Educated at Ayr A... he passed enough exams in-between sp... banker. After nearly 30 years in banking in London and New York he recently got a real job in industry. He is happily married to Ann and currently lives in exile between Harrow-on-the-Hill and Dublin. Since 1976 Clark has written and spoken on Scottish subjects internationally and is well known for performing at Burns Suppers every year, sharing his passion for the world's favourite poet and all things Scottish. He has delivered Immortal Memories around the world: in the last seven years travelling 166,000 miles (that's nearly seven times round the globe) with 100 speeches in 26 different cities in 12 countries.

His first book – *The Ultimate Burns Supper Book* – was published by Luath in 2006 and he contributed the afterword to *The Luath Kilmarnock Edition* in 2009. His latest book is *Out of Pocket: How Collective Amnesia Lost The World Its Wealth Again.*

# The Ultimate Guide to Being Scottish

CLARK McGINN

**Luath** Press Limited

EDINBURGH

www.luath.co.uk

*To Ann*

First published 2008
Revised edition 2013

ISBN: 978 1 908373 06 9

The paper used in this book is recyclable. It is made
from low chlorine pulps produced in a low energy,
low emissions manner from renewable forests.

Printed and bound by
Bell & Bain Ltd., Glasgow

Illustrations © A. Martin Pittock

Typeset in 10.5pt Sabon by 3btype.com

# Contents

Of all the small nations of the world,
only the ancient Greeks surpass the Scots
in their contribution to mankind.

There is only one thing wrong with Scotsmen.
There are too few of them.

*W.S. Churchill*

# *Thoughts on a Second Edition*

Scotland is a kaleidoscope: with many bright coloured parts, sometimes jagged, which change in evolving tartan patterns but which always throws up images that chime with those who live there, love there or leave there.

Sharing that fun is the purpose of this wee book and so this second edition is dedicated to everyone who love a piece of Scotland, particularly two gentlemen and friends of mine: Leonard Wallace whose enthusiasm for singing the Whisky Song (see p.193) brings a smile, and my newest reader, his grandson Findlay Howie, who has all the delights herein ahead of him.

*Clark McGinn*
Dublin November 2012

# Acknowledgements

I HADN'T EXPECTED to be writing another dedication, and so it's tempting to say that the acknowledgements from the first book are incorporated herein by reference.

But if you'll forgive me, I'd like to say thanks again, even if it's repeating myself. (Not for the first time, I hear from the back of the room.)

Thank you Ann, my Abu Ben Adhem, first and foremost in my life, my speaking and my writing. How many times have you heard these stories and yet never steal the punch line. A true partner – to you this book is dedicated, as am I.

And thanks to the payroll – all three daughters who inspire, annoy, and reflect my pride in them. To you Claire, Eleanor and Emma, whatever profits arise from this volume I may as well dedicate to you as you'll charm them out of my pocket anyway.

I had a fortunate early life, with Mum and Dad encouraging me not just to read, but to eat books and talk about them (sometimes too often and too much), particularly about our history, culture and tradition, and it was then that the peculiar (in both senses) culture of Scotland and the rich literature we give to the world captured my imagination. Growing up and exploring Scotland through Ayr Academy and via the Bursary Exams into Glasgow University, where the GU Union took me around our small country, book in one hand, glass in the other (and always speech notes in pockets), fostered a lively interest in all the different parts of our culture. Ferment this in the 30 years of friendships made in freshers' week and that distilled the spirit behind this book. Certainly many of the ideas came out of late night conversations with Douglas and Marion at Carson Towers, or from debating the Union with Murray.

Thanks to my friends and colleagues who have taken me to see many mad and merry aspects of life in Scotland, and to Charles (who taught me that Scotland looks best from the back of a taxi) for his insight in the foreword and Anne for capturing the book in its drawings. Thanks too to Gavin and the Luath team, perched atop the Royal Mile on a castle rock of manuscripts.

To the many guests and colleagues who have asked me over the years – just what is going on here? What is the essence of Scotland and the Scots? Well, to all of you, my thanks, and I hope I answer some of the questions.

*Clark McGinn*

# Foreword

'OH, THAT MINE ENEMY would write a book!' exclaimed Jo Grimmond of Harold Wilson's 1964–70 government memoirs. Well, I'm no Grimmond and Clark would not thank me for likening him in any way to Wilson – but with this offering my friend has produced another book and taken a sweep of quite enormous cultural and historical dimensions.

McGinn on Surviving Scottishness? (Surely a potential working title for the follow-up? Publisher please take note – our author is a senior banker and therefore needs every penny these days). In some respects it's a bit like letting King Herod loose in the maternity ward. Knowing the author and the subject-matter this is a guaranteed must read and an invaluable guide to keep on the shelf or by the bedside.

In asking me to pen a few words by way of introduction (strictly no sales, no fee basis) Clark encapsulates an essence of Scottishness which he neatly captures early on – that happy coexistence of contrasts and contradictions which keep us going, make us tick and which enable a global identity sales process which is at once remarkable and unique. Kennedy: Highlander, Roman Catholic, liberalish; McGinn: Lowlander, Presbyterian, conservative. Yet both Scots and seemingly comfortable in our skins. Each of us ply a trade in London and in years gone by have dipped our respective toes in time spent living in the United States. Neither of us, I think, get exercised about this sense of multiple or layered identity: Highland/Lowland, Scottish, British, European (well, to be fair, even the legendary McGinn sense of humour seems to evaporate when he contemplates my preference for a richly federal future within an ever closer European Union).

Am I allowed a personal plug? I tried to sum it up with the title of a documentary I made for BBC television on the 300th anniversary of the Act of Union. I called it 'A Chip On Each Shoulder.'

Years ago, in those depressing pre-devolution, Thatcherite days at Westminster I shared a Q&A session with Labour's George Robertson in front of an audience of visiting West Germans. They were puzzled indeed by our obvious sense of shared nationhood, yet coupled to the absence of an elected national legislature within and for Scotland. How so? George explained patiently the complications involved, remarking that the Scots were historically adept at running anywhere in the rest of the world – it was just that we were never so sure about running our own backyard. (He was later to prove the point by opting for the much cushier option of carrying responsibility for NATO's nuclear warheads in preference to administering Scotland).

The late, great Donald Dewar made a similar point when Malcolm Rifkind was recalled from the Foreign Office to become our Secretary of State. He would soon realise, Donald observed, how much easier political life was when you only had the rest of the world to worry about.

MacKenzie King, the Scots-born and phenomenally long-serving Canadian Prime Minister, remarked once in a moment of political frustration that the trouble with Canada was that it had too much geography and not enough history. Our own dear little land somehow seems to have more than its fair share of both.

In this utterly engaging book Clark manages somehow to convey just that conundrum – and a lot more wealth of fascinating detail along the way.

My friend must write yet another book...

*The Rt Hon. Charles Kennedy* MP

# Introduction:
# What Does it Mean to Be Scottish?

Away, ye gay landscapes, ye gardens of roses,
In you let the minions of luxury rove,
Restore me the rocks where the snow-flake reposes,
Though still they are sacred to freedom and love.
Yet Caledonia, belov'd are thy mountains,
Round their white summits tho' elements war,
Though cataracts foam 'stead of smooth-flowing fountains,
I sigh for the valley of dark Lochnagar.

Ah! there my young footsteps in infancy wander'd,
My cap was the bonnet, my cloak was the plaid.
On chieftains long perish'd my memory ponder'd
As daily I strode thro' the pine-cover'd glade.
I sought not my home till the day's dying glory
Gave place to the rays of the bright Polar star,
For fancy was cheer'd by traditional story,
Disclos'd by the natives of dark Lochnagar!

Years have roll'd on, Lochnagar, since I left you!
Years must elapse ere I tread you again.
Though nature of verdure and flow'rs has bereft you,
Yet still are you dearer than Albion's plain.
England, thy beauties are tame and domestic
To one who has roamed over mountains afar
Oh! for the crags that are wild and majestic,
The steep frowning glories of dark Lochnagar.[1]

THERE IS SOMETHING UNIQUE about being Scottish.
I've travelled around the world to meet Scots expats, descendants,

---

[1] *'Lochnagar', George Gordon, Lord Byron.*

employees, golfers, drunks,[2] usually in the guise of a Burns performer – celebrating that man, the greatest of the great gifts we have given the world – in the popular format of a Burns Supper. Sometimes in the corners of the US or Canada or parts of that former empire built on Scots capital, engineering and military bravery, the format of the evening is a St Andrew's Dinner – although those who wake up from the alcohol in the middle of this format probably assume it is a Burns Supper out of season. However you get involved, you can see in every member of the audience pride in having however tiny a percentage of tartan in the blood.

At other times you catch the glint of recognition in eyes across the world, or of smiles at remembered shared history. What is going on here? What is the essence of being Scottish and why does our culture and its celebration resonate across the world?

One of the oddest parts of coming from Scotland is the scale of our country. If you are in California (whose population is a six-fold multiple of Scotland's) or in Australia (a land mass that would fit in 96 Scottish mainlands with a bit to spare) it seems amazing that the Scots are recognised and applauded – how can this wee, old country stand out so?

What is it that makes a 'true Scot'? Is it just a question of adopting some peculiar habits?

- Stop wearing underwear.
- Grow significant amounts of hair on your knees.
- Drink more[3] than average.
- Exchange your food processor for a deep fat fryer.
- Find some bawbees and look after them well.
- Enjoy playing golf in the rain.
- Stop tipping.

Or is the qualification of being Scottish something inherent? And if so, what tests do we have to pass or what defining characteristics must be present to be defined as *Homo Caledonius*?

---

[2]   *Sorry, that should be 'malt whisky aficionados'.*

[3]   *Much more, actually.*

Is it a matter of BIRTH? And if so, is that defined as being born in Scotland, or of one or two Scottish parents, or will one Scottish granny carry you over the genetic scoreline? In some ways, RESIDENCY remains important – though we have a fierce and proud expatriate community; while AFFILIATION – by dint of marriage, education, taste in whisky or employment adds emphasis it doesn't intuitively grant full-blooded status.

In many ways, for me being Scottish is part genealogical but a great deal attitudinal. This book looks at Scottish attitudes through the prism of our history, culture and traditions, and above all our festivals and celebrations, to see how we, the Scots (in the broadest sense), act and interact with the wider world.

The most popular intersection of Scots, Scottophiles and non-Scot friends is, of course, the Burns Supper. On these convivial evenings everyone shares in our tradition, culture, cuisine and drink. But there are many other ways to throw a traditional party, and in this voyage together I hope we'll share a toast at some well-remembered but not-so-visited feasts, for it's the *joie de vivre* that can be seen in the people of Scotland and her festivals that is the true, nay the ULTIMATE guide to being Scottish!

## Scotland the What?

> Land of brown heath and shaggy wood,
> Land of the mountain and the flood,
> Land of my sires! What mortal hand
> Can e'er untie the filial band
> That knits me to thy rugged strand.[4]

---

[4]    'The Lay of the Last Minstrel', Sir Walter Scott.

The successful marketing of Scotland, built on the foundation of Burns's works by the energies of Sir Walter Scott and patronised[5] by Queen Victoria, encourages outsiders and visitors to see a unitary Scotland of kilted Highland warriors. But this is far too simplistic.

Scotland small? Our multiform, our infinite Scotland *small*?[6]

Sometimes our pride makes us define ourselves by what we are not: the English.

In the longest running[7] football match in history, these two kingdoms on one island have enjoyed[8] an on–off relationship that seems more soap opera than history. The Romans sensed this shortly after the birth of Christ. Having consumed the oysters of Colchester, subdued Boadicea[9] and built roads to York, the mighty legionaries of the imperial superpower came to the Scottish border. You can imagine these grim soldiers from the warmth of Italy peering into the typical drizzle of an August afternoon: debating whether the bare-bummed savages were scarier than the flying, biting midges.

At this point in history, we had neither whisky nor golf to offer tourists and so the Romans called it a day and built Hadrian's Wall – whether to mark the boundaries of Rome, or to create the world's first safari park, I'll leave you to judge. Traditionalists would assert that, with proto-*Braveheart*[10] ferocity, the eagles of Rome feared the foe in front and thus drew the line of boundary. I can't help but thinking that, after the sun-kissed shores of the Mediterranean and the gentle scent of tree-ripened citrus, the prospect of sitting in garrison under Scotland's

---

[5]    *In one, maybe two definitions of the word.*

[6]    *'Scotland Small?', Hugh MacDiarmid; a great Scottish poet of the 20th century, though his combination of communism/nationalism/pessimism alongside an ill-tempered attack on Burns Suppers has always left me wary.*

[7]    *And worst tempered.*

[8]    *If that's the word!*

[9]    *Or Boudicca, or more truly the ultimate cross mother. Could have been Scottish really…*

[10]   *At the risk of annoying the fans, it is an appalling historical train wreck.*

grey mist and rain was just too unappealing for the legions. And so, as the ancient history says, the emperor solved the problem:

> Ergo conversis regio more militibus Britanniam petiit, in qua multa correxit murumque per octoginta milia passuum primus duxit, qui barbaros Romanosque divideret.[11]

That architectural barrier defined, and still defines, our identity.

When I graduated in the dark, depressed days of 1983 there were few jobs in Scotland but I obtained a post in one of the English banks in London. A banker and in England; my Mum was so mortified she told everyone that I'd been committed to jail. Since the latest banking crisis she's promoted me to be the lead piano player in a strip club.

The rivalry has spawned many music hall jokes (and not a few political policies, now that you mention it):

|  | Scots view of | English view of |
| --- | --- | --- |
| The Scots | Prudent and thrifty<br>Generous hosts<br>Patriotic<br>Brave sportsmen<br>Rich literary heritage | Tight-fisted<br>Drunks<br>Bleating<br>Losers<br>Incomprehensible[12] |
| The English | Cold and aloof<br>Class conscious[13]<br>Rich football clubs<br>Morris dancing<br>Cold fish | Independent<br>Upwardly mobile<br>World-class sportsmen<br>Unique heritage<br>Stiff upper lips |

[11]   *'And so, having reformed the army quite in the manner of a monarch, he set out for Britain, and there he corrected many abuses and was the first to construct a wall, 80 miles in length, which was to separate the barbarians from the Romans'*, Historia Augusta, *Hadrianus, pars I, XI, 2 (Leob Classical Library, Vol. I p.35).*

[12]   *Even when sober.*

[13]   *'Snobby', actually.*

Truly, as Burns says:

> O wad some Pow'r, the giftie gie us,
> Tae see ourselves, as ithers see us...[14]

But I won't get involved – except to say that my professor expressed great pleasure when I moved from Glasgow to London – he felt it would raise the average IQs of both cities.

For centuries, the tussle of power ebbed and flowed across a band of land on either side of the present border. You might recall that Shakespeare[15] describes the meeting of the French Ambassador and King Henry V, where Westmoreland, one of the chief English nobles whose lands bordered Scotland, recalls the politics of war to his master:

> But there's a saying very old and true;
>   'If that you will France win,
>   Then with Scotland first begin':
> For once the eagle England being in prey,
> To her unguarded nest the weasel Scot
> Comes sneaking and so sucks her princely eggs,
> Playing the mouse in absence of the cat,
> To tear and havoc more than she can eat.[16]

The Ambassador insults Henry with a gift of tennis balls – suggesting that he was more fit for a game than a battle. How wrong they were! But this struck a chord, for the wars between Scotland and England were not unlike the formality of a tennis match – the Scots playing off a base line from Edinburgh to the Solway, and the English from

---

[14]  *'To a Louse' – one of the significant phrases of genius in Burns, directly linked to the moral philosophy of Adam Smith, who was a favourite author of R.B.*

[15]  *William Shakespeare (1564–1616), playwright, occupies a position in English letters not dissimilar to Burns's (without an annual dinner though). Interestingly, while Shakespeare's company of actors played for Good Queen Bess three times a year on average, after the accession of Scotland's own Jamie the Saxt the annual demand from the court rose to 13 performances.*

[16]  The Life of King Henry the Fifth, W. *Shakespeare, Act I, Scene II, Line 171.*

Newcastle to Carlisle. With each battle equivalent to a game, the sets of history fell thus:

| 832 | Athelstaneford | Scots win 1 game to love in the first set | |
|------|----------------|------|------|
| 937 | Brunanburh | 2 | love |
| 1018 | Carham | 3 | love |
| 1093 | Alnwick | 3 | 1 |
| 1138 | Northallerton (Battle of the Standard) | 3 | 2 |
| 1174 | Alnwick (II) | 3 | 3 |
| 1297 | Stirling Bridge | 4 | 3 |
| 1298 | Falkirk | 4 | 4 |
| 1306 | Methven | 4 | 5 |
| 1307 | Loudon Hill | 5 | 5 |
| 1312 | Durham | 6 | 5 |
| 1314 | 24 June – BANNOCKBURN![17] | Scotland wins the first set, beating the English by 7 games to 5 | |

So under the masterful management of King Robert 1 (he learned tactics, you'll remember, by watching the spider in his cave try and fail, try and fail and try once more to succeed[18]) the Scots lads go into the second set ahead, but maybe a bit of overconfidence creeps in.

---

[17] *Please sing along: 'O Flower of Scotland', 'Scots Wa Hae', etc., etc.*
[18] *Still the favoured way of playing sports in the blue jersey.*

| 1322 | Dupplin Moor | England win 1 game to love in the second set | |
|------|--------------|------|---|
| 1333 | Halidon Hill | Love | 2 |
| 1346 | Neville's Cross[19] | Love | 3 |
| 1388 | Otterburn | 1 | 3 |
| 1402 | Homildon Hill | 1 | 4 |
| 1513 | Flodden[20] | 1 | 5 |
| 1542 | Solway Moss | England wins the second set, beating the Scots by 6 games to 1 | |

The next set started off with a win for each side (Ancrum Moor[21] and Pinkie Cleuch[22]) but of course, following the death of the English Queen Elizabeth I in 1603, the Scots (represented by King James) won the third set and the match without having to go into battle.

VI GAMES TO I

---

[19]  *Is he?*

[20]  *Now you have to sing 'The Flowers o' the Forest' and other laments... 9 September 1513 wasn't a good day: amongst the dead on Scotland's side were: the king, the archbishop, nine earls, 14 lords, three Highland chiefs, and 10,000 men.*

[21]  *1545.*

[22]  *1547 – although this might have been a disease, not a battle...*

## Land of the Mountain and the Flood

There are hills beyond Pentland and lands beyond Forth,
Be there lairds in the south, there are chiefs in the north!
There are brave duniwassals, three thousand times three,
Will cry 'Hoy!' for the bonnets o' bonnie Dundee.[23]

The mistake that is made is to see the whole northern nation within our islands as a single defined culture. Oh no. It is much more complex.

The most obvious divide is that between the Highlander and the Lowlander.[24]

The Highland line, which isn't just a straight line east to west, at times seems more a division in age rather than geography. You could look at it as the north containing traditional, pre-industrial (almost mythic) values compared to the commercial, industrial and agricultural certainties of the 'modern' Lowlands.

Still, some of my favourite stories are those told about that culture clash: the Highland laird who boasted of his estates that he could drive his car for the whole afternoon without getting to the boundary, and the Glasgow man who replied 'I had an old car like that too'.

Or what about the Edinburgh banker who went to the remote Highland shop to buy the *Financial Times*? The nice lady gave him yesterday's edition. 'But I wanted today's paper', he spluttered. 'A weel ye'll have to come back tomorrow', she admonished him.

It is interesting that while the industrial revolution and the collapse of the clan system changed the economics of the Highlands and saw many

---

[23] *'Bonnie Dundee' – good song, great tune, complex history. This is the version arranged by Scott. A duniwassal is a tenant of the chief who owes feudal fighting service.*

[24] *With sincere apologies to my Aberdonian friends, who inhabit an independent corner outwith this dichotomy. They will, however, have the opportunity to see themselves as others see them in a later tome ('Scotland on Five Pounds a Day – with £4.95 Change'). I sincerely hope they will not be offended when they see these comments when they borrow this book!*

leave (voluntarily or, I am ashamed to say, often involuntarily[25]), much of the image of Scotland internally and abroad is a function of the history of the Highlands.

## East, West, Hame's Best

Glasgow plays the part of Chicago to Edinburgh's Boston.[26]

The formerly tense relationship across the Highland line has few real repercussions nowadays. It's within the Lowlands that the greatest rivalry is spawned: Glasgow vs Edinburgh. The slug-fest between the Capital City and the Great Industrial Powerhouse[27] carries on through TV and radio, rival newspapers (*Scotsman* vs *Herald*[28]), football teams[29], even the weather: warm and wet[30] in the west or chilly blue skies[31] in the east. The people, the architecture[32] and the culture are noticeably different but perhaps the rivalry has somewhat of the fake about it.

---

[25] *In the Highland Clearances, after it was proven that the best economic return on the hills could be obtained by demolishing the subsistence farms and villages and populating the land with sheep. Ironically, the emigration of Scots to Australia to work in the wool industry there contributed to the collapse of the Highland flocks, many of the hills becoming shooting estates.*

[26] In Search of Scotland, *H.V. Morton, London, 1929.*

[27] *Although the last few years have seen Glasgow diminish economically while Edinburgh has regained some of the political apparatus of government once more.*

[28] *Formerly the* Glasgow Herald *but now reaching out beyond the city.*

[29] *Though the real rivalry is inside each city: Rangers vs Celtic and Hearts vs Hibs.*

[30] *And the smell of the Glasgow Subway – or, as it's affectionately known by its denizens, the Clockwork Orange.*

[31] *And the damp, cold potato smell of the hops brewing in the beer which wafts across the Capital. As redevelopment takes these industrial eyesores out of town, let's hope there's a way to keep the distinctive aroma!*

[32] *Edinburgh is a world-class beauty, but Glasgow has many fine buildings – it used to be said 'if you want to see Glasgow – look up' and it was the cast-iron buildings in a grid pattern that inspired the Chicago School of architects and changed the world with the skyscraper.*

One of the greatest periods in Scottish cultural history was the Enlightenment at the end of the 18th century:

> Really it is admirable how many Men of Genius this country produces at present. Is it not strange, that at a time when we have lost our Princes, our Parliaments, our independent Government, even the presence of our chief Nobility... Is it not strange, I say, that in these Circumstances, we should really be the People most distinguished for Literature in Europe?[33]

In the 25-odd years from 1776, mainly in Edinburgh,[34] the power and energy which would have gone into government, parliament or court intrigue were channelled instead into pure thought – but pure thought with a very Scottish twist – it was done with a practical use and outcome in mind.

Not just philosophies and inventions but whole new sciences sprung out of the salons. Adam Smith founded economics, David Hume remains the greatest moral philosopher in the English language, Hugh Blair was the first professor to teach English literature, Adam Ferguson created social science, Hutton set geology on a scientific footing, Black revolutionised chemistry, Hunter took surgery from the barbers and John Millar brought the first elements of what we'd recognise as MBA training into his commercial law lectures. Outwith the universities, the Adam brothers changed architecture, Walter Scott created the historical novel, Burns was an early romantic and Byron a late and naughty one, and Cochrane was admiral of five navies.[35] The list is if not endless, at least boastful.[36]

No wonder so many foreigners visited and expressed praise and wonder. Ben Franklin opined that:

---

[33] *'Letter', David Hume to Gilbert Elliot of Minto, July 1757.*

[34] *But with sound input from Glasgow and Aberdeen!*

[35] *UK, Chile, Venezuela, Brazil and Greece. Chile sends an annual honour guard to lay a wreath at his monument in Westminster Abbey.*

[36] *The intellectual base was so strong that the great James Watt, it must be remembered, was not even a professor, but the lab technician at Glasgow University!*

> Did not strong connections draw me elsewhere, I believe Scotland
> would be the country I would choose to end my days in.

While Voltaire famously complimented us by saying:

> It is to Scotland that we look for new ideas nowadays.

It's fair to say that the rivalry hasn't diminished over the years: Glasgow won the title European City of Culture and Mr Happy (adopted as the city's mascot) trudged around Edinburgh trying to find a nice comment.[37] Edinburgh has had a boost in the re-founded, devolved parliament and has the trappings of a political capital city for the first time in many long years. Glasgow's industries are turning more entrepreneurial; Edinburgh makes good money for all of us in the financial services sector (or has done for hundreds of years until now). Edinburgh held the Commonwealth Games in 1986 with Glasgow to follow in 2014; Edinburgh was named UNESCO City of Literature, then Glasgow was made a UNESCO City of Music. Ping Pong. One remains cold, the other damp. The only links are incomprehension and rivalry![38]

## A Tale of Two Cities: the Old and the New

> Stately Edinburgh, throned on crags[39]

Of course, those of you who know Edinburgh will recall that she is in so many ways two towns conjoined as twins.

In the south beyond the railway line from Glasgow we have the Old Town, a gem (albeit somewhat unpolished) all hugger-mugger and helter-

---

[37]   *Unsuccessfully.*

[38]   *I am plainly biased (though I love Edinburgh, where my two elder daughters studied at that very nice but post-Reformation institution, the University of Edinburgh). So the appendix has some objective evidence from a unique Scottish viewpoint: William Topaz McGonagall, widely believed (with quite a lot of objective evidence too) to be the worst poet in the world.*

[39]   *'The Excursion', William Wordsworth. Ironically, although the poet liked Edinburgh, the affection was not reciprocated. The influential* Edinburgh Review *panned this poem with the immortal put-down, 'This will never do.'*

skelter, with hidden stairs and steep cobbled slopes linking the brooding castle with the part-time palace. Now fortunately cleaner than ever in history,[40] you can still feel the ancient heart of our capital.

On the right side of the tracks[41] is the greatest piece of urban planning in Europe – the New Town – a triumph of elegant Georgian houses in geometrical street patterns, set around with pretty gardens, squares and churches,[42] the epitome of the rationalism of the Enlightenment.

This juxtaposition of two towns was cultural as well as architectural. The old, douce, smelly folk on the hill looking down at the effete modern manners of the parallel streets below. The modern-thinking, outward-looking people embracing the 19th century opposed to the backwardness found in towering shared blocks of flats, stuck like limpets on the castle rock.

There was one man who exemplified this – he's commemorated by a pub on the Royal Mile[43] – called Deacon Brodie.

What a character.

He was the third most important magistrate in the city and lived up in the eyrie of the Old Town. As a cabinetmaker and locksmith he made a pile of money in fitting out the New Town. He also, alas, made a copy of the key whenever he sold a lock. At night, off with the magistrate's three-cornered hat and into a black mask – for the Deacon was a burglar bold!

He got caught – over-reaching ambition as usual – and an irony which he found quite funny[44] was that he was executed on a modern drop gallows that he'd invented and sold to the council.

---

[40]  *The Old Town had virtually no drainage for centuries and so the inhabitants used to empty their bedpans out of their windows at night into the street. You had to watch your feet in the gutters, but especially your head – the neighbours would shout* 'GARDY LOO'! *(from the French* 'gardez-l'eau' – 'beware of the water'*) and then out it went from the upper-storey windows! Edinburgh's ancient nickname was 'Auld Reekie' – linked to the reek or smoke from its myriad chimneys. It became progressively reekier by dint of the rather quaint hygienic approach referred to here.*

[41]  *Actually it's on the left as you come in from Glasgow Queen Street.*

[42]  *Then bank branches and now all-day pubs. Can't win them all.*

[43]  *And there's no greater honour than that.*

[44]  *He literally died laughing about it!*

Whoops.

The real gratitude I have to the old Deacon was that his life of two halves, hat by day and mask by night, stimulated Robert Louis Stevenson's imagination, where it came out in a slightly different story:

Doctor Jekyll and Mr Hyde.[45]

## That's the Point

> I learned to recognise the thorough and primitive duality of man;
> I saw that, of the two natures that contended in the field of my
> consciousness, even if I could rightly be said to be either, it was
> only because I was radically both.[46]

I think it's that duality, which Stevenson expressed so well, that is the interesting thing about Scotland and the Scots. You can see it in hundreds of ways:

- Scots and English in one United Kingdom.
- Highlanders and Lowlanders.
- East and West.
- Old Town and New Town.
- At Home and Abroad.

The essential element in our Scottish psyche is this: our mindset, which is passionately partisan yet can hold both the pro and the contra in its hands and juggle with them.

Yes, a small physical plot was granted to us to build our nation. Yes, there are relatively few of us in the balance of the population of the world. Yes, we are relatively poor in physical resources, assets and wealth. Yet overarching this is that recognition that we are one and that duality is not a bar to unity.

---

[45]  *Although set in London, if you know Edinburgh, you can see that's the city
      being described by Stevenson.*

[46]  The Strange Case of Dr Jekyll and Mr Hyde, *R.L. Stevenson, 1886.*

Scotland is only as small as each of us wants her to be.

> On with the new coat and into the new life! Down with the
> Deacon and up with the robber!...
> There's something in hypocrisy after all. If we were as good as we
> seem, what would the world be? The city has its vizard on, and
> we – at night we are our naked selves. Trysts are keeping, bottles
> cracking, knives are stripping; and here is Deacon Brodie flam-
> ing forth the man of men he is! – How still it is!... the night for
> me; the grimy cynical night that makes all cats grey, and all hon-
> esties of one complexion. Shall a man not have HALF a life of
> his own? – not eight hours out of 24? Only the stars to see me!
> ... I'm a man once more till morning. (*GETS OUT OF THE
> WINDOW.*)[47]

---

[47]  Deacon Brodie or The Double Life: A Melodrama in Five Acts and Eight
      Tableaux, *W.E. Henley and R.L. Stevenson, Act I, Scene IX.*

# I

# Hogmanay All The Way

So may the Auld year gang out moanin'
To see the New come laden, groanin',
Wi' double plenty o'er the loanin',
    To thee and thine:
Domestic peace and comforts crownin'
    The hale design.[1]

IF FESTIVALS ARE WHAT define a culture, then marking the end of the old year and bringing in the new is a fundamental thread in Scots DNA. For even if you never wear tartan, can't abide whisky and hate the TV shows of geriatric Scots performing on accordions or guitars, I bet every Scot[2] undertakes some festive ritual to welcome in the New Year in style.

Now, when Christmas is the biggest religious, quasi-religious and commercial event globally,[3] it is almost unimaginable that until 1958, Christmas Day was an ordinary working day in Scotland. The post was delivered, the courts sat in judgment, the bakers baked, the offices hummed (slowly); the English and other 'heathen nations' might well dance in their blindness, but in pure Scotland there was no backsliding[4] and no festal joy would taint our Holy Days.

However, the powers-that-be couldn't bottle in the natural enthusiasm of the whole Scottish nation, so the celebration of starting a New Year became the focal point of an entire country, and even today, when most Scots homes will have a Christmas tree, a turkey and stockings hanging at the mantelpiece, our national festival remains overnight on 31 December into 1 January – Seeing in the New Year. This remains a cornerstone of what it is to be Scottish.

---

[1]   *'Verses to Collector Mitchell', Robert Burns.*

[2]   *And I'm starting to use this in a pretty wide and inclusive sense.*

[3]   *In ascending order of importance.*

[4]   *More of that in a later chapter; I don't want to spoil a good story.*

First things first. We call New Year's Eve 'Hogmanay'[5] – but here's a confession: I have absolutely no idea where this funny word came from – nor what it actually means![6] Just about everyone else in the country has an idea (or two) about the etymology: the *Oxford English Dictionary* says:

> Hogmanay: corresp. in meaning and use to OFr. Aguillanneuf
> last day of the year, new year's gift (given and asked for with
> the cry 'aguillanneuf') of which the Norman form hoguinané may
> be the immed. source of the Eng word.[7]

Other equally inadequate theories depend on mispronunciations of other languages: could it be the Gaelic for 'a new morning' ('*oge maidne*')? But there are 365 or more new mornings a year, so I don't think that's a persuasive idea.[8] Or the Anglo Saxon could have given us '*haleg monath*' or 'Holy Month', but that's the opposite problem – now it's too wide a time period. The theory that the French party around the mistletoe ('*au gui*') must have been invented by lovers of Asterix.

Some rely on guesswork: on the Edinburgh Hogmanay website they quote a writer from 1824:

> I think Hog-ma-nay means hug-me-now[9]

Which stands the test of time in my opinion. In my last book, I thought that it might be the future tense of the verb 'to be hungover'[10] but that's just making up a cheap laugh.[11]

---

5   *Pronounced 'HUG-manay'.*

6   *Assuming it means something.*

7   *With thanks to* The Shorter OED. *But their argument is not very convincing, even though many Scots words are directly influenced by the French – a great shame it was the cookery words we stole, not the cookery style.*

8   *Though I bet you didn't know that the tune for Cat Stevens's 'Morning has Broken' is an old Scottish hymn tune written by an old lady from Mull – my Uni friend, Murdo Macdonald from Lewis, taught me that in between pints.*

9   *John Mactaggart – bright chap. Unfortunately I lost the reference to this quote, so I don't know if he said cleverer things or not.*

10  *See* The Ultimate Burns Supper Book, *p.119,* FN 191 – *at last I have footnotes on footnotes.*

11  *And using it twice.*

What about the lads and lassies who make up the body o' the kirk? What do they say? They say Hogmanay means a great, great party.

And one unique to Scotland.[12]

## Preparation is Everything[13]

Now that's over, we have some hard work to do. A very significant part of the celebration at New Year is the preparation.

The obvious part is in cleaning the house. For those of you who believe (like Quentin Crisp) that dust ceases to accumulate after the first inch, this is going to be bad news. Every corner of your home, whether it's a but-and-ben[14], a tenement[15] or a castle,[16] has to be scrubbed, dusted and polished.

Imagine the scene: an Edinburgh dowager was inspecting the house before the Bells and called the housemaid down to the parlour to berate her for not dusting well enough in the run-up to midnight:

'Look Bessie – I can actually write my name in the dust on the sideboard – what have you to say about that?'
'There's nothing like a good education, ma'am.'

---

[12] *Sometimes causing a bit of snippy backchat from our southern neighbours: one of the first printed records about Hogmanay is a scurrilous book from London in 1693 called* Scotch Presbyterian Eloquence Display'd, *which was designed to ridicule the Scots preachers. It says: 'It is ordinary among some Plebeians in the south of Scotland, to go about from door to door upon New Year's Eve, crying Hagmane.'*

[13] *So if you are reading this at quarter to midnight – better luck next year!*

[14] *A wee cottage (the 'but' is the public room at the front door, with the bed at the back in the 'ben').*

[15] *A tenement building need not be a squalid existence – it's an architectural style rather than a social quality: it has a common entrance ('the close' – or if you are posh and have a tiled entrance it's properly called a 'wally close') leading to the central staircase with (typically) two flats/apartments opening on each landing. A bit like an Oxford college, really.*

[16] *Whether Castle Urquhart or Castlemilk.*

Particular care has to be paid to the fireplaces. Remembering our ancient worship of fire, some bright spark has taught us that the hearth on this night becomes again our link with the mysteries of nature. All ashes have to be emptied out the back door, while the grate and irons are polished to glisten in the flames. When you light the fire that's going to warm you through the last hours of the dying year into the new hope of next year, it mustn't be allowed to die down (or heaven forefend, go out) until the New Year is safe in. When it does expire naturally, the ashes can be read by the wise to foretell the joys and travails of the upcoming 12 months: if the ashes form a pattern like a foot with the heel closest to the room, then someone is going to walk away from the house (typically a death); while if the foot can be discerned with the toes pointing into the room, a new arrival will be at the fireplace at the next Hogmanay.[17]

After preparing the food and drinks for your family and guests, the kitchen gets the same treatment[18] and all the bins and wastepaper baskets in the house need to be emptied.

While this was going on, in the old times, the children were thrown out of the house to get out from under mum's feet so she could make a good cleaning from top-to-bottom.[19] These happy bands would marauder the streets calling out for sweeties to celebrate the Hogmanay. This has its roots in French traditions from the time of Mary Queen of Scots,[20] along with the sheer practicality of shifting idle hands out the house. (The men would still be at work – or down the pub!)

There were a number of traditional street rhymes, all now defunct I think, that the children would chant:

> Rise up gude wife an shak' yer feathers,
> An dinna think that we are beggars,
> We are bairns come oot to play,
> Rise up! An gie's oor Hogmanay!

---

[17]   *So just be careful how much fun you have at the party… and with whom…*

[18]   *Which is quite practical – and gets rid of all those hairy green moulds which lurk in the bottom back corner of the average fridge.*

[19]   *Not sure when the weans were cleaned…*

[20]   *The OED was right on that point. Mind you, it was started by a Scotsman.*

The day will come when ye'll be deid;
Ye'll neither care for meat nor breed;
Rise up! Guid wife an' dinna spare
Ye'll hae less an we'll hae mair!
Up stocks! Doon stools![21]
Dinna think that we are fules,
We are bairns come oot to play
Rise up! An gie's oor Hogmanay![22]

Now it's time to prepare yourself!

On the 31st, in years gone by, the working men and merchants would go round their business colleagues and would pay up any monetary debts or repay any favours, to stand free and clear at the New Year's dawning.[23] Now it's just a question of getting home sharp, and as the sun goes down, we all have to wash and wear new clothes to greet the New Year as a party guest.

I forgot to mention one crucial taboo: you must NEVER talk about the New Year ahead of time. When wishing people 'A Good New Year' in advance of midnight, you should always hedge you bets by adding 'when it comes' or some other phrase as it is most high presumption to assume that the gifts of the New Year will be given to us. In the strictest regimes (including the hard-line element of the McGinn household[24]), you wouldn't write in the upcoming year's diary if you had one, which for the more forgetful amongst us usually causes some social mishap in the first few days of the New Year. (It might just be practicality; if you don't make it to midnight your executors might manage to take the diary back to the shop and exchange it!)

---

[21] *Encouraging play (with sticks) rather than sitting on the schoolroom stool.*

[22] *Ancient traditional – I have no idea where from! A shorter version is 'Ma feet's cauld, Ma sheen's din, Gies ma cakes and lets rin!'.*

[23] *As recently as the '90s, the manager of one of the major Edinburgh bank branches told me that his farming customers would pay off their overdrafts. A custom that, until my girls left home, was a pleasant but definitely historical tradition for me.*

[24] *i.e. me, but widely ignored by the children.*

## The Bells[25]

Now it's close to 11.30pm and we are in our nicest clothes, before our flaming logs and with a glass in our hands, it's time to reflect on the last year. But before we move into the height of the celebrations: just before midnight the father of the house has a very important ritual duty. The back door (or a back window if there's but one door) must be unlocked and opened so that any bad luck lying in the house will fly away.

I'll drink to that!

TEN…

NINE…

EIGHT…

SEVEN…

SIX…

FIVE…

FOUR…

THREE…

TWO…

ONE…

!!!!!!!!!!!!!!!!!!!!!!!!!!!!!!!!!!!!!!!HAPPY NEW YEAR!!!!!!!!!!!!!!!!!!!!!!!!!!!!!!!!!!!!!!!!!

I'm not a big counting down sort of a chap, but in a big crowd or party, there will inevitably be those excited enough to chant out the Old Year.[26] Then pandemonium breaks out.

This moment is traditionally called 'The Bells' because all the bells of Scotland ring from church towers, town halls and chiming clocks with the twin purposes of 'seeing in' the New Year and creating a clamour to scare away the lingering vestiges of bad luck that we didn't throw out hard enough from our back doors.

There is nothing as poignant as hearing the bell in a wee kirk ringing out the good news as you walk along on a cold, icy night, with the

---

[25]   *The Bells have made me deaf but Johnny Walker has kept me going strong.*
[26]   *Or at least to prove themselves sober enough to count backwards from ten.*

coal-black sky scattered with starry dia-monds above your head.[27] In Glasgow, in its role of the shipyard of the Empire,[28] all of the ships berthed along the Clyde and the harbours of Greenock and Gourock would sound their horns and whistles for minutes and minutes of naval cacophony.[29]

Interestingly, in the Reform-ation, while the church organ and musi-cal instruments were abandoned, the use of bells to mark the times of worship remained, so our New Year bell ringing is an old, old tradition. One of my favourite bell inscriptions is on the Great Bell of Glasgow Cathedral. This is written on its awesome 12-foot one-inch circumference:

---

[27] *Wee kids will often be scooped out of bed and have a woolly jumper thrown over them so they can join with sleepy eyes the fun before being bundled off to sleep.*

[28] *Now, alas, virtually gone, though there are still a few to carry on at the time of writing, so that the romantic and the acute of ear will hear a memory of the great days through Glasgow windows on the night.*

[29] *In the Algonquin Hotel, New York City, in a crazy mésalliance between Chinese New Year and Hogmanay, the entire staff charge through the lobby dressed as ghosts with sheets over their heads, banging pots and pans together to scare away demons. There's hasn't been banging like that in the hotel since the late great Dorothy Parker passed away. Or at least was last laid (to rest).*

In the year of grace
1594,
Marcus Knox,
a merchant of Glasgow,
zealous for the interests of the reformed religion,
caused me to be fabricated in Holland
for the use of his fellow citizens in Glasgow,
and placed me with solemnity
in the tower of their cathedral.
My function
was to announce, by the impress on my bosom,
(Me audito venias doctrinam sanctam ut discas;)[30]
and
I was taught to proclaim the hours of unheeded time.
195 years had I sounded these awful warnings,
when I was broken
by the hands of inconsiderate and
unskilful men.
In the year 1790,
I was cast into the furnace,
refounded at London,
and returned to my sacred vocation.
Reader,
thou also shall know a resurrection,
may it be to eternal life.
Thomas Mears fecit, London, 1790.[31]

---

[30]   *Trans: 'Hear me and come, that ye may learn holy doctrine.'*

[31]   *Thomas Mears came from the greatest family of bell founders, whose company, the Whitechapel Bell Foundry, still trades today. America's Liberty Bell was cast there, and a group of Americans wrote a complaint 200 years after its delivery in 1776 to demand compensation for the most famous cracked bell in history. The Managing Director at Whitechapel wrote by return with profuse apologies that his family's product had failed to please. He would of course refund the customers' money in full (if they would only return the bell, in its original packaging and with the receipt, to the office).*

## Auld Lang Syne: Should Auld Song Lyrics Be Forgot?

After the bells, whistles, possibly fireworks and certainly cheering, every-one in the world sings Robert Burns's famous song, 'Auld Lang Syne'.[32]

There's a running argument over which is the most sung song in the world: 'Auld LS' or 'Happy Birthday to You' and a few hold out for 'For He's A Jolly Good Fellow'. But I think that you have to say there is a bit more poetic ability in the former. Certainly ALS takes a bit more effort and has had a number of quite disparate uses. In Japan it is often used as the signal that a department store is closing; it was even the national anthem of Mauritius for a while. Now it is famed as the signa-ture tune of the Hogmanay celebrations all over the world.[33] Every Scot knows the words.[34]

It does have its own set of problems. Not least of all – what is it going on about?

What exactly does 'for auld lang syne' mean? The connotations run deeper than the literal translation of 'for old long ago'. It's a very Scottish thought, which appealed to Burns as soon as he heard it – and there are many, many examples of the emotional response to the way that Scots carry the fond remembrance of old friends, old landscapes and glories gone by.

My old school, Ayr Academy (where Burns himself attended a few lessons under the aegis of his friend, John Murdoch), knows a bit about the ages gone past, having been founded in 1233;[35] the school motto is

---

[32] *Both Alan Ramsey in his 'Tea Table Miscellany' ('Should auld acquaintance be forgot/Tho' they return with scars?/These are a noble hero's lot,/Obtain'd in glorious wars;/Welcome, my Varo, to my breast,/Thy arms about me twine,/And make me once again as blest,/As I was lang syne.') and the great Semple of Belltrees had used the phrase in poems before it caught Burns's eye and he created the immortal version we know today.*

[33] *Mainly, to be fair, popularised by the Guy Lombardo, the famous Canadian big band leader, who used it in his New Year's Eve broadcasts from 1929.*

[34] *Well, roughly.*

[35] *Just giving the masters time to get to the pub for one o'clock.*

'*Respice Prospice*'[36] – which could do as a Latin translation of our song at a pinch.

For those of you – the silent majority – who are still neither sure, nor impressed, I hope this new verse translation will be helpful:

SHOULD auld acquaintance be forgot,
 And never brought to mind?
Should auld acquaintance be forgot,
 And auld lang syne!

*Chorus—*
For auld lang syne, my dear,
 For auld lang syne.
We'll tak a cup o' kindness yet,
 For auld lang syne.

And surely ye'll be your pint stowp!
 And surely I'll be mine!
And we'll tak a cup o'kindness yet,
 For auld lang syne.
*Chorus*

We twa hae run about the braes,
 And pou'd the gowans fine;
But we've wander'd mony a weary fit,
 Sin' auld lang syne.
*Chorus*

We twa hae paidl'd in the burn,
 Frae morning sun till dine;
But seas between us braid hae roar'd
 Sin' auld lang syne.
*Chorus*

*Should our old friendship be forgot,*
 *And memories never grow?*
*Should our old friendship be forgot,*
 *From long, long ago?*

Chorus—
*For long, long ago, my dear,*
 *For long, long ago.*
*We'll share a toast in friendship now,*
 *For long, long ago.*

*So gather up your full flagon!*
 *And my own beer will flow!*
*We'll share a toast in friendship now,*
 *For long, long ago.*
Chorus

*We two have run around the hills,*
 *And picked the daisies, so*
*We've trudged a good few weary miles,*
 *Since long, long ago.*
Chorus

*We've both been playing in the stream,*
 *From dawn to sun's last glow;*
*But seven seas had sundered us*
 *Since long, long ago.*
Chorus

---

[36]   '*Look Back: Look Forward*', or as the School Song captures the theme: '*Age cannot stale thee, nor years ever rob us/of memories stored in the noontide of youth,/Still may our thoughts of thee/On to life's ending/Keep our feet steadfast in hope, love and truth./Floreat Semper Academia!*'.

| | |
|---|---|
| And there's a hand, my trusty fiere! | *And there's my hand, my own true friend!* |
| And gie's a hand o' thine! | *And on me your hand bestow!* |
| And we'll tak a right gude-willie waught, | *We'll find goodwill in a shared glass,* |
| For auld lang syne. | *For long, long ago.* |
| | |
| For auld lang syne, my dear, | *For long, long ago, my dear,* |
| For auld lang syne. | *For long, long ago.* |
| We'll tak a cup o' kindness yet, | *We'll share a toast in friendship now,* |
| For auld lang syne. | *For long, long ago.* |

So really it's not that opaque. The very good news is that only the first verse and last verse are sung nowadays, with the chorus after each,[37] so when we start, stand up (either round your table or a big circle on the dance floor) and join in!

I hate being bossy[38] but so many people just get the song wrong. It is one of those shibboleths that annoy true Scots, so these are the things you must NOT do if you want to keep your status:

- Pronounce 'Syne' as 'Zine' – it HAS to sound like the trigonometric term 'Sine'.[39]

- Introduce the spurious and egregious words 'For the sake of' – they just don't exist in the lyrics, so leave them out.

- Cross your arms across your chest all through the song – this isn't how it's done. Start off the song by holding hands normally, side-by-side.[40] ONLY when you sing out 'And there's a hand, my trusty fiere' do you cross arms across your chest and grab the

---

[37]  *In bold above.*

[38]  *I've learnt my lesson, as one reviewer of my last book gave a very kind write-up but chided me for using 'footnotes as a running line of supposedly off-the-cuff witticisms, erring occasionally on the side of fogeyish exasperation'. So I've been trying to rein it in – no pipe, no slippers and haven't had a pink gin in months. But this time it's important. Dammit!*

[39]  *For the non-mathematical, it's fine to rhyme with 'line'.*

[40]  *There's a classic photograph of the Queen looking especially unhappy as a former PM and his wife get 'Auld Lang Syne' completely wrong. In retrospect, like so many things.*

opposite hands of the people on either side.[41] Then you pump your crossed hands up and down in time to the music. Don't worry; a few people don't have arms long enough to do this[42] – just try your best and go with the flow!

At a dance, particularly of young people, the band will play a few extra choruses and the circle will run in and out[43] on the dance floor like a child's party game, which is rather jolly and exhilarating. It's also a good way to burn off some calories[44] to give you a second wind for the next part of our celebrations.

## Food and Drink (Especially Drink)

Whyles dullness stands for modest merit,
And impudence for manly spirit;
To ken what worth each does inherit,
Just to try the bottle;
Send round the glass, and dinna spare it,
Ye'll see their mettle.
Oh, would the gods but grant my wish,
My constant prayer would be for this:
That love sincere, with health and peace,
My lot they'd clink in,
With now and then the social joys
O' friendly drinkin'.[45]

Whether you are celebrating round a dinner table (at home or in a restaurant) or milling about (indoors or at the street party) or dancing the night away, you will need a bit of sustenance. Here the great Scottish trait of being hospitable comes into play. As Scott says:

---

[41]  *When you think of it, it makes the circle smaller and signifies us all coming closer together in our shared hopes and memories.*

[42]  *Due either to short arms or big tummies.*

[43]  *And bounce up and down like Teuchter Tiggers.*

[44]  *And units (of alcohol).*

[45]  *'An Invocation', Robert Tannahill.*

Each age has deemed the new-born year
The fittest time for festal cheer[46]

The drink is easy – it is the host's duty to see that everyone gets his/her Ne'erday[47] – the first social drink[48] of the year. This needn't be a dram[49] – as a good host you should offer your guest his or her favourite tipple. In my boyhood, people would carry sports bags with bottles of whisky, brandy, rum, vodka and gin as they went round different houses to greet their friends and share the first toast to each other and then to the New Year – both the day and the drink are called 'the Ne'erday'.

One of the dangers in my university days in Glasgow was that you'd bump into some old drunk guy beside the park benches with his half bottle and he'd offer you a swig from it as a Ne'erday toast – it would be rude (and potentially dangerous) to refuse but equally hazardous (or at least noxious) to partake.

So the drinking is really no big shakes.[50] What about the nibbles? If you are going to be up all night (until the wee sma' oors) you need some carbohydrate to keep you going.

Assuming that you are not having a formal dinner (or you are just looking to have a buffet sideboard to regale your friends and guests), the traditional foods for Hogmanay are oatcakes and local cheese accompanied by sweet biscuits and cakes.

The staple is shortbread – archetypal to the point of cliché! Wherever you wander[51] you'll find tins of shortbread: Harrods to Honolulu, Myers of Keswick in New York's East Village to Japanese stores. And virtually every duty-free airport shop in the Western world sells this taste of Scotland in a box. These tins have a lot to answer for – invariably tartan with twee pictures (a Jacobite gentleman in starched linen and

---

46   *'Marmion', Sir Walter Scott.*

47   *The Scots for 'New Year's Day' – pronounced 'newer day'.*

48   *Or 'swally' in Glaswegian.*

49   *The traditional euphemism is often heard: 'a wee nippy sweetie'.*

50   *If there are any shakes, then you do have a problem. Mind you, as the former Dundee MP Sir Winston Churchill famously pointed out: 'I've taken more out of drink, than drink's taken out of me!'*

51   *Or wherever you roam.*

trews kissing the hand of a ruddy-cheeked Scots dairymaid; more pictures of Rabbie or Charlie than you could shake a stick at; or one of those ruined castles – everyone knows the one, but can't recall the name) – I am sure you've seen them a hundred times or more. The shortbread tin was designed to keep Scottish food fresh, but inadvertently acted to keep Scotland's culture stale.

That being said, good shortbread gives the sugar boost you need tonight. You'll see it in big rounds (with traditional thumb pinches around the circumference – representing the new sun's rays on this New Year's morning) or wee round or finger biscuits, or the classic 'petticoat tails' – a thin roundel scored across several diameters to break into kite shapes – which the romantics claim look like the tails of the lady's undergarment.[52]

But in many ways, shortbread is the easy way out... real Scots eat the mighty BLACK BUN. A good black bun is a wondrous sight: a thick mass of raisins and currants squashed into a pastry sandwich. It weighs a ton and would meet any normal person's weekly calorie intake – but it's the dark, pressed, slightly spicy squashed fruit that takes you aback when you first see it – I can only say that the weans call it the 'flies' graveyard'.

There is a thinner commercial equivalent called the Garibaldi biscuit, a favourite of the English tea table, which was invented by Peake Freans in London after the Italian freedom fighter Guiseppe Garibaldi visited that city in 1861 and created quite a stir. It seems[53] that the biscuit was created by a young Scotsman called John Carr. I bet you he carried his family recipe south and made his fortune by creating an English-sized black bun.[54]

---

[52]   *The Francophiles amongst us think that 'petticoat' might be a mispronunci-ation of* 'petite gâterie', *a small friandaise or treat for a child. As this phrase is now used in France as a euphemism for a sexual practice (an auld alliance indeed), I'll stick with the first thought.*

[53]   *With thanks to the superb website www.nicecupofteaandasitdown.com – a kindred spirit if ever I saw one.*

[54]   *There is some discussion about the Eccles cake too – but you'll have to buy the book on Lancashire festivals* (Hot Pots and What Nots) *when I get round to writing it. Enough of the biscuits already.*

If this is all too much, there are various local traditions for ginger-bread or current or fruit loaf – I think by now you will have worked out what's needed: a good bit of soak-it-up sugar.

So your sideboard is groaning with fine festive food and drink – but there's time now for the most important tradition of all – first footing.

## First Footing

This is the one tradition that I take very seriously. The entire fortune and fate of your family for the forthcoming year depends on the person who first crosses your threshold after the Bells. This person is your 'First Foot'.

Fortunately[55] the divination of whether you will have good luck or bad is very easy.

- Good luck comes if your first foot is tall, dark (ideally an adult male[56]) and bearing gifts.
- Bad luck comes if a red-haired person first foots you!

There's been a lot in the papers lately about the persecution of red-haired people in Britain – it doesn't seem common in other nations or cultures, where red hair can signify a good fighter in a man or great attractiveness in a woman. But the fear comes from further back than this – to have a red-haired Viking or Norseman burst across your Dark Age door wouldn't have been a bundle of fun[57] and although we whipped the Norse finally at the Battle of Largs in 1263, the memory, as is its wont, lingers on. So an absolute prohibition exists on having a red-haired first footer.[58]

---

55  *Pun intended.*

56  *Strictly speaking a female cannot first foot, but that might change as we all grow less gender aware.*

57  *He's not there for your black bun, I'll tell you.*

58  *I'd be canny about strawberry blonds and generally light-haired folk – even under expensive security lights, there might be enough red in the colour to ensure that you get bunions, or bump the side door of the car – not devas-tating, but bad enough.*

So a tall, dark-haired man is your safest bet.[59] If you are tall[60] and dark-haired enough then you will be in good demand this night! You, as the first footer, have duties too, though. We're only halfway there to good luck, as even a good six foot and jet-black hair can let a house down if he comes in empty-handed.

The old tradition was to carry food, drink and coal to signify enough to eat, the joy of fellowship and fire to warm the family in the coming year. There are regional variations: fishing communities often bring a fish to presage a year of full nets and happy returns, while farmers create short-breads with special ingredients – Pitcaithly in Fife used almonds and caraway seeds, while Yetholm in the Borders mixed in stem ginger. In St Andrews, bakers vied with each other to bake beautiful cakes and give them away to the children – so New Year's Eve there was often called 'Cake Day'.[61]

Even some families would have a particular tradition[62] of having a unique gift to mark each year. These gifts 'handsel'[63] the home and give the family the symbols of the good luck ahead. Now I'd recommend

---

59   *While writing this, I started to worry about bald guys. Is that good or bad? Does it depend on what his lost hair colour was? Can you tell from eyebrows? This is a very worrying question that I wish I hadn't raised. I'm going to stick to people with a good head of black hair. Not that I'm really superstitious (touch wood).*

60   *And this is a relative term; the average male height in Glasgow is 5ft 3in.*

61   *Sounds like a tradition worth reviving!*

62   *I know of someone who always brings that year's* Broons Annual.

63   *We'll find this concept of handsel through the year in particularly old festivals. Handsel is to give a gift to another at an important moment. Burns, in his autobiographical song 'There Was a Lad', described the storm on his birthday which blew down the chimney, saying it 'blew hansel in on Robin'.*

bringing any gift of food or drink; it's hard to lay your hands on a lump of coal nowadays, so you can be excused that part of the equation.[64]

Under the strict rules of first footing, the residents of a house cannot leave the house after the Bells until the first foot arrives. If you are worried that no one will call for a few days, there is an extraordinary derogation allowed: a suitable man on the premises is allowed to go out[65] ahead of midnight. Then he can be your first foot by making the ceremonial re-entry through the front door.

You greet your first foot – and in fact all mankind on New Year's Day – with a handshake and/or a kiss and wishes for a Good New Year. The kissing is an interesting custom. As England became a more formal society it became taboo to kiss, while in Scotland a greater latitude was permitted, especially at New Year.

> Alack and alas! for our stiff humanity. Here in England [the kiss] is reserved for children and girls. Well, it is a beautiful old custom and if we were not so wicked in this 19th century, we should have more of it. This privilege is now reserved for our Scotch cousins, who make a very free use of it![66]

The army has an interesting variant on first footing.

When the Scottish Regiment mounts guard on Hogmanay, the pipers march out of the camp gates 'playing out the Old Year'. After the strokes of midnight, they return with more cheerful tunes, to be challenged as usual:

| | |
|---|---|
| GUARD | Halt, Who Goes There? |
| PIPER | The New Year! |
| GUARD | Pass, New Year, For All's Well. |

---

[64] *Though in a modern twist I have seen people bring candles.*

[65] *Preferably using the back door.*

[66] The Habits of Good Society *by The Gentleman in the Club Window, Jas Hogg & Co, 1860?, p.276.*

And then a good dram is had by all in the warmth and comfort of the guardroom.[67]

## Street Parties[68]

In times gone by, New Year's morning saw the town councils send out huge copper kettles full of hot toddy to warm the citizens.[69] Carried by stalwart men, the cry of 'Het Pint' roused the weary to come to the street corner and, with the neighbours, greet the year and toast the politicians for the honour and good fortune of the burgh. Some took it to great lengths:

> But the magistrates [of Ayr] themselves were jovial fellows. They ate, drank, and spent the funds of the burgh, all for the 'honour and glory' of the good town – making stated peregrinations through the most delectable of the taverns. The town was in such a bankrupt state [in 1724] that the clear income of the burgh only amounted to £469 1s 4d which was less by £11 13s 8d than the sum spent in supporting 'the honour and dignity of the burgh in the public houses'.[70]

Glasgow's version sounds as if it would take a strong man to have half a pint: boil up ale with grated nutmeg, eggs and sugar; add a quarter as much of whisky and boil again – that's guaranteed to warm the cockles of your heart. Egg nog with attitude!

In Edinburgh it was more decorous: made from red wine and spices

---

[67]  *The massed pipes and drams, I suppose...*

[68]  *Or 'clamjamfreys' in Scots.*

[69]  *Can't see that being paid out of the council tax nowadays!*

[70]  *'Auld Ayr', Anonymous (undated Victorian)*, Why Called the Wicked Town of Ayr.

[71]  *Many people believe that the Scottish word 'slug' for a sip or measure of drink comes from the great legal case of Donohue vs Stevenson (1932) AC 562 (HL), where a decomposing snail was discovered (belatedly) in a bottle of ginger beer.*

heated through with a good slug[71] of French brandy. In Aberdeen (not because they were mean, but because they liked it) het pint was a simple mix of oat husks and ale.

While free booze is off the menu, in the last few years the traditional Glasgow and Edinburgh rivalry has burgeoned into rival Hogmanays,[72] with street parties in both cities. Edinburgh's is certainly the larger and gets increasingly elaborate, and at its peak over 100,000 people congregate in the streets around Princes Street to hear music, dance and gasp at one of the largest pyrotechnic displays in the world. It's very popular (although weather dependent – twice in the last five years wind and rain have caused parts of it to be cancelled) – but you should book tickets well in advance for you'll need a pass to get into the party (though you can see the fireworks from further afield!), unless of course you are already in the city centre by the time it is cordoned off.

Glasgow's celebration centres on George Square under the bulk of the magnificent City Chambers, with a large pop concert leading up to the Bells. Across Scotland, more and more towns and communities are following – with what is really a new communal first footing.

## The First Two Days of January

And what's going to happen for the rest of Ne'erday?

> We are na fou, we're nae that fou,
>  But just a drappie in our e'e!
> The cock may craw, the day may daw,
>  And ay we'll taste the barley bree![73]

There will come a point at which it's best to make off to bed and get a wee rest from the excitement. Then after a suitable period of recuperation, as your stamina and sore head permit, cast a pink eye over the duvet cover

---

[72] *If anyone knows what the plural of Hogmanay is, please call me...*

[73] *'Willie Brewed a Peck o Maut', Robert Burns.*

in time for a brunch or lunch. Or even better, a full Scottish breakfast!

If you are rather more vigorous, mad or just want to end it all, get down to Queensferry for the Loony Dook – where the locals have for 20 freezing years bared (almost) all and swum in the Firth of Forth. There must be better hangover cures![74]

And don't forget that 2 January is[75] a bank[76] holiday[77] in Scotland too – so you can catch up on your sleep then.

HAPPY NEW YEAR my friends! And many of them!

---

[74]  *Irn Bru and a roll and Lorne sausage are personal recommendations.*

[75]  *Rather wisely.*

[76]  *The Scottish Banks are still stalwarts of tradition (even in these sad and troubled times). Hardly surprising with Bank of Scotland (founded in 1694), The Royal Bank of Scotland (1727) and Clydesdale Bank (1838) each still printing their own banknotes. And very handsome they are! RBS is the last to still print the popular green £1 note, while all three have blue fivers, brown tenners and a bright scarlet £50 note. Every UK bank once had this privilege, but under The Bank Charter Act 1844 any English bank which changed ownership automatically lost that right. The Scots banks were exempted (thanks to Sir Walter Scott's essays – for which derring-do he remains on the BOS notes today). One by one the English fell, and today only Messrs C. Hoare & Co. of No. 1 Fleet Street remain banca intacta, and so the Old Lady herself prints literal Monopoly Money. We still have our notes (hooray!) but for every pound note in excess of the number of pounds on issue in 1844, we have to hold an equivalent number of Bank of England notes (boo!). As BOE was also founded by a Scot, they make it easy for us by having very special £1,000,000 notes for the purpose.*

[77]  *This is one of the very keenly felt traditions in Scotland. At devolution, The Scotland Act 1998 (Part II of Schedule 5) granted the right to set bank holidays in Scotland to the Scottish ministers based on the statutory provisions of The Banking and Financial Dealings Act 1971 (Schedule 1), which allows both extra days (fat chance) or the nomination of the following Monday should the Bank Holiday fall on a Sunday; however, if it falls on a Saturday there needs to be a royal proclamation! There was great outcry when the Scottish clearing banks sought to abolish the second day at New Year. After industrial action, a compromise was reached.*

An indescribable cheerfulness breathes about the city; and the well-fed heart sits lightly and beats gaily in the bosom. It is New-year's weather. New-year's Day, the great national festival, is a time of family expansions and of deep carousal. For at this season, on the threshold of another year of calamity and stubborn conflict, men feel a need to draw closer the links that unite them;

they reckon the number of their friends, like allies before a war... Auld Lang Syne is much in people's mouths; and whisky and shortbread are staple articles of consumption. From an early hour a stranger will be impressed by the number of drunken men; and by afternoon drunkenness has spread to the women. Before night, so many have gone to bed or the police office, that the streets seem almost clearer... when once the New Year has been rung in and proclaimed at the Tron railings, the festivities begin to find their way indoors and something like quiet returns upon the town. But think... of all the senseless snorers, all the broken heads and empty pockets![78]

---

[78]  Picturesque Notes, *Robert Louis Stevenson, Chapter* IX *'Winter and New Year', 1879.*

# 2

# New Year and New Fire

The Norseman's home in days gone by
Was on the rolling sea,
And there his pennon did defy
The foe of Normandy.
Then let us ne'er forget the race,
Who bravely fought and died,
Who never filled a craven's grave,
But ruled the foaming tide.

The noble spirits, bold and free
Too narrow was their land,
They roved the wide expansive sea,
And quelled the Norman band.
Then let us all in harmony,
Give honour to the brave
The noble, hardy, northern men,
Who ruled the stormy wave.[1]

IN SOME WAYS ALL the Hogmanay rite is the tip of a cultural iceberg. Understanding it is certainly a necessary condition to be Scottish, but it's not enough on its own!

Man has been fascinated by fire since our common ancestor found a lightning-struck bush and brought it home to show the missus. From Ug the caveman to the neds round Glasgow bus station flicking matches at each other – man's desire to play with fire and not get burned proves that there is a pyromaniac gene inside us all.

I come from the rainy part of Scotland (the Wet Coast as it's known),

---

[1]   'The Norseman's Home', words of obscure origin with a traditional Norwegian melody from Up Helly Aa.

but the top half of our country is more characterised by the short days of winter and the long summer nights. If you add the mystery of fires with the dark winter nights you get the natural desire to chase away the gloom.[2] That's why there are a number of very ancient fire ceremonies which still occur in northern corners of Scotland to mark the New Year. Thrilling shows to cheer chilling nights.

So, will you have to miss Hogmanay to see these? The odd answer is 'probably not', for these traditions are older than our modern calendar so fall not on 31 December, but in early January.

## A Digression

Whereas the legal supputation of the year of our Lord in England, according to which the year beginneth on the 25th day of March, hath been found by experience to be attended with divers inconveniences, not only as it differs from the usage of neighbouring nations, but also from the legal method of computation in Scotland, and from the common usage throughout the whole kingdom, and thereby frequent mistakes are occasioned in the dates of deeds and other writings, and disputes arise therefrom: And whereas... The Julian Calendar, hath been discovered to be erroneous,... And whereas it will be of general convenience to merchants and other persons corresponding with other nations and countries, and tend to prevent mistakes and disputes in or concerning the dates of letters and accounts, if the like correction be received and established in his Majesty's dominions:[3]

---

[2]   *It's now called* SAD, *'seasonally adjusted disorder' by the doctors. Or 'The Glums'. There was a homeless guy they found in San Francisco a few years ago who was diagnosed with deep clinical depression. After all treatments failed he was signed up for a nice refreshing zap of* ECT. *By good fortune, the nurse attending was from Glasgow and explained to the doctors that their patient wasn't ill and depressed, he was just Scottish. (From Motherwell, actually, if you need further corroboration.)*

[3]   *Calendar (New Style) Act 1750 c. 23. Known as Lord Chesterfield's Act.*

It all comes down to the difference between the Scots and the English[4] but it's an old story.

The Romans had defined each year as commencing on 1 January,[5] however the rise of Christianity encouraged some states to find an appropriate Christian festival to start the annual cycle. In the 12th century, the two British kingdoms adopted 25 March or Lady Day[6] as New Year, while continental Europe maintained the old form. Scotland (being Scotland) had it both ways, by maintaining Hogmanay at the old Roman year end.

This is confusing enough, but the mathematics of the Julian calendar had meant that the legal year was slipping out of tune with the seasons. Pope Gregory[7] calculated that the two were ten days adrift[8] and boldly brought the New Style[9] into kilter by abolishing ten consecutive days: 4–13 October 1582. And as an afterthought, being a true Roman at heart, he decreed that throughout the world, 1 January was back in as the one and only New Year's Day.

There's a famous British newspaper headline: 'Storms in Channel: Europe Isolated'. Pretty much our approach here. In England, Queen

---

4    *As usual.*

5    *Named after the god Janus – the god of doors and boundaries – two-faced, so the titular deity of doorkeepers and politicians. In Scotland the school caretaker is entitled 'Janitor' or in the demotic: 'ra Janny'.*

6    *That's the Annunciation, not the jazz singer.*

7    *A great guy in so many respects.*

8    *Julius Caesar had responded to a similar crisis before by creating an extra day* (dies bisextillis – *there were lots of rumours about Julius, 'a husband to every wife and a wife to every husband', but this Latin word only means a second 6th of the second month) every four years. His calculations were based on the Earth's orbit of the Sun (he thought it was the other way round, but it doesn't affect the maths) of 365¼ days. By Pope Gregory's more refined calculations it was slightly less than that, so he changed the formula for leap years so that century years would only be leap years if exactly divisible by 400 – so 2000 AD is a leap year whereas neither 1900 nor 2100 are (neither of which particularly affect the current readership).*

9    *Or Gregorian calendar. Not everyone adopted that, mind you. Ethopia only celebrated the millennium in September 2007!*

Elizabeth I (having been excommunicated) wasn't in the mood to take advice, while in Scotland the Reformation was too busy to reform the diary. So we carried on with the Old Style but often dated letters and documents between January and March as, say, '1598/9' to cover both options.

That being said, the Scots always preferred New Year in January, so in a carefully worded law[10] of 1599:

> The Kingis Majestie and Lords of his Secrit Counsall, undir-standing that in all utheris weill governit commoun welthis and countreyis the first day of the yeir begynnis yeirlie upoun the first day of Januare, commounlie callit new yeiris day...[11]

This determined forever that the next New Year's Day was on 1 January 1600.[12]

Even after the union of the crowns of England and Scotland in 1603 and that of the two countries' parliaments in 1707 we had a United Kingdom with two different New Years!

By the middle of the 18th century[13] this was a complete muddle and Lord Chesterfield (the noted wit, raconteur and letter writer) suggested cancelling the eleven days between 2 and 14 September.[14]

---

[10]  *Avoiding any suspicion that we were taking advice from Rome!*

[11]  *Privy Council of Scotland Resolution, 17 December 1599.*

[12]  *Don't forget that 1600 would be a leap year everywhere – but 1700 would only be a leap year in Scotland, England and the Orthodox Countries (who maintain an unorthodox Old Style calendar to this day).*

[13]  *And it was a long 18th century, take it from me.*

[14]  *Lord C.'s own birthday was 22 September, so he carefully avoided losing his own party and presents!*

|  | New Year's Day | Old Style | New Style |
|---|---|---|---|
| Europe | 1 January | 10 January | 1 January |
| Scotland | 1 January | 11 January[15] | 1 January |
| England | 25 March | 6 April[16] | 25 March |
| Proposed UK |  | 1 January |  |

Unfortunately, many ordinary folk found the loss of eleven days confusing – but the loss of eleven days' pay was insulting.[17] So, particularly in the country, the community hung to the Old Style, especially round the turn of the year. Which brings us home to the burning topic of this chapter.

## The Comrie Flambeaux

Perthshire is one of the prettiest and most prosperous of our counties[18] and on Hogmanay the village of Comrie[19] explodes into a festival[20] of music, fancy dress and great cheer.

The whole village gathers in the square. At the chimes of midnight eight men appear with long fiery torches called flambeaux[21] – each is responsible for making his own[22] – and, bearing these six-foot-long beacons aloft,

---

[15]   *The extra day is because of the revision of the leap year rule above.*

[16]   *Ditto.*

[17]   *The government was determined to get a full year's tax and even now the UK tax year starts on 6 April – eleven days after a Lady Day New Year!*

[18]   *Only this week I was talking to a bright young legal graduate, just about to go south, whose real ambition is to marry the only son of a Perthshire farmer. Old traditions die hard!*

[19]   *Which has won prizes for the prettiest village in Scotland many times.*

[20]   *In fact two – one in the early evening for the children and one later for the grown-ups.*

[21]   *French for 'fiery torch' = 'flambeau' (plural 'flambeaux').*

[22]   *The secret is to cut the wood on the Sunday after Remembrance Sunday, wrapping the business end in sacking or hessian, and soaking that end in a bucket of paraffin for the next 12 weeks. I'd be careful where you go for a smoke in Comrie in November!*

accompanied by the local pipe band, they lead a procession of revellers around the village, visiting each point of the compass before returning to the square for the judging of the fancy dress competition.[23] That concluded, they march to the Dalinglas Bridge and all eight flambeaux are cast into the waters of the River Earnall and extinguished.

I'm not sure if Comrie's good luck manifests itself in a higher than average number of Lottery winners but if you are there at Hogmanay you'll be guaranteed the good fortune of a great party!

## Biggar's Bonfire

For centuries[24] the old town of Biggar in Lanarkshire has brought in the New Year by building a huge bonfire on the High Street. After a torchlight procession of the townsfolk, the oldest resident uses his or her[25] torch to light the great fire, ensuring that there's a good blaze going at midnight.

This is a proudly defended tradition – it even carried on through the dark days of World War II. The bonfire would have been a dangerous beacon for the enemy bombers heading for the Clyde shipyards, so the good folk of Biggar enacted their celebration with a candle inside a tin on the bonfire site – keeping their tradition alive and alight.[26]

After the war, in the period of austerity that we faced across Britain after expending so much in the defence of the free world, Scotland was heavily rationed, and that included coal and other fuel. The powers-that-be decreed that there should be no bonfire in Biggar that year, but upon vocal appeal by the townsfolk, they condescended to permit a small fire (after all it would have been unfair of HM Government to break the

---

[23] *Dressing up is an important Scottish tradition – have a look at Hallowe'en for more about this – it's not as childish as it seems!*

[24] *Locals would say this tradition stretched back to pre-Christian and even pre-historic times.*

[25] *Biggar is refreshingly inclusive.*

[26] *Bonfires were a common festival but few communities have maintained the ritual as steadfastly. Dingwall, Campbeltown, Invergordon and Newton Stewart still celebrate. If I've missed anyone – sorry!*

tradition when the Enemy hadn't managed to). The government inspector[27] came to check up and gazed admiringly at the barbeque-sized bonfire before toddling off to his comfy home to see in his own New Year.[28]

No sooner had he left, the burghers of Biggar came from all corners to add truckloads of coal and wood and old furniture and the blaze burned for five whole days![29]

Independence of mind – that's an essential trait in the Scots!

## The Stonehaven Fireballs

Further north in the fishing community of Stonehaven in Aberdeenshire, the theme is taken up with gusto and a fair bit of terror.

While only formally recorded since 1909, the locals are sure this is a ritual performed by the ancient fishermen, who sought to overcome the cold, cruel sea and so created a ceremony of fire – the opposite natural element – to propitiate their gods.

As the fishing community declined, there were fewer participants and in the 1960s Stonehaven had few swingers indeed.[30] Fortunately, the

---

[27]   *Biggar has a chequered relationship with government. In the '80s a Scottish Secretary of State was replying to a letter from the Minister of Biggar. His trainee typist misaddressed the envelope to:*
*The Minister*
*The Manse*
*Bugger*
*In exasperation, the cabinet minister shouted 'Make "Bugger" "Biggar"!' – you can imagine the poor old Rev.'s shock when next day he received a formal letter On Her Majesty's Service addressed thus:*
*The Minister*
*The Manse*
*BUGGER.*

[28]   *No doubt with a weak cup of tea and a small biscuit.*

[29]   *The spirit of compromise in these festivals is important, and in the modern world, towns and villages see a greater mix of people residing within them. This is often true of pretty towns within striking distance of the cities, so there have been issues, but always successfully resolved – lang may Biggar's bonfire reek!*

[30]   *An ironic state of play in that decadent decade.*

community banded together to ensure that their unique approach to Hogmanay stayed out of the history books and alive on their High Street.

Wherever the idea came from, now between 10 and 12 thousand people gather in the streets,[31] being entertained by the local pipe band while waiting for one of the most impressive sights you'll ever see. At the striking of midnight by the town hall clock, up to 50 locals[32] parade from the old Mercat Cross to a cannon bollard at the harbour, swinging huge balls of fire[33] round and round their heads. After half an hour or so the flaming spheres are hurled finally into the harbour to expire in steam and sizzle.

It's a dramatic sight in the dark and the spectators are right in the middle of the action.[34] But the heroes are the swingers. The balls are wire cages a couple of feet in diameter with long wire handles (watch this closely – the shorter the handle the hardier the swinger – that's a lot of heat to have four foot away from your hair). Each swinger has developed their own secret recipe for the fuel inside the cage – you want something that will burn  evenly, keep alight for 40 minutes and not have too many sparks. When it's all packed up it weighs a good 20 pounds, so a combination of decent upper body strength and a fair bit of skill is needed in the handling!

Rumour has it that some of the most successful 'recipes' include coal and wood, old socks and jumpers soaked in paraffin, pine cones and pine branches – whatever can add to the blaze. The Stonehaven Fireball Committee, who organise the event, keep an eye on each fireball; they all have to be passed for safety before being lit. The committee also awards a prize for the most impressive fireball of the year.[35]

---

[31]  *The normal population of the town is only 11,000 souls!*

[32]  *Traditionally it would have been local men, but now there are some women too.*

[33]  *Goodness gracious!*

[34]  *So don't wear your best clothes – you usually go home with a few burn holes! And wrap up warm – that's one cold coastline!*

[35]  *A prize for burning ambition.*

## The Burghead Clavie

On Old New Year's Day – 11 January – in the small town of Burghead in Moray (north of Stonehaven), an even older ceremony is enacted. It is entrusted to one local man, 'the Clavie King', and his nine elected helpers, 'the Clavie Crew',[36] who are typically members of the burgh's fishing fleet.

The Clavie is a large barrel packed full of peat and wood.[37] The King and his crew set it up outside the old provost's[38] house in the town and it's from the provost's fire that the barrel gets lit. The Clavie King then picks it up and carries it on his shoulders and starts the procession clockwise around the town – symbolising the journey of the Sun. Every so often, the procession will stop at a house[39] to offer a burning stick to the residents to light their New Year's fire – a great honour which brings great good fortune.[40] One of the crew will then take over the carrying for a spell.

Once the town is circled, the Clavie is attached to the old fort on Doorie Hill (always using the same nail[41]) and is refilled so that it will burn away for the rest of the night, with fire trickling down the hill. When the fire burns itself out, that's the cue to join in the food, drink and music in the town's hotels and bars.

The fire ritual of lighting your own hearth from some central solar

---

[36]  *Interesting echoes of the Krewes responsible for the Mardi Gras parade in New Orleans.*

[37]  *Ancient tradition would have this as a herring cask – all that fish oil would certainly burn, but in reflection of the change in the economy, it is an old whisky barrel that's now used, probably sealed with a bit of creosote.*

[38]  *The provost is the mayor of a Scottish burgh; in cities a lord provost.*

[39]  *And in the old times, every boat in the harbour too. It was thought to be propitious to name a new boat during this ceremony; the last recorded was the* Doorie *in 1875, but then the marine insurers began to get cold feet about having a burning barrel on a wooden boat.*

[40]  *In fact, people will scramble for any embers that fall from the barrel – so they too can start a fire from the Clavie. Even a cold ember kept in the house will bring luck.*

[41]  *They know the value of a good nail up in Moray!*

substitute appears to be ancient and reminiscent of Celtic rites, so this ceremony looks to be very old indeed – we do know that the local kirk tried to suppress it in 1704, worried that the whole thing was:

> idolatrous, sinfule and heathenish[42]

But unfortunately[43] that only encouraged the fisherman on to more fun![44]

## Uphill Struggles

We Scots like our mountains, and the chance to build a cairn or bonfire on the top of one is hard to resist. It is a long-standing convention that one should never pass a cairn without adding a stone. I think that Jews place pebbles on graves, as opposed to flowers, and maybe there's some link in the philosophy. Certainly the apogee of cairn architecture was in the reign of Queen Victoria[45] – Albert had a good run in the manly Scottish pursuits (fishing, shooting stags and birds, and gathering rocks) and when he popped his royal clogs in 1861, the disconsolate queen basically hid herself in Balmoral, wrapped in the comforting tartan excess of their joint creation and planning a countrywide commemoration of her late

---

[42]  *Kirk Session Minutes, Burghead.*

[43]  *From the minister's viewpoint at least.*

[44]  *Although, in a nod to the organised religion, the ceremony is never held on a Sunday. If the 11th is on the Sabbath, the Clavie is burned on the Saturday before.*

[45]  *Her first foray was on 11 October 1852, to mark taking possession of Balmoral: Her Late Majesty recorded: 'I then placed the first stone, after which Albert laid one, then the children, according to ages. All the ladies and gentlemen placed one; and then everyone came forward at once, each person carrying a stone and placing it on the cairn. Mackay played; and whisky was given to all... it took, I am sure, an hour building [and] some merry reels were danced on a stone opposite. At last, when the cairn [was] seven or eight feet high... Albert climbed up to the top of it, and placed the last stone; after which three cheers were given... I felt almost inclined to cry... the whole so gemütlich',* Leaves from the Journal of Our life in the Highlands: From 1848 to 1861, HM *Queen Victoria, Folio Society, 1973, pp.63–5.*

husband. Amongst the Scottish memorials to her hero[46] the great Cairn an Lurchain on the Balmoral Estate is best worth seeing.

Lighting fires at the tops of hills and bens continues today, most notably on great occasions like the Queen's jubilee or the millennium, but one village still celebrates its New Year in an old fashioned hill-fire ceremony. Falkland in Fife is the pleasant village nestling beside Falkland Palace.[47] It's famous for two reasons – rather improbably it has a cricket team which has won the British Village Cricket Cup several times[48] and it has a Hogmanay hill walk. In the run-up to midnight all the village men climb the Lomond Hills behind the village, each carrying a candle, to bring in the New Year.

---

[46]    *As if the Albert Memorial and Royal Albert Hall in London were not monumental enough, the Queen's grief spilled into a statue of Albert in kilt (Cliveden, Bucks); another in Perth; a memorial tablet on the spot he shot his last stag in Balmoral – nothing for the stag, mind you; equestrian statues in Charlotte Square, Edinburgh and George Square, Glasgow; while in the Royal Mausoleum in Frogmore near Windsor, the queen and her prince lie in sarcophagi of Aberdeenshire granite. (Let alone the Albert Docks, the Albert Bridge, the Albert Embankment and, most famous of all, Albert Square in Eastenders.)*

[47]    *A former royal timeshare.*

[48]    *Although cricket is quintessentially English, some with Scottish links have captained the English national team – Mike Denness (Ayr Academy, Essex and MCC); Douglas 'bodyline' Jardine (Winchester, Oxford U, MCC) – albeit with varying degrees of lack of success, or lack thereof.*

## Up Helly Aa

The northern archipelagos of Orkney and Shetland hold themselves very different to the Scots of the mainland. Historically, genealogically and culturally, the inhabitants of these islands are descended from the Nordic kingdoms. They became part of the Scottish crown by quite an odd route, these lands having been pledged as security for the dowry of one of the Scandinavian princesses upon her marrying James III. Things didn't work out as planned, for the tide of history had turned against the mighty Vikings, as the old rape-and-pillage business wasn't yielding the cash that it once did. They fell behind in their payments, blotted their credit record, and the two sets of islands were foreclosed upon to settle the debt.[49]

Whatever the passport carried, the culture remains rooted in the Norse sagas. And the biggest example of that is Up Helly Aa – without a doubt *the* fire festival to see.

For centuries the lads of Shetland's capital, Lerwick, got their New Year kicks by rolling tar barrels[50] up and down the rather narrow streets, to the discomfort of the more genteel inhabitants (and with the loss of the odd finger or two in the process). The middle classes got their way after a good 50 years of whingeing and the last tar rolling was in 1870, replaced by what was planned to be a more sedate torchlight procession.

They hadn't accounted for the exuberance of the lads, though! The first 10 years saw a fairly traditional (i.e. noisy) fancy dress parade with torches, then in 1880 someone had the bright idea to reach back into the warlike history of the Vikings and include a mock longboat in the procession. By 1906 the modern festival had taken shape.[51]

The festival is presided over by the Guizer Jarl,[52] who will have served on the organising committee for at least a dozen years. In a closely-guarded secret, he will choose to dress as one of the heroes of the Sagas

---

[49]  *Some maintain that Norway would have the right to repay the original debt plus interest and get the title deeds back, but no one really wants that.*

[50]  *Ablaze, of course!*

[51]  *And even the middle classes enjoyed it.*

[52]  *'The Fancy-Dress Earl'.*

and will build a team of 50 chums to be the Jarl's Squad – his body-guard for the day. Each of them will be dressed in the trappings of a great Norse warrior.

This underestimates the preparation – for the Guizer Jarl shares the stage with a perfectly-built 30-foot-long replica Viking longboat, which has to be built from scratch in four months.

On the last Tuesday of January, all the preparation comes to fruition – regardless of wind or weather.[53] At 7.30pm a warning flare is fired and the Guizer Jarl appears, in helmet and shield and bearing a mighty battle axe, to take his proud place at the helm of his dragon-prowed longboat. Nearly a thousand men,[54] all in fancy dress – these are the Guizers[55] – each carrying a huge burning torch, drag the land-bound ship to its Ragnarök[56] through the throngs of cheering onlookers.

After a hard pull of 30 or 40 minutes, the ship arrives at the burning place and the Guizers march round her until the signal is given for the Guizer Jarl to leave his ship to her fate. He joins his men on the ground and, as the bugles signal, each and every Guizer hurls his flaming torch into the boat until she is entirely engulfed in fire – recreating the traditional Viking funeral, which took the war chiefs of old straight to the halls of their gods – Valhalla.

And the whole crowd sings – five or six thousand people[57] join in the traditional songs.

The rest of the night centres on the many parties set up in the halls and hotels of Lerwick – they are mainly private, but there are a few where tickets are sold to outsiders. Food and drink flows, and each of the Guizer companies visits each venue to put on a show – a political or

---

[53] *Lerwick is as far north as Greenland and Siberia, but the festival has never been cancelled through inclement weather (the two world wars did cause a lull, but that's because the warriors were really bearing arms in those dark years).*

[54] *Gender equality was not a traditional attribute of Norse society – though the Valkyries did their bit – but I'm not getting into an argument with a beefy guy and a battle axe...*

[55] *We'll pick this theme up at Hallowe'en.*

[56] *Or Götterdämerung, for Wagner buffs.*

[57] *And not many dry eyes!*

cheeky skit on current affairs.[58] Importantly, to get a drink, each Guizer
has to dance with one of the womenfolk present. It's a long and happy
night, so it's just as well that dawn is late in the Northern Islands!

It's hardly a surprise after this, the flaming Mardi Gras, that the next
day is a public holiday in Lerwick.[59]

So here our northernmost isles again assert their individual culture
and heritage, which reflects the unique links Scotland has with the
Scandinavian countries.

> The king sits in Dunfermline town,
>  Drinking the blood-red wine;
> 'O where shall I get a steely skipper
>  To sail this ship o' mine?'
>
> Then up and spake an eldern knight,
>  Sat at the King's right knee:
> 'Sir Patrick Spens is the best sailor
>  That ever sailed the sea.'
>
> The King has written a broad letter,
>  And sealed it with his hand,
> And sent it to Sir Patrick Spens,
>  Was walking on the strand.
>
> 'To Noroway, to Noroway,
>  To Noroway o'er the foam;
> The King's daughter of Noroway,
>  'Tis thou must fetch her home.'

---

[58]  *On the morning a satirical 'Bill' is stuck to the Market Cross – it's usually a
good tease on local politicians and worthies.*

[59]  *Although most have got their second wind by then and join in the dance at
the Guizers' Hop that night. Over the following weeks every squad of Guizers
holds its own squad party for its wider family, and then, before you know it,
it's time to start planning next year.*

The first line that Sir Patrick read,
 A loud laugh laughed he;
The next line that Sir Patrick read,
 The tear blinded his ee.

'O who is this has done this deed,
 Has told the King of me,
To send us out at this time of the year,
 To sail upon the sea?'

'Be it wind, be it wet, be it hail, be it sleet,
 Our ship must sail the foam;
The king's daughter of Noroway,
 'Tis we must fetch her home.'[60]

---

[60]   'Ballad of Sir Patrick Spens', Traditional. The remaining verses tell of the tragedy of Sir Patrick and his crew, drowned in the winter storms.

# 3

# The Burns Supper

On my lonely walks, I have often thought how fine it would be
to have the company of Burns. And indeed he was always with
me, for I had him by heart. On my first long walk from Indiana
to the Gulf of Mexico I carried a copy of Burns' poems and
sung them all the way. The whole country and the people, beasts
and birds, seemed to like them... Wherever a Scotsman goes,
there goes Burns. His grand whole, catholic soul squares with
the good of all; therefore we find him in everything everywhere.

*John Muir*[1]

BURNS NIGHT IS SCOTLAND'S greatest celebration bar none[2] and so I have
little shame in devoting a chapter to it here, having already assaulted the
reading public with *The Ultimate Burns Supper Book*,[3] which promoted
my long-held theory that Burns Suppers had become too formulaic at times
and that all you really needed to do was follow McGinn's three precepts:

- Have as many or as few people as you want to invite.

- Have as much food and drink as you can afford.

- Have as much or as little formality as you all feel comfortable
  with (but don't forget the three essential elements: a haggis,
  a poem or song and a toast to Robert Burns).

However, some friends and readers did point out that many Burns Suppers
follow as fixed a journey as a train, and while I might recommend that a

---

[1]  *The great conservationist often said that a perfect day was throwing a loaf
of bread and the works of Burns in a knapsack and climbing over the back
wall into the wilderness.*

[2]  *And I do mean 'bar'...*

[3]  *Available in good bookshops or on Amazon – if you are looking for a
second-hand copy, go for an unsigned one – they're much rarer and hence
more valuable.*

small group travel by taxi, a lot of folk like the familiarity of the railway journey.

So here is an analysis of a traditional[4] format for the evening at which you will have more fun than you've ever had – and if you are a laddie, that's without wearing a pair of trousers, too.

Burns, the National Bard of Scotland and a man of very ordinary upbringing, was born in a cottage in Alloway beside the town of Ayr on 25 January 1759, and it's on or around this day we party.

That being said, the 'season' really runs from about 15 January to the end of February[5] due to a combination of (a) people preferring Thursday/ Friday/Saturday nights and (b) the explosive growth in people wanting to attend Burns Suppers. But in the spirit of trying to find the common theme, you'll probably be invited on the nearest Thursday, Friday or Saturday to the date of the 25th.[6]

The amazing thing is that more people celebrate at Burns Suppers across the globe every single year than there were people alive in Scotland in Burns's time. An extraordinary thought, for Burns left Scotland only once, for a short trip from Newcastle upon Tyne to Carlisle. He was pretty disenchanted because his horse got a 'parking ticket' in the latter town, so he went home and stayed in Scotland for the rest of his life. Yet after death, he's visited every corner of the globe.

So – how do we start?

- If you've never been: Have a quick look through this guide and, if you have time and access, read a bit about Rabbie and maybe listen to a CD of his songs.

---

[4]  *Dangerous word; perhaps 'typical' or for the statistically-minded 'median' (for no Burns event could ever be mean).*

[5]  *Our Welsh friends celebrate St David on 1 March and it would be churlish to interrupt their leeks and daffodils – even if St David was probably born in Scotland…*

[6]  *Some big events have a formula to help you plan ahead: the Scottish Bankers – the largest Burns Supper in the world – is always held on the fourth Friday of January in the Grosvenor House Hotel in London; that could be as early as the 22nd or as late as 28th. If you hold it on the last Friday, it could be as late as the 31st.*

- If you are a regular: Sponge the stains off last year's kilt, polish your brogues to a dazzling sheen and look forward to another great evening.
- Everyone: Arrive at the appointed time, following Raymond Chandler's dictum: to be 'neat, clean, shaved and sober'.[7]

Whether the dinner is being held in a grand banqueting room or the local church hall, the evening will often begin with the seated guests clapping as the organisers and the speakers are piped in procession to their seats at the top table. At that time, the chairman of the evening will welcome everyone and will ask for heads to be bowed so that Grace can be said.

Many people think of Burns as a confirmed atheist, but they are very wrong. Throughout his short life he kept his faith, although he reserved the right[8] to question the ecclesiastical follies perpetrated by ordained but ordinary men in God's name.

One of the themes he often returned to was giving thanks – in every way – for the gifts he had been given. Gifts of food – and drink – as well as of life, babies, friendship and poetry. So it's not surprising that our evenings will start with a local member of the clergy, or the dinner chairman, asking the company to say Grace.

Almost universally, the words will be the Selkirk Grace:[9]

Some hae meat, and canna eat,
And some wad eat but want it;
But we hae meat, and we can eat,
And sae the LORD be thankit.[10]
AMEN

---

[7]  The Big Sleep, *Chapter 1. Chandler was a Burns fan.*

[8]  *As many of us do still.*

[9]  *Listen to the words and see how they cover our human situation, regardless of gender, faith or race.*

[10] *Many people are unhappy with this attribution as a Burns poem. It is certainly a version of an older prayer, in my opinion crafted by Burns into this form. It is now hallowed by tradition. 'Some have food but cannot eat, and some who hunger have none; but we have food and the appetite too, bless us Lord, every one.' Please note that 'meat' is any food – 'butcher meat' or flesh would have been relatively rare compared to the vegetables and porridge of the ordinary folk.*

Increasingly, the words are printed on the menu, so the company can join in, and at the end, in either case, those moved to do so will join in the 'amen'.

Most Burns Suppers will err on the simple side when it comes to choosing the menu. Starter followed by haggis (compulsory[11]), then a robust main course, rounded off with pudding and cheese.

But it's fair to say one course attracts all the attention – or do I mean fear?

## The Haggis

The 'Great chieftain o' the puddin' race'[12] is one of the few mandatory parts of any Burns celebration. Our poet used to call on some friends who were so poor all they could afford to serve him for dinner was haggis every time. One day, the wife's apologies caused Rabbie to compose the mock-heroic poem addressing the haggis as the epitome of Scotland, to the pride and joy of his friend, who was never ashamed again. The rest, as they say, is history.

To be fair, there is a considerable proportion[13] of people – even in Scotland – who regard the Addressing the Haggis tradition as 'the incomprehensible followed by the inedible', but that's unfair. Better by far to think of the haggis as an oatmeal-based sausage rather than the sweepings of the butcher's floor. Just as you get premium sausages and horrible ones,[14] so you can get delicious haggis and pedestrian ones. There are two schools of haggis production:

- Lighter-coloured ones where oatmeal predominates.
- Darker versions, where the liver is the leading ingredient.[15]

---

[11]  *I expect you to clean your plate!*

[12]  *I don't have to tell you this reference – do I?*

[13]  *A majority?*

[14]  *When asked why more than half his sausage was breadcrumbs and binding, the English butcher is famed for saying that business was bad and so it was hard to make both ends meat...*

[15]  *And sometimes made with pork, not lamb.*

My preference is for an oatmeal-heavy haggis, but one with a good peppery kick of cayenne.[16] Whatever you choose, you'll serve this either as a 'taster' in between the starter and the main course or, as in the old days, a full main-course portion,[17] along with the traditional accompaniments:

- Champit tatties – as 'mashed potatoes' is translated.
- Bashit neeps – puréed turnips.[18]

There will very often be a dram of whisky beside your plate – you can pour it over the haggis (and take away the taste) or just drink it in one (and take away the fear).[19] Don't forget though that you'll need something in your glass as we are about to enjoy the first of the entertainments of the evening.

## Addressing the Haggis[20]

Before the plates of *delicious* haggis arrive at your table, the sound of the pipes will signal the ceremony of addressing the haggis. To rousing[21] tunes and the clapping of the audience, the piper leads in the chef, carrying a huge haggis on a silver salver, suitably festooned with greenery. The procession weaves its way through the room to the table where the ceremony will be performed. There stands the addressor.

---

[16] *Veggies and kosher or halal chefs will create acceptable variants nowadays, too.*

[17] *Usually this shows a foolhardy bravery or a keen desire to keep the food budget low.*

[18] *As I am still getting letters written in green ink on the controversy about what is a turnip and what a swede, I'll leave you to look it up in Volume 1. Just to remind you, we're cooking here with the large root vegetable that is orangey-yellow inside and cooks to an orange mush.*

[19] *Though purists often frown at the former – but let them sneer if they want to!*

[20] *There is a great tradition of the mock-heroic in Scottish poems – Burns and Robert Ferguson are notable in this genre. The important point is that it is 'mock' or tongue-in-cheek.*

[21] *Pretty loud in an enclosed banqueting room; it will take you a few minutes to get your hearing back.*

This lady or gentleman has the duty of reciting Burns's own 'Address to a Haggis' from memory – to the terror of the audience and the extinction of the haggis. Many nowadays turn this into a hugely enjoyable act – with gestures, noises and actions. Joking apart, I find these help people understand – roughly speaking – what's going on in the poem. But equally traditionally, you can find a quieter approach, which looks to deliver the music of the poetry by a simple exhortation of the words.

If you wanted, you could summarise the whole thing in a quick mnemonic condensing each verse to one line:

CHIEF of sausages
With mighty BUM
KNIFE to slice you
And set off SCRUM
GRIEF over stews
Makes foreigners GLUM
LIFE is better
If the haggis COME.[22]

The one obligatory point[23] is that a knife is picked up and wiped clean (either on the cloth or, most likely, the addressor's sleeve) at the verse starting 'his knife' and then the haggis is stabbed at the words 'an' cut ye up'.[24] This can cause some collateral damage if the haggis was stuffed too full – so make sure you are sitting quite far away!

At the end of the poem, to cheers and applause, the chairman will give the addressor, the piper and the chef their glasses of whisky and then lead them and the whole audience in toasting the haggis.

That's the cue for the piper to start up and for the chef to pick up the last mortal remains on his tray, both retiring to the kitchen to plate it out with the mash and neeps, giving us all a chance to eat.

---

[22]  *See the interesting discussion 'Thirteen Ways Of Glossing To A Haggis',
Mark Watson (IJSL Issue 6).*

[23]  *I'm not sure if that's a pun or not.*

[24]  *Highlighted in the poem below.*

## Address to a Haggis[25]

| | |
|---|---|
| Fair fa' your honest, sonsie face, | *You've an honest, round and jolly face,* |
| Great chieftain o' the puddin' race! | *Great chieftain of the sausage race!* |
| Aboon them a' ye tak your place, | *Above them all you take your place,* |
| Painch, tripe, or thairm: | *Offal, tripe, or lamb:* |
| Weel are ye wordy of a grace | *You are most worthy of a grace* |
| As lang's my arm. | *As long's my arm.* |

The groaning trencher there ye fill,
Your hurdies like a distant hill,
Your pin[26] wad help to mend a mill
In time o' need,
While thro' your pores the dews distil
Like amber bead.

*The groaning platter there you fill,*
*Your buttocks like a distant hill,*
*Your skewer could help mend a mill*
*In time of need,*
*While through your pores the dews distil*
*Like amber bead.*

His knife see rustic labour dight,[27]
An' cut ye up wi' ready slight,[28]
Trenching your gushing entrails bright,
Like onie ditch;
And then, O what a glorious sight,
Warm-reeking, rich!

*His knife is wiped with rustic might,*
*To cut you up with ready sleight,*
*Digging up gushing entrails bright,*
*Like out a ditch;*
*And then, O what a glorious sight,*
*Warm, steaming, rich!*

Then horn for horn, they stretch an'
    strive:
Deil tak the hindmost, on they drive,
Till a' their weel-swall'd kytes belyve
Are bent like drums;
Then auld guidman, maist like to rive,
'Bethankit!' hums.

*Then spoon for spoon, they stretch out*
    *fast:*
*On they drive – hell take the last,*
*Till all the swollen guts so vast*
*Are tight as drums;*
*Then old grandpa, most fit to burst,*
*'Thanks Be!', he hums.*

---

[25] 'Address to a Haggis', Robert Burns, a new verse translation by Clark McGinn: reprinted as so many people ask for an explanation in detail.

[26] This needs some more explanation – the old way of handling the cooking haggis was to tie the ends to a long wooden pin, so it could be lifted in and out of the boiling pan.

[27] Get your knife out here and give it a rub.

[28] And now give the haggis a belt with the knife: a gentle stab or a backhanded blow – your choice!

Is there that owre his French ragout,
Or olio that wad staw a sow,
Or fricassee wad mak her spew
Wi' perfect scunner,
Looks down wi' sneering, scornfu' view
On sic a dinner?

*Who, with a plate of French ragout,*
*Or pig-sickening oily stew,*
*Or fricassee to make you throw*
*With real distaste,*
*Looks down with sneering, scornful view*
*On such a feast?*

Poor devil! see him owre his trash,
As feckless as a wither'd rash,
His spindle shank a guid whip-lash,
His nieve a nit;
Tho' bluidy flood or field to dash,
O how unfit!

*Poor devil! see him eat his trash,*
*As feeble as a withered rush,*
*His skinny legs a mere whip-lash,*
*His fist a nut;*
*Through bloody flood or field to dash,*
*O how unfit!*

But mark the rustic, haggis-fed,
The trembling earth resounds his tread,
Clap in his walie nieve a blade,
He'll make it whistle;
An' legs, an' arms, an' heads will sned
Like taps o' thrissle.

*But mark the rustic, haggis-fed,*
*The trembling earth resounds his tread,*
*His big fist holds a knife of dread,*
*He'll make it whistle;*
*Chopping legs, arms, and every head*
*Like tops of thistle.*

Ye pow'rs, wha mak mankind your
  care,
And dish them out their bill o' fare,
Auld Scotland wants nae skinking ware,
That jaups in luggies;
But if ye wish her gratfu' prayer,
Gie her a Haggis!

*You powers, who make mankind your*
  *care,*
*And dish them out their bill of fare,*
*Old Scotland want no soupy ware,*
*To splosh in dishes;*
*But if you wish her grateful prayer,*
*Give her a Haggis!*

## The Loyal Toast and the Pit Stop

By now you should feel pretty stuffed;[29] the staff will fill your glasses and we move back into the formal proceedings.

At very formal events, there is a longstanding rule that the health of Her Majesty the Queen should be drunk as the first toast. The chairman

---

[29]   *TTT as my Auntie Peg used to say – 'Tummy Touching Table'*

will rise, call for silence and ask everyone to stand with a glass in their hand. Simply then, he proposes a toast: 'The Queen'[30] and everyone repeats the toast and drinks.[31]

The Loyal Toast[32] has a subordinate but important role too: to signal the break of 15 minutes to allow everyone to nip out to the loo[33] before the entertainment starts. Make sure that you are back in your place by the appointed hour, or face the wrath of the chairman!

## Speeches and Entertainment

I would always prefer to say 'entertainment including the speeches', as I do hope the speakers will provide enjoyment too! A chairman once asked an audience I was about to address the chilling question: 'Lads are ye ready for the boy tae start his speech, or would ye like to enjoy yersels a few minutes mair?'

Ever since the first Burns Supper, one guest has risen to present his or her view of an aspect of Burns's life, works or story in the toast 'To the Immortal Memory of Robert Burns'. It's a difficult speech to get right; in fact Abraham Lincoln – no slouch on the podium – famously declined to give the IM, writing:

---

[30]  *In the Scots Guards and some Gaelic societies, the toast is 'Deoch slainte ne bhan Righ' (doch slaye van ree) or 'God give health to the king'.*

[31]  *If you are observant, you'll notice that some don't. Some nationalists in Scotland with romantic attachment to the lost cause of the Stuart monarchy will wave their glasses over water jugs to toast not the crown in London but the 'crown over the water'; while there are left-wingers who are anti-monarchical, preferring the tyranny of party politics to that of primogeniture.*

[32]  *Internationally, you'll find two toasts, one to the queen as monarch of Scotland and, out of courtesy, one to the head of state in the host country – so watch out and don't empty your glass on the first toast!*

[33]  *John (US), possibly Cludgie (Glasgow) or Netty (Newcastle). In the US this is called a 'comfort break' – linguistic difficulties abound! When I first was met off a plane in the US, my hosts asked if I needed to visit the rest room. 'It's OK,' said I, 'I'm not tired at all.' Blank looks…*

> I cannot frame a toast to Burns. I can say nothing worthy of his generous heart and transcending genius[34]

Too many times have I seen the audience adopt the rhetorical 'brace position': fill your glass and slump back in your chair fearing the next 45 minutes. It shouldn't be like that!

The Immortal Memory should be in tune with the audience – a function of how well they know Burns and how light the evening is. In the bad old days, the Immortal Memory was accorded the reverence due to Sunday's sermon in the kirk and – alas! – had to be longer. I believe it's much better to have 15 minutes that can be understood and appreciated by all than to have an endurance competition.[35] The speaker and the speech should always match the audience.

Writing a good speech is like making a haggis. Many are scared at the size and composition – but if you get the mix correct – it's melt-in-the-mouth. Try blending these traditional ingredients:

- Oatmeal: this simple Scottish fare is the story of Robert Burns himself, with a focus on his life and loves – and fills the tummy comfortably.

- Liver: adds a strong taste. The look at the texts and writings of the man – harder to digest in general, but the right proportion adds colour and flavour.

- Cayenne pepper: spice up the mixture with a good few[36] jokes and witticisms.

- Whisky: round it all off with the warmth and tradition of Scottish hospitality – a nice-sized dram but not too much at once.

---

[34] *From the* Forbes Collection of Presidential Autographs. *Lincoln famously could recite all of Burns by heart. His fellow busts on Mount Rushmore agreed: Jefferson called Burns 'my favourite still by far'; Washington was pleased to be the subject of one poem; and, of course, Teddy carried Burns in his knapsack in the Badlands.*

[35] *Of course, there are specialist dinners where the academic approach is essential, but please don't take Sunday ramblers up the Eiger!*

[36] *Or at least a few good.*

At the end, the speaker will ask everyone to fill their glasses and stand, to join in the toast 'TO THE IMMORTAL MEMORY OF ROBERT BURNS'.

Cheers all round and a few quick glasses for the speaker, now happily off duty.

## Sangs an' Ploys

In a change of pace after the applause[37] has died down there will usually be a performance of some of Rabbie's works.

> See the smoking bowl before us,
>   Mark our jovial, ragged ring!
> Round and round take up the chorus,
>   And in rapture let us sing[38]

Typically in the evening you will have some of his songs, a recitation of his poetry, maybe exhibitions of Scottish country dancing, or a solo performance from the piper or a virtuoso on the fiddle or the accordion.

These pop up in between the speeches – giving some respite to the listeners and a little longer to panic for the next speaker up.

My preference is to have some singing after the Immortal Memory (as it's the longest speech), and what a collection of songs there is to choose from. One of the legacies of Burns is that he worked tirelessly to capture the folk songs of Scotland in his later years. Sometimes he'd transcribe a whole traditional lyric and its music, other times all he'd have was a fragment, which he'd lovingly rebuild.

His songs stir our hearts in many ways still: songs of love, of course, such as 'My Luv Is Like A Red, Red Rose', 'Ye Banks An' Braes' or 'Ae Fond Kiss'; but there are many others: songs of valour like 'Scots Wa' Hae' and songs which call across the world: 'A Man's a Man'.[39]

---

[37] *Polite or hearty – or horror: the slow handclap.*

[38] *'The Jolly Beggars'.*

[39] *Which so memorably was sung by Sheena Wellington at the opening of the Scottish Parliament.*

If you are really lucky, you might be at one of the old Scottish suppers where the singing becomes communal, with song sheets at each table – something rather special and quite in keeping with our poet's style.

Turning to the poems (which you'll hear shortly, after the next speech), the first thing that everyone worries about is: will I understand them?

Certainly to a greater or lesser extent Burns revels in the Ayrshire dialect of his day, a dialect that was already at that point beginning to crumble in the 'globalisation' of English.[40]

If you relax and 'go with the flow' you'll start to pick up the gist of the poem – particularly if you have an accomplished performer who can help with a clear voice, well-stressed metre and perhaps hand gestures to point you in the right direction. Not unlike a good haggis addressor, the performer of the great poems can call upon the mimetic arts to create a theatrical illustration of whatever he's reciting.

Two favourite poems are often performed: 'Holy Willie's Prayer' and 'Tam o' Shanter'.

**'Holy Willie'** Fisher was a God-fearing Elder of Mauchline Church by day and an absolute hypocrite by night.[41] Burns knew him, but only came into warfare when Holy Willie attacked one of our Poet's mentors. This is a coruscating poem of invective and still makes us laugh today. You'll find a performer, dressed in Willie's nightshirt, night cap and candle, about to say his prayers in the 'privacy' of his chamber (with us as merry eavesdroppers) – and what a prayer: a combination of spleen against his enemies and confession of his own sins (repeated sins!) of lust and drink.[42]

**Tam o' Shanter** on the other hand is one often most expansive poems

---

[40]   *My edition of the old warhorse of Reference,* Brewer's Dictionary of Phrase and Fable, *has the memorable entry: 'Broad Scotch (Braid Scots). The vernacular of the lowlands of* SCOTLAND; *very different from the enunciation of Edinburgh and from the peculiarity of the Glasgow dialect' (Centenary Edn, 1952).*

[41]   *Actually he was a stinker in the day, too! Not as fun as Deacon Brodie...*

[42]   *Art often imitates life, and vice versa. Fisher fell off his horse (drunk in charge of a quadruped) and was so intoxicated that he froze to death. He still lies in Mauchline churchyard as he lied in life; but were his prayers answered, or did he thaw out in a very much warmer place?*

in the canon. Burns's avowed masterpiece takes us through an evening with Tam, an up-country farmer. After market day is over, and in defiance of his wife's stern injunctions, he blows a goodly proportion of the day's takings in the warmth of the pub. Fortunately, Meg, his old grey horse, can find the way home better than her drunken master and they set off in the storm to go home. But evil portents are all around and as Tam approaches the ruins of Alloway Kirk he hears music – Satan himself playing the bagpipes, with witches and warlocks dancing.[43] Tam, transfixed, notices one pretty witch with longer legs (and a shorter shroud) and forgets himself, calling 'Weel done Cutty Sark!'[44]

This is not a good idea, as Tam now has to flee for his life and soul, chased by the hosts of hell. Cutty Sark is the fastest, but Meg and Tam know that witches cannot cross running water. Just as Meg gets to the brow of the Brig o' Doon, Cutty Sark catches her tail, but Meg jumps forward bringing Tam to safety – but she never had a tail on her rump again!

Burns can't help thinking of the moral to the tale – one that affects him, Holy Willie and Tam – and, hand on heart, many of us:

> Now, wha this tale o' truth shall read,
> Ilka man and mother's son, take heed:                    [Each]
> Whene'er to Drink you are inclin'd,
> Or Cutty-sarks rin in your mind,
> Think ye may buy the joys o'er dear;
> Remember Tam o' Shanter's mare.[45]

The possibilities for acting this out are, like the witches, legion. Costumes (hats[46] and wigs), props (a grey hobby horse) and/or special effects (flashing the lights on and off for the lightning![47]), the poem carries you along like Meg carries Tam.

---

[43]  *Scottish country dances, of course.*

[44]  *'Well danced the lassie in the short shirt!'*

[45]  *'Tam o' Shanter', final stanza.*

[46]  *Including, of course, a blue 'Tam o' Shanter' hat – with or without an attached fake wig of orange hair, as the 'Tammie' evolves into the 'Jimmy'.*

[47]  *But be careful – in 2006 an enterprising chap doing this fused the entire New Club in Edinburgh!*

## The Toast to the Lassies and the Reply to the Toast to the Lassies

Probably in between some songs and some poems we'll hear this next pair of speeches, celebrating the relationship, love and rivalry between the sexes. They use a tradition that's less that a hundred years old, but is a really pleasing part of the evening,[48] being totally light-hearted; and of course, Rab was a bit of an expert on the subject!

> Auld Nature swears, the lovely dears
>  Her noblest work she classes, O:
> Her prentice han' she try'd on man,
>  An' then she made the lasses, O.[49]

The idea is simple – Boys in the blue corner and Girls in the red come out for a bit of verbal boxing.

The Toast to the Lassies (or Lasses) is a humorous look at womankind. It need not be anchored in Burns (though he knew more about women that most of us) and so a great deal of freedom is permitted to create a funny speech.[50] After the Laddie toasts all the ladies (only the men in the audience rise to this toast), the Lassie takes the floor to reply, using the last word to good verbal and witty effect. For years, this second speech was a thank you, but increasingly it's developed into the Toast to the Laddies, and all the lassies present will toast the lads.

A good pair of speeches will show some common themes and will be like a verbal tennis match. Over my 30 years, I've yet to see the Laddie win![51]

---

[48]   *They are not really mandatory, and it's better to miss them out if you can't find a good pair of speakers.*

[49]   *'Green Grow the Rashes O'.*

[50]   *Please note that it must not be a 'blue' speech.*

[51]   *And if that isn't a moral, I don't know what is.*

## Auld Lang Syne

We've talked about the origins and meanings of ALS already in Hogmanay (but maybe you were too drunk that night to remember – nip back to the first chapter and check to refresh your memory). Burns was captivated by the words of this song and ALS will draw this great Burns Supper to its formal close.

Just time after, perhaps, for a last few handshakes, a fare-thee-weel kiss or that last dram before turning in, refreshed in the company and the genius of a man who lived for all of us and wrote for each of us.

For me (and many Scots of blood or sympathy) this is truly our greatest celebration of the year. And it's odd; I think Burns foretold this. One day he said to his loving (and long-suffering) wife Jean Armour, 'they'll think mair o' me in a hunner year that they do today'. How true that is, for today (which is 250 years on) Burns manages both to be definitively Scottish and to reach out across the world.

## Hangover

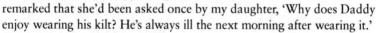

Not an obligatory part of the proceedings, but I have noticed a statistical correlation. At one of my own Burns Suppers, a good friend[52] remarked that she'd been asked once by my daughter, 'Why does Daddy enjoy wearing his kilt? He's always ill the next morning after wearing it.'

> A last request permit me here,—
>   When yearly ye assemble a',
> One round, I ask it with a tear,                    [toast]
> To him, the Bard that's far awa.[53]

---

[52]  *Linda Sutherland from Aberdeen.*

[53]  *'The Farewell to the Brethren of St James's Lodge, Tarbolton', Robert Burns. Written as Burns was expecting to emigrate to Jamaica and a slave planta-tion, but look at it as an injunction that has been followed every year – to drink to our Bard who is awa' but whose legacy of genius inspires us.*

# 4

# The Scottish Diet
# (And Other Oxymorons)

*And it's ill speaking between a fou man and a fasting.*[1]

PHILOSOPHERS HAVE SAID that 'you are what you eat'. Where does that leave the Scots?

There used to be a nationalist slogan 'It's Scotland's oil', referring to the North Sea; I always thought it referred to deep fat frying!

For many years Scottish cooking was looked at in pretty much the same light as Scottish football[2] – occasional glimpses of divine genius based on limited raw materials, but in the end, more unsatisfactory than not. Cynics abroad[3] despaired that the Scottish diet was rooted in a culture of 'kill it quickly and fry it deeply'. Our great national resource of fish was mainly enjoyed battered and fried with chips, well endowed with salt and vinegar.[4]

As the world globalised, international cuisine established itself in the fast food restaurants of Scotland. The Chinese came first, bringing cross-cultural favourites such as fried balls of Cantonese sweet and sour chicken and chips; the Indians contributed the pakora, the samosa and the bhaji to the fry basket (and of course curry sauce as a side order for your chips); and the Italians, already masters of the ice cream trade, realised that the only way to sell their native pizza was to quarter it and give it a good fry.

---

[1]   Redgauntlet, *Letter 11, Sir Walter Scott.*

[2]   *'Soccer' as called in some countries – a 1920s Oxford slang ellipsis: just as breakfast became 'brekkers' so Rugby football became 'rugger' and Association football, 'soccer'. The slang finally collapsed under its own weight and most words ended up in the wagger pagger bagger (sc. waste paper basket).*

[3]   *And a fair few cardiologists at home…*

[4]   *Or 'saut an sauce' as they prefer in the east.*

Now, the good news is that there is nothing quite as enjoyable as a fish supper[5] from a traditional chippie. The ideal location is in a bus stop after closing, with rain running down the walls, eating it with your fingers out the paper. All else is posh.

The bad news is that our love of frying (plus smoking and drinking[6]) led to an epidemic of heart disease that is still a trend, albeit thankfully declining.[7]

Our other contribution to the Oscars of fried food is the full Scottish breakfast. Yes our southern neighbours have their full English, but we have added our own national charm to it. Who could resist:

- A couple of rashers of **fried** Ayrshire bacon.
- One slice of **fried** Lorne sausage.[8]
- Two **fried** pork sausage links.
- Two or three **fried** eggs.
- A **fried** tattie scone.
- **Fried** Stornoway black pudding.
- A wee portion of **fried** haggis.
- A big dod of **fried** mushrooms.
- A nice **fried** tomato or two (with extra tomato sauce).
- And baked beans (not because we like them, just to prove that not everything we eat is **fried**).

Of course, you could be good and have a hot bowl of porridge instead. This is the ur-food of my country. As Burns calls it:

the halesome porritch, chief of Scotia's food[9]

On a winter's morning there is no better start to the day than a steaming

---

[5] *Fish supper = fish and chips. You can get a nice haggis supper, too.*

[6] *And a belief that exercise was watching the football.*

[7] *Glasgow's life expectancy is now just better than much of sub-Saharan Africa's.*

[8] *aka square sausage.*

[9] *'The Cottar's Saturday Night', Robert Burns.*

bowl of porage.[10] Traditionally it is made with water and salt, of course,[11] and in the oldest families always eaten standing up, in wooden bowls with horn spoons. Oddly enough this recipe is as good for your heart as every other is bad!

Nowadays Scotland's cuisine has moved away from the fry on the one hand and the high tea[12] on the other. When I was a lad, the only link to the Michelin style was the shape of the average consumer of pie, beans and chips, although as the years progressed intrepid souls moved through the deep-fried pizza, followed by similarly-cooked pakora, to the ultimare: the deep-fried Mars Bar. Now we have starred restaurants.[13]

That being said, our re-found cookbook can sometimes be a hard sell. It's another case of the Good (which people forget), the Bad (which we've just seen above) and the Ugly (our national dishes of haggis and boiled sheep's head feature prominently here!).

But what about the Good? – and there is plenty of it around today.

## Good Scots Fare

Leaving aside cliché (even true cliché), let's look at the real meals of quality that will fill the Scots tummy to fuel enthusiasm, enlightenment or empire building.

Our starters tend to be simple (largely because not many could afford them!). The most popular traditional soups are cock-a-leekie (a thin broth[14]

---

[10]   *There is a great controversy about how to eat this dish, but even more acrimony about how to spell it.*

[11]   *No sugar, certainly no honey.*

[12]   *Which is fried fish and chips or a fried mixed grill along with a three-tiered cake stand – toast at the bottom, scones in the middle and cream cakes at the summit.*

[13]   *Even in Leith Docks, until very recently the destination for a completely different social experience.*

[14]   *Broth is a general Scottish word for soup: Two Scotsmen opened a pub, which was doing very badly. The cleverer Glasgow lad said to his rather more posh and naïve Edinburgh partner that the only way to save the business was to turn it into a brothel. The reply came back: 'If they won't come in for whisky, why would they come in for broth?'*

with leeks and pieces of chicken[15]) and Scotch broth[16] (a lamb-based soup, thickened with heavy barley – this is often cooked three days in advance and tastes the better for the keeping!).

> I've supped gude bree i' muny a howff
>  Wi'in Auld Reekie,
> But nane wi' siccan a gusty gowff
>  As cock-a-leekie[17]

Other alternatives at the start of dinner might be our plain but high-quality Scottish fish,[18] such as our excellent salmon – typically smoked or maybe cured in whisky. A delicious alternative now is hot smoked – a pinker, flakier version of the standard.

The main course[19] is very often beef or steak for the carnivores. There's a lot of venison about, too. It is good to have a taste of Scotland's red meat, which was needed for red-blooded deeds!

> On siccan food has mony a doughty deed
> By Caledonia's ancestors been done[20]

It's fair to say that Scottish vegetarian cooking is still pretty primitive[21]

---

15  *Sometimes a prune or two is added. Legend has it that Mary Queen of Scots was fairly partial to a prune and so added them to this soup. However, I think it's more likely that there's been a confusion over the French word for a leek (le pruneau).*

16  *One of the few acceptable uses of the spelling 'Scotch' rather than 'Scots'. See also trifle, collops and woodcock (but not on the same plate).*

17  *Traditional rhyme.*

18  *As our patron saint is a fisherman, that's a nice symbol.*

19  *I am thinking about writing a cookery book on airline food called* Chicken or Beef? *(Not a choice, rather a question after you've eaten it...)*

20  *'The Farmer's Ingle', Robert Ferguson.*

21  *Although clapshot – one of Orkney's great gifts to the world – is superb: Boil two pans with equal amounts of potatoes and of turnip. When ready, take a bowl and mash both together with some butter (or for non-veggies, beef dripping from the butcher's) and salt and pepper to taste.*

but that being said, our salmon, trout and deep-water fish (and of course, our superlative shellfish) are excellent and there are a few ancient recipes which are worth looking out for – how about herrings in oatmeal or oven-roasted wild salmon, or maybe some big fat diver-caught scallops?[22]

Scottish people have a sweet tooth[23] and so much more effort and imagination has been spent in creating puddings. Scotch trifles, Edinburgh Fog, Blairgowrie Flummery, Athole Brose and the perfect Crannachan are superb (and often helpful words to know when playing Scrabble). Or for an alternative, there is an increasing availability of local hand-made cheeses, which, when eaten with oatcakes,[24] are a great way to participate in the new Scotland in terms of food.

Scottish cheese has changed radically in the last decade. No longer a choice between red cheddar, yellow cheddar or bright-yellow processed cheddar slices, this is a real home industry, exemplified by true artisans throughout the country.

I like to see a plate or board (of wood or maybe slate) with contrasting cheeses:

- Hard (like Dunlop) against soft (maybe one of the Crowdies or Caboc rolled in pinhead oatmeal).

- Sheep's milk cheese (try small rounds of Arran Crottin) versus goats' milk (from Galloway).

- Strong cheddar (from Isle of Mull) compared to one of the mild cheddars (from Orkney perhaps).

- Blue cheeses – Lanark Blue – the great revival of sharp blue sheep milk, measured against the cows' milk-made Dunsyre from Ayrshire.

---

[22]   *Fat scallops that is, not fat divers.*

[23]   *More accurately, given the national statistics on dental decay, 'had' a sweet tooth…*

[24]   *Sometimes described on the menu as 'kebbuck' (sc. cheese) and 'bannocks' (sc. oatcakes or buns).*

Add to these some onion marmalade or chutneys, a selection of oatcakes (some rough, some smooth, some salty), and apples, celery and grapes and your cheese board will have a real Scottish welcome to it.

## The Dark Corners of the Scots Cupboard

Haggis, and to a lesser extent[25] sheep's heid, aren't as bad as they sound.[26] I'd strongly suggest you give everything a quick try (you can always ask for an extra dram if you want to take the taste away!). If the chef gets the balance right, there will be a great choice of fine unfried local produce (and then you can have a fish supper on the way home if you're still hungry).

Eat well!

Imprimis, then, a haggis fat,
Weel tottl'd in a seything pat,
Wi' spice and ingans weel ca'd thro',
Had help'd to gust the stirrah's mow,
And plac'd itsel in truncher clean
Before the gilpy's glowrin een.
Secundo, then a gude sheep's head
Whase hide was singit, never flead,
And four black trotters cled wi' girsle,
Bedown his throat had learn'd to hirsle.
What think ye neist, o' gude fat brose
To clag his ribs? a dainty dose!
And white and bloody puddins routh,
To gar the Doctor skirl, O Drouth!
Whan he cou'd never houp to merit
A cordial o' reaming claret[27]

---

25  *i.e. it makes a nice soup.*

26  *On balance.*

27  *'To the Principal and Professors of the University of St Andrews, on their Superb Treat to Dr Samuel Johnson'. This is from one of Robert Ferguson's gems, and a suitable broadside to the man who is the most famous critic of the Scots, in both his conversation and his famous Dictionary.*

# 5

# Celtic Calendars

The smiling Spring comes in rejoicing,
  And surly Winter grimly flies;
Now crystal clear are the falling waters,
  And bonie blue are the sunny skies.
Fresh o'er the mountains breaks forth the morning,
  The ev'ning gilds the ocean's swell;
All creatures joy in the sun's returning,
  And I rejoice in my bonie Bell.[1]

THE MODERN WORLD WHEECHS around in nanoseconds[2] – instant calls, emails, sell-by dates defined to the second. The traditional Scottish year takes a more leisurely pace, measuring eternity in yearly cycles.

The early history of our country is enveloped (appropriately) in a grey misty fog. No one is quite sure what became of our Pictish ancestors and the Celtic religion of druids and rituals. While other parts of our United Kingdom, notably Wales and Cornwall, join in modern resuscitations of the druidic/bardic rites – which are now used to epitomise the core of ancient culture of those locales – in Scotland we do not have that. But our legal and practical calendar stands pretty much foursquare with the high days of those mysterious ancient folk, who used a lunar calendar to follow the cycle of the seasons.

Their New Year's Day[3] started with the fires of Samhain on 31 October as they settled down for the winter; this was followed by Imbolc at the end of January (the end of winter and the start of lambing time); then through

---

[1]  *'Song: My Bonie Bell', Robert Burns.*

[2]  *A nanosecond is defined as the smallest potential measurement of time, i.e. the gap between the plane wheels touching down and the switching on of the mobile phone.*

[3]  *Or really night, for the Celts' day started at nightfall.*

three more months to Beltain(e) in May (the fires of summer and abundance – and sex); and then at harvest time, Lugnasadth in our August.

Our legal and commercial forebears copied the ancient Celtic cycle of the land; our years were broken up to reflect the four seasons[4] and all agreements whether to lease land, hire staff or pay interest fell on one of the four 'quarter days'.[5] Here, as in so many things, Scotland and England differed!

| English Quarter Days | | Scottish Quarter Days | |
|---|---|---|---|
| Christmas Day | 25 December | Candlemas | 2 February |
| Lady Day[6] | 25 March | Whitsunday | 15 May |
| St John the Baptist[7] | 24 June | Lammas | 1 August |
| Michaelmas | 29 September | Martinmas | 11 November |

The old traditions and festivals still linger on their old days and we will look at each of them. One running theme that you'll see is that they all hark back to our pagan prehistory.

---

[4]  *In the west of Scotland the seasons are: spring (characterised by refreshing rain); summer (warm rain); autumn (heavy rain); and winter (cold, icy rain). George Orwell famously said that to live in Scotland 'one should be amphibian'.*

[5]  *In practice, Scotland had some six-month contracts, which were renewed on the May and November quarter days. For that purpose they were called the 'term days'.*

[6]  *The Feast of the Annunciation and, as discussed elsewhere, old New Year's Day in England.*

[7]  *Effectively Midsummer's Day.*

## Candlemas: February

> Gin Candlemas day be dry an' fair
> The half o' Winter's to come an' mair.
> Gin Candlemas day be wet an' foul
> The half o' Winter's gone at Youl[8]

After the cold hard winter, where by good fortune you and your family had stored enough food to live through the cold and snow, the first signs of spring were the signs of hope and fresh food. Thus was held the festival of Imbolc,[9] which we kidnapped and rebranded as Candlemas on 2 February annually.

The ancients were celebrating the lambing (on or about 31 January) and the name Imbolc itself comes from the Gaelic for 'ewe's milk'. The Christian Candlemas, too, has maternal connotations as it commemorates the traditional rite of purification under Mosaic law, when Mary visited the temple 40 days after the birth of Jesus.[10] The old man who saw them called the child 'A light of revelation',[11] and this text was linked to the opening line of the Prophet Zephaniah ('I will search Jerusalem with candles'[12]) – hence our name for this special day.[13]

The main interest in Candlemas is that there was a very old (now extinct) Scottish custom that if hedgehogs came out of hibernation on Candlemas day and saw their own shadow in the sunshine they would return to the burrow as a further six weeks of winter lay ahead. On the other hand, if it were an overcast day then the back of winter had been broken.[14]

---

8   *Traditional rhyme. Youl = Yule = Christmas.*

9   *Pronounced IM-bulk (or sometimes EM-bulk). As there are no living Picts, it seems a bid theoretical to worry about pronunciation!*

10  *For the law, see Leviticus xxii, 1–8; for the presentation of Mary and Jesus, Luke ii, 22.*

11  *Luke ii, 32 ('Nunc Dimittus').*

12  *Zephania i, 12.*

13  *We'll see regularly how the early Christian missionaries wove much of the old into the new – not just in Scotland, but across Europe. Imbolc's tutelary deity was a virgin, too.*

14  *When you think of the practicality, sowing the seeds too early and losing them in the frost could cause the starvation of the family.*

This of course was taken from Scotland to the USA in the days of the Highland Clearances – the first recorded mention of what is now Groundhog Day in Pennsylvania was in 1841. There they transferred the prophetic power from the hedgehog to the groundhog[15] and so, to this day, television cameras chase[16] this poor beast in the name of prophecy. Fame has fallen on the rather extraordinarily-named Punxsutawney Phil from Punxsutawney, Pennsylvania, but many other towns across North America have their own mascots. As to the accuracy of the predictions? I'd just be guessing.[17]

All the older traditions have died: this was a day for clearing gorse by burning in the Candlemas Bleeze, or to give gifts – initially candles for the schoolroom, but latterly money – to the village schoolmaster, with the most generous pupil being crowned 'king' and carried by two pupils round the school in a fourhanded chair to share in a bowl of punch served by the teacher.[18]

In the Hebrides until relatively recently, corn dollies were made and cribbed by the women folk, following rituals intoned to St Bridgit (or 'Bride'), which we believe were the selfsame incantations made to 'The Maiden' goddess of yore.

In some rural communities blessings of seeds and tools – notably the plough – were common and Candlemas Day was the start of a probationary type of marriage called 'handfasting' – the couple would have their hands tied together in a ceremony and would act as if married for a specified period (often a year and a day), after which if there were no progeny on the way either side could terminate the arrangement without shame. This does seem an odd idea in the context of the relatively small communities – you'd be bumping into your ex on a daily basis, not something I'd relish.

---

[15]  *Hedgehog*: erinaceus europaeus; *groundhog*: marmota monax.

[16]  *Or badger, perhaps.*

[17]  *A bit like the groundhogs.*

[18]  *Heaven knows how many health-and-safety rules that breaks; no wonder such fun is no longer found.*

There are a few old events which are still current at this time of year. If you visit Lanark on 1 March, go along to St Nicholas's Church to watch 'The Whuppity Scourie'. At 6pm a bell is sounded and all the local schoolchildren race three times around the kirk anticlockwise,[19] shouting and cheering and hitting each other with balls of paper attached to strings. At the end of the third lap the local councillors have a 'scramble', which is the old Scots custom of throwing pennies[20] in the air for the children to collect.

## Whitsunday: May

> As I was a-wand'ring ae morning in spring,
> I heard a young ploughman sae sweetly to sing;
> And as he was singin', thir words he did say,—
> There's nae life like the ploughman's in the month o' sweet May.
> The lav'rock in the morning she'll rise frae her nest,
> And mount i' the air wi' the dew on her breast,
> And wi' the merry ploughman she'll whistle and sing,
> And at night she'll return to her nest back again.[21]

Given our weather, the ancient Celts celebrated the commencement of summer in the feast of Beltane on 1 May. Here we had another fire festival, for Beltane means 'the fires of the god Bel', and bonfires were lit on the tops of the largest hills in the neighbourhood and celebrations of fertility[22] lasted the night.

> At Beltane when ilke bodie bownis
>   To Peblis to the play
> To heir the singing and the soundis
>   The solace suth to say[23]

The tradition died out, but was rekindled in the 1980s by the Beltane Fire Society in Edinburgh, who have, since then, held a boisterous festival every year on the night of 30 April/1 May on top of Calton Hill at the bottom of

---

[19]  Or 'widdershins' – by and large not a safe thing to do.

[20]  I think coins of a higher denomination are now used.

[21]  'The Ploughman's Song', Robert Burns.

[22]  Often rather practical celebrations of fertility!

[23]  'The Kingis Quair', James I – I have no real idea what it means.

Princes Street.[24] A procession of fire and music is formed by various groups, some symbolising the four elements[25] and some throwing back to the pre-Christian days: the White Warrior Women (who guard the May Queen), the Blue Men (who are druid spirit guides) and the lusty and lustful Red Men (who spread mischief). They pass through a gateway of fire and process round points representing the other elements before the symbolic arrival of the Green Man heralds summer's beginning – then party continues until one o'clock, when the ancient laws of the druids have to contend with the more mundane laws of the City Licensing Board.

Sacrificing people – or pretending to – in the fire was an important part of the ritual. In rural communities young boys would jump over a bonfire (not usually in kilts!) or run in between two fires, and these sacrificial remnants have spurred many stories – John Buchan's eerie novel *Witch Wood* or the more modern cult film, *The Wicker Man*.

This still captures the imagination. In Edinburgh in 2006 some gifted modern performance artists created the Mantilla Foundation, which collected works of art from artists worldwide – but only those pieces regretted by the creator. The Foundation Members took these embarrassing cast-offs to the Isle of Colonsay in 2007 and burned them on a great cleansing fire while dancing around the pyre.[26]

Across the wider countryside, special bannocks would be baked – the *Bannoch Bealtainn*. The most common tradition was to prepare oatmeal bannocks with nine square knobs on top. When the bannock was baked everyone would face into the fire and in turn break off a knob, cast it back over their shoulder and ask for a blessing or protection from a particular predator. In Badenoch they made larger round bannocks, marked on one side with a cross and on the other with a circle. These were rolled down the hill[27] and if yours came to rest at the hill foot with the cross downward, that was a bad omen for the year.

---

[24] *If you see what I mean... The organisers warn of 'nudity and some uninhibited behaviour' but it's not an area I've completed my research in (yet). Research is often a hard taskmaster – two more personal inhibitions to jettison then I am up for it all!*

[25] *Earth, Air, Water and Fire.*

[26] *www.mantillafoundation.com.*

[27] *Whether like a wheel or an egg, I know not. It certainly seems to have links to egg rolling at Easter time.*

Looking over from Calton Hill[28] in Edinburgh you'll see the great lion-shaped rock known as Arthur's Seat.[29] One (not exclusively Scottish) custom was to climb this hill at dawn on May Day and wash your face in the morning dew. This, too, links into the druids, for dew was their holy water. The dew falling after Beltane must have been powerful enough to grant anyone who washed their face in it happiness, maybe a wish, and certainly for a young girl, a beautiful complexion for the year.[30] Edinburgh went into this in a big way, with early morning parades – firstly the servants and then later, after their richer slumbers and finer breakfasts, the gentry, often accompanied by pipers and drummers. The custom fell into disuse after a number of enterprising liquor salesmen got to the top first and sold buckets of whisky to the celebrants![31]

All this was just too much fun for the powers-that-be, and so the legal quarter day became the nearby Christian festival of Pentecost (or Whitsun).[32] While theologically this made a lot of sense, there was a particular technical problem. Whitsun is the 50th day after Easter, and as Easter changes every year, it's not a fixed date. So a compromise had to be reached[33] and it was decided that the legal Whitsun would henceforth be fixed.[34]

---

[28]    *If you can tear your eyes away from the uninhibited nudity...*

[29]    *This extict volcano lowers over Edinburgh to an extent greater than its height of 832ft merits.*

[30]    *Cheaper than Botox.*

[31]    *Similar bacchanals were seen on Ben Ledi (Callander), Kinnoull Hill (Perth) and Tinto Hill (Lanarkshire).*

[32]    *Celebrating the arrival of the Holy Ghost to the Apostles (Acts ii, 2).*

[33]    *Particularly as house rentals ran traditionally from Whitsunday – so 15 May was often known as 'flitting day'.*

[34]    *Removings Act 1693 (c. 40): 'Our Soveraigne Lord and Lady The King and Queens Majesties with advice and consent of the Estates of Parliament ... Statute and Declare that the Fifteenth day of May ... shall be in all time comeing in place of the former Terme of Whitsunday to all effects whatsoever as well as to Removeings'. Recently, though this law remains valid, the Term and Quarter Days (Scotland) Act 1990 (c. 22) set the date to 28 May (and the other quarter days, too, are now the 28th of their respective months).*

What makes Auld Reikie's dames sae fair,     [Edinburgh's]
It canna be the halesome air,
But caller burn beyond compare,                    [fresh stream]
  The best of ony,
That gars them a' sic graces skair,
  And blink sae bonny.

On May-day in a fairy ring,
We've seen them round St Anthon's spring,
Frae grass the caller dew draps wring
  To weet their ein,
And water clear as chrystal spring,
  To synd them clean.

O may they still pursue the way
To look sae feat, sae clean, sae gay!
Than shall their beauties glance like May,
  And, like her, be
The goddess of the vocal Spray,
  The Muse, and me.[35]

---

[35] *'Caller Water'*, R. Fergusson.

## Lammas: August

It was upon a Lammas night,
 When corn rigs are bonie,
Beneath the moon's unclouded light,
 I held awa to Annie;
The time flew by, wi' tentless heed,
 Till, 'tween the late and early,
Wi' sma' persuasion she agreed
 To see me thro' the barley.

[*Chorus*] Corn rigs, an' barley rigs,
 An' corn rigs are bonie:
I'll ne'er forget that happy night,
 Amang the rigs wi' Annie.[36]

The taking in of the harvest was of paramount importance in the rural world of early Scotland and so the celebration of Lammas on 1 August, when the first fruits of the harvest would be ground and baked into bread, became our third quarter day. The standard explanation of the name is that it is a contraction of 'loaf mass', but some believe that the name is Celtic, derived from the god Lugh[37] and as usual adopted, camouflaged and quietened down as a Christian feast. As it was after the harvest, many towns held a special fair, but these have died out with a few exceptions, such as St Andrews and Kirkcaldy.[38]

Some other towns preferred Marymass on 15 August as their celebration, because it is the traditional birthday of the Blessed Virgin Mary (Lammas had no spiritual sponsor). This was another day of special bannocks but the tradition is virtually extinct, with a few examples left in the north such as Inverness and Caithness, where the ancient custom has been grafted on to a modern fair.

About ten days later, on the second Friday of August, if you are at the

---

[36] '*Corn Rigs and Barley Rigs*', *Robert Burns.*

[37] *The sun god, or 'shining one', after whom Lyons in France is named.*

[38] *The Kirkcaldy fair is, I hope, a free-market economy in honour of that town's most famous son, Gordon Brown (sorry, I meant Adam Smith).*

Forth Bridges[39] take a slight detour into the town of South Queensferry, where you may think that you've fallen into some sci-fi scenario as a tall humanoid figure totally covered in green spikes lurches through the town.

Meet the Burryman.

From the 14th century[40] to today, each year has seen a local male resident make a suit of flannel clothes then painstakingly[41] gather by himself the prickly burrs of the lesser burdock[42] and delicately sew hundreds and hundreds of the little blighters on to his outfit, so that his whole body is covered in them.[43] He augments this with a sash around his middle (currently the lion rampant flag is used!) and, with wildflowers tied around two sticks to help him walk, he is guided by his two supporters, rather thankfully wearing their own ordinary clothes.[44]

He then has a seven-mile route to cover[45] with his arms painfully stretched out, observing total silence as he goes. He stops at the house of the provost and then at shops, factories and houses (public and private), where the owners are obliged to give him drinks of whisky.[46] But beware looking directly into the Burryman's eyes! Who knows what fate will befall you if you look into his soul.

It is quite surreal and the rationale is lost to time. Some believe that he is a scapegoat or a sin eater – those burrs catch the sins of all the parish members and he bears them for all, relieving everyone of the burden. Others more mundanely think it's to enhance the coming season's fishing catch; perhaps the fish will stick to the nets as the jaggy burrs do to the clothes.[47]

---

[39]  *Only two of them, to the confusion of non-native speakers.*

[40]  *The first written record is from 1687 but this has all the hallmarks of being very old.*

[41]  *Literally – prickly fingers!*

[42]  *Dandelion and burdock was a popular precursor in Scotland to Coca-Cola (well, at least it was widely available).*

[43]  *The current Burryman estimates that it takes 11,000 to cover the suit.*

[44]  *Maybe a small bit of Velcro.*

[45]  *Often taking nine hours to complete the cycle.*

[46]  *And provide a straw so that he can get to it!*

[47]  *It probably has links too to the various Green Man myths across England.*

It's a hard job,[48] and whatever the initial purpose was, it must have been a strong one for this traditional festival to have run for well over 700 years![49] I think it's a reflection of the hard and dangerous lives that the fisher folk and their families endured to bring fish on our table. It's still a hard life, with great financial worry in the complex world of catch quota and tied-up days. We owe a debt of gratitude.

> Baloo-loo lammie, noo baloo my dear,
> Does wee lammie ken its daddie's no here?
> Ye're rockin' fu' sweetly on minnie's warm knee,      [mummy's]
> But daddie's a-rockin' upon the saut sea.             [salt]
>
> Noo hush-a-ba, lammie, noo hush-a my dear,
> Noo hush-a-ba, lammie, ain Minnie is here;
> The wild wins is ravin', and minnie's hert's sair,
> The wild wind is ravin', and ye dinna care.[50]

Of course, our fishermen, too, had their festivals. For centuries Scotland had the largest fishing fleet in Europe, dedicated to catching the herring – or 'silver darlings' as they were known to the community. The catching and the preserving of this oily fish was a major source of revenue, employment and food for the population across Scotland. It remains a popular traditional dish today, although its days of glory are no longer.

In early July, the Eyemouth Herring Week[51] sees parades and dances culminating in the crowning of the elected Herring Queen. At the later part of the quarter, on 29 September, the Feast of St Michael (as patron saint of the sea) was a noisy time on the west coast, where the fisher-

---

48  *An endeavour not unlike 'painting the Forth Bridge', although modern technology will see that painted to last from 2010.*

49  *Fraserburgh did something similar until 1800, and there are records of this happening ad hoc in Buckie round that time, but only if the herring fishing had been poor.*

50  *'Fisherfolk's Cradle Song', Lady Nairn,* Lays from Strathearn, *1846.*

51  *Eyemouth is also known as the site of one of the great fishing tragedies. On Black Friday 1881, nineteen boats and two hundred men perished within sight of the harbour in a tremendous storm. You should see the poignant monument if you can. Herring Week, though, is a happier recollection, which developed out of a picnic to welcome the men of Eyemouth returning safely from the war in 1919.*

folk and farmers would dance and share the special cakes called Struan Michaels[52] which were baked by the women without using any iron implements at all – only if untouched by metal would the eating of this bring prosperity and success in the year.[53]

The late summer/early autumn is a lovely time in Scotland, as the harvest is gathered and we often see a spell of fine weather, but the evenings turn very quickly and soon the dark nights will be upon us, with their own stories and parties.

> Now westlin winds and slaught'ring guns
>   Bring Autumn's pleasant weather;
> The moorcock springs on whirring wings
>   Amang the blooming heather:
> Now waving grain, wide o'er the plain,
>   Delights the weary farmer;
> And the moon shines bright, when I rove at night,
>   To muse upon my charmer.
>
> We'll gently walk, and sweetly talk,
>   Till the silent moon shine clearly;
> I'll grasp thy waist, and, fondly prest,
>   Swear how I love thee dearly:
> Not vernal show'rs to budding flow'rs,
>   Not Autumn to the farmer,
> So dear can be as thou to me,
>   My fair, my lovely charmer![54]

---

52  *Made of oats, barley and rye, fired and then glazed three times over, with batter and soft fruits added.*

53  *Also, carrots were distributed as a rather-too-visual emblem of male fertility – the first carrots pulled were given by the women to their men. Orange-coloured Viagra?*

54  *Now Westlin' Winds', Robert Burns. This is the first and last verse of Burns's second-earliest work on record, written in his sixteenth year, and I think it's one of the undiscovered gems of his output – capturing the Burnsian themes of the ordinary, honest rural man, his symbiotic place within nature and the love of women.*

## Martinmas: November

> It fell about the Martinmas time,
> And a gay time it was then O
> That our gudewife had puddings to make,
> And she boiled them in the pan O.[55]

As those nights grew longer and the pasture became exhausted, this was the date the Celts set to butcher the livestock, make pies and sausages and salt the rest of the meat so that the family could eat through the winter months.

Christian religious life[56] came to Scotland in the 4th century with Ninian,[57] who was taught by the famous St Martin of Tours, so it is appropriate that the only saint honoured in a quarter day is St Martin,[58] on his feast day of 11 November. The acute amongst you will have noticed that if we jump back into the Julian calendar this takes us to Samhain,[59] so we are still cycling round the Celtic calendar.

Round about this time, there are relatively few celebrations – the nights

---

[55] 'Bar the Door', Traditional.

[56] You do get a few doubts about the strictness of the old religious life – 'Macpherson' means 'son of the parson', 'Mactaggart', 'son of the priest', 'Macnab' is the 'son of the abbot' and 'Buchanan' is 'son of the canon' (a canon is a big shot in the Church).

[57] Most people think of St Columba as the apostle of Christianity in Scotland. Certainly his iconic and truly moving choice of the isle of Iona to build his church is a keystone of the mythic history of Scotland. The real history is that, while Columba was still a spoilt and rather vengeful Irish warrior prince, St Ninian had introduced the worship of Christ into the town of Whithorn in Galloway in the south west by building a small white chapel, the candida casa, which adds the 'white' in 'Whithorn' to this day. One of my Dad's friends was the Minister of Whithorn, who once rather confused the Archbishop of Canterbury by pointing out his parish was older than Canterbury by two-and-a half centuries!

[58] As well as his teaching, he is famed for tearing his coat in half to share it with a frozen beggar. That night Jesus came to him wearing the selfsame torn cloak and Martin became a Christian. He was baptised by St Hilary, who, coincidentally, is one of the English legal/university term days.

[59] I should have mentioned this earlier, but it's pronounced SA-vane. Most of its traditions have stuck on our Hallowe'en – that's another chapter.

encourage us all home early! If you were in the Royal Burgh of Rutherglen a few weeks before, on 18 October, you could have participated in Sour Cakes Day, where a local lass is chosen 'Queen, the Bride of the Toaster' and, to mark the Feast of St Luke, she and her handmaidens bake cakes to an old recipe, which are distributed and eaten with sour cream.

We in Scotland, as across the UK, celebrate Guy Fawkes Night – or Bonfire Night as it is often known now – marking the saving of James VI & I on 5 November 1605, when Fawkes and his conspirators filled a basement in the Houses of Parliament with enough gunpowder to blow up the king.[60] But this festival of fireworks, bonfires and burning the stuffed dummy or 'guy' has its explicitly Scottish side, too.[61]

There is another, sombre British tradition that I do want to mention as it affected Scotland profoundly.

On Martinmas Day, 11 November 1918, at the 11th hour of the 11th day of the 11th month, the guns fell silent at last, bringing World War 1 to its close. All of Europe had suffered dreadful losses, but the military Scots took a heavier than average toll.

It brings it home to me to think of the 510 former pupils and staff of Ayr Academy who joined up, with 115 dead (a casualty rate of 23 per cent); or of the young men from the Scottish universities, from whence 2,026 students left their books to serve in the forces with 15 per cent killed in action; or of the Royal Bank of Scotland employees, where of a male staff of 901, two-thirds of them (602) volunteered to serve the colours, with 84 (or 14 per cent) never returning to the tills from which they marched.[62]

In every town and village in the country, you'll find a monument to

---

[60]  *And just to be sure, HM still has her Beefeaters search the cellars of Westminster on the day of the opening of parliament. Rather dangerously, they search for gunpowder with an old-fashioned candle-lit lantern.*

[61]  *'Remember, Remember the Fifth of November, Gunpowder, Treason and Plot.' Fawkes memorably claimed that the plot 'would blow the Scots back to Scotland' – this was one of the least friendly welcomes a Scot has been given in London. The story of how we Scots have run London in the subsequent centuries is found in David Stenhouse's book,* On the Make *(Mainstream, 2004).*

[62]  *In context, at the time of writing RBS had 135,000 staff – if you apply the same percentages then 90,000 would volunteer and we would have to bury 18,900. Think on that, as it explains the shock and effect of the hecatomb.*

these men, and their successors (male and female) in wars since, who have given 'their tomorrow, for our today'. Whether from the formality of the Scottish National War Memorial in Edinburgh Castle, or from a simple Celtic cross in the middle of a Highland village, we will remember them.

The pipes in the street were playing bravely,
 The marching lads went by,
With merry hearts and voices singing
 My friends marched out to die;
But I was hearing a lonely Pibroch
 Out of an older war,
'Farewell, farewell, farewell MacCrimmon,
MacCrimmon comes no more.'

And every lad in his heart was dreaming
 Of honour and wealth to come,
And honour and noble pride were calling
 To the tune of the pipes and drum;
But I was hearing a woman singing
 On dark Dunvegan shore,
'In battle or peace, with wealth or honour
MacCrimmon comes no more.'

And there in the front of the men were marching,
 With feet that made no mark,
The grey old ghosts of the ancient fighters
 Come back again from the dark;
And in front of them all MacCrimmon piping
 A weary tune and sore,
'On the gathering day, for ever and ever,
MacCrimmon comes no more.'[63]

---

63 'Cha Till MacCruimein, Departure of the 4th Camerons', Lt Ewart Alan Mackintosh MC, 4th Bttn Seaforth Highlanders, kia Cambrai 21 November, 1917 (aged 24). Quoted in Anthem For Doomed Youth, ed. Lyn Macdonald, Folio Society, 2000.

# 6

# Check Out the Tartan

The fighting sheen o' it;
The yellow, the green o' it;
The black, the red o' it;
Every thread o' it.
The fair have sighed for it;
The brave have died for it;
Foemen sought for it;
Heroes fought for it;
Honour the name o' it;
Drink tae the fame o' it –
THE TARTAN![1]

IS THE SIGHT OF a Scot striding down the street in the kilt a cliché or a source of pride?

Is it a tartan comfort blanket or a sharp-edged statement of identity?

Does tartan tie us to looking backwards or empower us to march forwards?

Even within Scotland there is no unanimity of view. In fact, I'd say there's more tosh talked about tartan than almost any other Scottish subject,[2] reflecting its status as the ultimate image of the Scots.

The real truth about the kilt though is that tartan is recognised throughout the world as the colours of Scotland and her people. Regiments in old Empire dominions, Japanese schoolgirls, golfers in slacks and families on picnic rugs, shortbread tins and Scotty dogs' collars – you

---

[1] *This traditional(ish) rhyme is very popular in North America but isn't really authentic – though it was read into the Hansard report of the Nova Scotia legislature (Res 2917 of 2002) by the Hon. Ronal Chisholm. I don't know who the author was – some talent inspired by Rabbie but unfortunately taught by McGonagall.*

[2] *Except maybe the national football team, but that's not uncommon.*

don't need to travel far from home to find this most pervasive of Scottish exports.[3]

I think that it's fair to say that the kilt is now the national dress of the whole of Scotland, and not just the preserve of the old Highland clans – yet the story of how we all got to wear these beautiful fabrics is a pretty complex pattern in its own right!

Of course, the ability to design and weave checked patterns is not unique to the Scots. You can find tartan-like patterns throughout the Celtic nations: Ireland, Brittany, northern Spain, Wales and Cornwall; and some commentators even maintain that tartan was invented in China three millennia ago.[4] Whoever came up with the bright idea, it was the Highlanders of Scotland who pursued it with vigour.

Like the other great Scottish clichés, kilts and tartan generate a fair amount of bar-room controversy, laced with a fair degree of urban myth. Let's sit down and pop a few of them (both in terms of history and dress sense!).

The best way to understand the whole story is to consider it in four periods:

- The Clans.
- The Military.
- Balmorality.
- Today.

## The Clans

Civility seems a part of the national character of Highlanders. Every chieftain is a monarch, and politeness, the natural product of royal government, is diffused from the laird through the whole clan.[5]

---

[3]  *A recent Scottish executive estimate was that about 200 businesses employing 7,000 people in the tartan industry added £350m annually to the country's GDP.*

[4]  *Though they would have had to have made time in between inventing gunpowder, paper, etc. The oldest remnant of Scottish tartan is the 'Falkirk Tartan' in the Royal Scottish Museum, which dates from the second or third century AD but looks like a bit of doormat chewed by the dog today.*

[5]  Journal, *Samuel Johnson, pp.21–2.*

Life in the historical Highlands was hard. A family's existence might depend on the outcome of a well-executed cattle raid to fill the larder at the year's dark times, or they might be wiped out in an unexpected snow fall which cut the village off. Naturally, family groupings were important, but the extended family – or clan – assumed a great practical role on the society – in return for obedience, the head of this grouping – the chief – as King, Father, Banker and General, would lead the fortunes of his people in a military mutual society.

It was a hierarchical and historical contract. At the peak of the ben stood the chief, in whose person resided the legal power to command and to punish his people[6] – the right of 'pit and gallows'.[7] He was supported in his administration by his officers – the chieftain (his trusty No. Two), the sennachie (his bard, genealogist and registrar of births, marriages and deaths), his ghillies (the servant lads and hunting companions) and, when in full war structure, the tacksmen[8] – the heads of families who held land in lease from the chief directly and in return owed military service, having to 'bring out' a certain number of men. Beneath them were the clansmen – the ordinary folk. These would mainly carry the name of their clan, but not exclusively, as there's a geographical element to this, and an outsider who by marriage or inclination accepted allegiance would be as much a clansman as his named brethren.

Clans could be huge like the Mackenzies or tiny like the Napiers, as rich as the Campbells or as poor as the Ruthvens. Some were confined to one small island like the McLeods, while others were a mighty confederation of Macdonalds[9] across swathes of Scotland. But each kept its own pride and its own traditions.

---

[6]    *Adam Smith mentions this in* Wealth of Nations: *'Mr Cameron of Lochiel without being so much as a Justice of the Peace, used notwithstanding to exercise the highest criminal jurisdiction over his own people... with great equity, though without any of the formalities of justice.'* II.iv8 (p.416, Glasgow Edn).

[7]    *Or fossa et furcam – the right to throw recalcitrants into a pit or dungeon, or just hang 'em. I suppose if you were cross enough you could try both. There was a chief who had a clanswoman tied to the seashore rocks by her hair to drown at high tide as a punishment for theft!*

[8]    *Or 'duniwassals'.*

[9]    *The Macdonalds being five clans under a high chief.*

Chiefs have a number of personal rights, jealously guarded. They wear three eagle feathers in their hats.[10] Each has an oral genealogical history (often encapsulated in a Gaelic soubriquet) and a chiefly title (which can be linked to the family, the estates, or both), and most have a unique right or privilege. Here are a few:

| Clan | Chief | Gaelic | Unique Right |
|------|-------|--------|--------------|
| Chisholm | The Chisholm | Siosalaich | Only three men were traditionally called 'The': the King, the Pope and the Chisholm[11] |
| Cameron | Cameron of Lochiel | MacDhomnuill Duibh | The bells of the City of Glasgow are rung if Lochiel enters the city[12] |
| Campbell | His Grace the Duke of Argyll[13] | MacCailein Mor | Hereditary Admiral of the Western Isles[14] |

---

[10] *Recently, with animal rights legislation, chiefs are advised to carry a certificate proving no wild eagles were harmed in the collection of the feathers.*

[11] *Now others avail themselves of the definite article by permission, maybe Chisholm should be 'THE the'.*

[12] *Lochiel stopped his Highlanders from robbing the merchants of Glasgow in 1745 and they established this right for 'Gentle Donald' and his descendents forevermore.*

[13] *To reflect the political success of the Campbells, the current duke is not only 6th Duke of Argyll (in the UK), but also 13th Duke of Argyll (in Scotland). His business card must be rather large, for he is also: 13th Marquess of Kintyre and Lorne; 22nd Earl of Argyll; 13th Earl of Campbell and Cowall; 13th Viscount of Lochow and Glenyla; 23rd Lord Campbell; 22nd Lord Lorne; 16th Lord of Kintyre; 13th Lord of Inverary, Mull, Morvern and Tirie; 9th Baron Sundridge, of Coomb Bank, Kent; 10th Baron Hamilton of Hameldon, Co. Leicester; and 15th Baronet. Not all chiefs have shared in the largesse of British establishment titles; some are legally mere 'misters'. Try telling them that makes a difference!*

[14] *The current duke is not just an inheritor of honours – he also successfully captained the Scottish elephant polo team to victory twice. (Don't laugh – that and curling are the old two sports where Scotland has been world champion over the last decade!)*

| Clan | Chief | Gaelic | Unique Right |
|------|-------|--------|--------------|
| McNeill | McNeill of Barra | MacDhomhinuill | Has the right to eat dinner ahead of any potentate in the world |
| Macleod | Macleod of Macleod[15] | MacLeòid | Owns the 'Fairy Flag', which can be waved to vanquish the enemies of the clan[16] |
| Murray | His Grace the Duke of Atholl | Am Moireach Mor | Commands the only legal private army in the UK[17] |

Despite this highly structured social grouping, the pattern of the tartan the clan wore did not reach a uniform design in this early period. This was a poor society and, while the natural dyes from a given area would tend to be used, giving some colour palette in common, there was no definitive rule which defined the pattern. Each clan identified its fellows in battle or on the march by a sprig of a particular plant carried on the bonnet, not by the pattern and colour of the tartan worn.

This social structure operated for centuries, until the succession of rebellions in the UK over the joint crowns of Scotland and England, known as the Jacobite rebellions.[18] Then, to the great joy of romantic

---

[15] *Please be careful: some chiefs repeat their names – the ultimately repetitious being the late Sir Gregor McGregor of McGregor – while some families dislike the repetition and call themselves 'Of that Ilk' (Moncrieffe of that Ilk, rather than Moncrieffe of Moncrieffe).*

[16] *The fairies who gave this flag said that it could be waved three times to vanquish the enemies of the Macleods; it worked in 1490 and 1580, so there's still one go left. Consideration was given to waving it in 1940!*

[17] *The Atholl Highlanders, fighting since 1562 but recognised by Queen Victoria, who gave them Colours in 1845.*

[18] *Or the Fifteen and the Forty-Five. The whole Jacobite (meaning a Stuart supporter – from the Latin for James, 'Jacobus') saga is very complicated and based on a combination of anti-Catholiscm and the irritating personality of James VII & II. He ascended to the throne after his brother's death but quickly annoyed everyone (partially, but not exclusively, because he was a very committed Roman Catholic). He did a bunk in 1689 with his second wife and*

18   *their new-born son, so the Protestant establishment invited his Protestant daughter (Mary II) and her husband (William III) to rule jointly in what the victors called 'the Glorious Revolution', which established the form of constitutional monarchy we still have in Britain today. James returned to reclaim his crown, but his defeat at the Battle of the Boyne sent him back to France (and William on his White Horse into the troubled iconography of Northern Ireland). After James's death in 1701, his son (scurrilously known as 'the warming pan baby', as it was rumoured that he had been substituted in the birthing chamber to ensure a male Catholic heir) was recognised by France and the Vatican as the de jure King James VIII & III, although the history books call him 'the Old Pretender' (in the sense of a claimant to the throne). The warming pan story is patently false, for James was his father's son in so many respects, all of them making him unfit to rule. After the Union of the Parliaments had caused resentment in Scotland, and with German Geordie (George I, Elector of Hanover and a grandson of the daughter of James VI & I – distant, but legal and certainly Protestant) taking the throne after his cousin Anne's death in 1714, the OP struck out with a rebellion in Scotland: the Fifteen. Hindered by the death of his ally the Sun King (and the near bankruptcy of the French state after the gilded honeyed years of Louis XIV), his personal inability to lead, and his chief supporter the Earl of Mar's jumping the gun and starting the rising too early, this rebellion was doomed. A no-score draw at the Battle of Sherrifmuir and a defeat at Preston saw James OP exiled in Rome with rather more Scotsmen that he'd set out with. There were a few flurries, plots and plans over the next decades but he waited to see his two sons grow. The younger (Henry) decided to build himself a treasure in heaven by becoming a priest. Fortunately in the politics of the time it was expedient to make him a cardinal (of York – though he never quite got there...) and as luck would have it he got a free treasure on Earth, too. It was his older brother, Charles Edward, who took his father's sword home to lead the last battles on British soil. The story is too well known, with the brave and handsome lad landing in his home Highlands with a few friends (the Seven Men of Moidart) to find hesitation in the clans, but by his personal charm calling the great fighting tail out from the heather and then carrying the campaign against the Hanoverians even unto Derby (allegedly Geo I by that stage was using the services of Jas VII's old travel agent for an awayday saver to safe old Hanover). Then fatal weakness stole the dice from the young gambler. His youth could not stop his generals from bickering and, fatally, they resolved to fall back to Scotland. A cancerous retreat followed, harried by Butcher Cumberland (George's son), until that last grey April morning in 1746 when the cousins faced each other over Drumossie Moor, when the professional army closed the history books with the blood of the*

novelists and film producers, on 16 April 1746 the last warlike clans charged armed with swords and axes against the muskets and artillery of the loyalist troops[19] and ran across the moor of Culloden to join in the last battle fought on British soil, and thence into the land of legend.

## The Military Phase

And wild and high the 'Cameron's Gathering' rose!
The war-note of Lochiel, which Albyn's hills
Have heard, and heard, too, have her Saxon foes:—
How in the noon of night that pibroch thrills,
Savage and shrill! But with the breath which fills
Their mountain-pipe, so fill the mountaineers
With the fierce native daring which instils
The stirring memory of a thousand years,
And Euan's,[20] Donald's fame rings in each clansman's ears![21]

The retribution following Culloden was barbaric under the wrathful

---

*Highlandmen. The Prince's bravery in escape is a legend, but escape it was, never to return and never to be a political force. On his father's death the Pope refused to recognise him as Charles III and he sunk sadly into an alcoholic court of his own imaginings. His death, after that of his only (illegitimate) daughter, left the old cardinal as the last of the Stuarts until his own death in 1807. They now sleep under a marble tomb by the great Canova in the Vatican itself – a tomb paid for by King George III.*

[19] *As many of whom were Scots as were English. Several of the cleverer clans hedged their bets and put one son into each opposing army – in the smoke of Culloden's battle, the Earl of Kilmarnock fell in with the Hanoverian troops, thinking that they were his fellow Jacobites; the officer who arrested him and escorted him off the field (in the first steps to his execution in the Tower of London) was his own son and heir, Lord Boyd. Both men were in tears.*

[20] *The great Sir Euan Cameron of Lochiel, who killed the last wolf in Scotland and famously, when wrestled to the ground in battle, bit the throat of his English opponent right out. It was he said, 'the sweetest morsel ever tasted'.*

[21] *'The Eve of Waterloo' in 'Childe Harold's Pilgrimage', Canto III, Lord Byron.*

eye and direct order of HRH the Duke of Cumberland,[22] and the safely-enthroned King George II could no longer risk the ancient right of the clan chiefs.

The political decision was taken to extirpate the clans and transfer power to the loyalist chiefs, but in a new role as local landowners and magnates, not as feudal lords.[23] The ordinary folk were banned from owning weapons and even the production and wearing of tartan was outlawed in 1746. But the real change came with the laws breaking the feudal service of the tacksmen (the chief's sub tenants) and vassals[24] so that the lease rental was the only contractual link between the chief as landowner and his folk as mere tenants. Equally ruinous for the chief, his feudal rights of justice were quashed.[25]

---

[22]   *Known universally by the soubriquet 'Butcher Cumberland' – even the arch English Tory, Dr Johnson, called him 'the heavy hand of a vindictive conqueror'* (Journal, *p.69*).

[23]   *Although bits survived in the feudal law book until they were finally squashed on 28 November 2004 under the Abolition of Feudal Tenure etc. (Scotland) Act 2000.*

[24]   *The Tenure Abolitions Act 1746 (c.50). The key provision was: '21. And whereas it hath been frequently practised in Scotland, to let lands to tenants or tacksmen, reserving or expressing, over and above the certain rents and duties payable for the same, services used and wont, or services indefinitely, or other general words of the like nature, without specifying or ascertaining the same; which practice is liable to be abused, ... no tenant or tacksman ... in Scotland, ... shall be obliged or liable to perform any services whatsoever to his heretor or landlord other than such as shall be expressly and particularly reserved and specified, and the number and kinds thereof enumerated in ... writing, and signed by the parties thereto, or some persons authorized by them, any former law or usage to the contrary notwithstanding.'*

[25]   *The Heritable Jusidictions (Scotland) Act 1746 (c.43). The Act's opening words make the politics pretty clear: 'For remedying the inconveniences that have arisen and may arise from the multiplicity and extent of heritable juris-dictions in Scotland, for making satisfaction to the proprietors thereof, for restoring to the Crown the powers of jurisdiction originally and properly belonging thereto, according to the constitution, and for extending the influ-ence, benefit, and protection of the King's laws and courts of justice to all his Majesty's subjects in Scotland, and for rendering the union more complete.'*

In a stroke of genius, the process was handled with full legal honours – the Acts were voted through by Scots and English legislators in the Lords[26] and the Commons, and the Scots justices were set to evaluate the monetary recompense due to each chief. The clever part, though, was that the chiefs who had followed the prince were disbarred from receiving their lump sum, which went instead to the pockets of the Campbell. Power and money were now aligned.[27]

So all seemed quiet in London. The Campbells were asked to arrange a regiment to support the garrison troops – and as a signal honour, were allowed to wear the tartan, but a strictly-defined pattern: the Government Sett or, as both the regiment and its plaid became known, the Black Watch. The bravery of this regiment led Prime Minister Pitt to see a solution to the stretch in the army – an early surge in op tempo – caused

---

[26]   *The Earl of Kilmarnock, Lord Lovat and Lord Balermino neither had votes nor, by that point, heads. The odd way our constitution works was seen in 2008 in the House of Lords, where this exchange took place:*
*The Earl of Mar and Kellie: My Lords, is the noble and learned Lord aware that the Scottish Independence Convention is this morning launching a petition to the Scottish Parliament for a referendum on political independence?*
*Lord Davidson of Glen Clova: My Lords, until a few minutes ago that question fell to be answered in the negative…*
*The Countess of Mar: My Lords, will the noble and learned Lord learn from my noble kinsman's and my joint ancestor, who failed in the 1715 rebellion? Perhaps our family is not the one to take advice from.*
*Lord Davidson of Glen Clova: My Lords, I will note that suggestion.*
*House of Lords Hansard, 24 January 2008, Column 331.*

[27]   *Over time, the exiled chiefs returned to Scotland and to the new regime. Oddly enough, nowadays more chiefs live abroad voluntarily than were exiled after the Forty-Five! The chief of the Lamonts is a priest and teacher in New South Wales, The Chisholm owns a scaffolding business in England and the Duke of Atholl is in the South African sunshine, just to mention three of the thirty-odd who live away from home.*

by the Seven Years War[28] and soon several Highland forces were on the march. Each in a distinctive regimental tartan.[29]

These are two crucial developments: (a) a fighting Highlander who was a source of pride in the United Kingdom, no longer the bogeyman of rebellion; conjoined with (b) a scientific description of a tartan linked to a body of men.

## Balmorality

> I thought the drawing room at Osborne was the ugliest in the world until I saw the one at Balmoral. The ornaments are strictly Scotch and the curtains and covers are of 'dress Stuart' tartan. The effect is not very pretty.
>
> Lord Rosebery[30]

Walter Scott created the literary tradition of the historical novel and in so doing captured the romance of 'old Scotland'.[31] He was a complex

---

28  *'I sought for merit wherever it could be found; it is my boast that I was the first minister who looked for it, and found it, in the mountains of the north. I called it forth and drew into your service a hardy and intrepid race of men – men who, when left by your jealousy became a prey to the artifices of your enemies, and had gone nigh to have overturned the state in the war before last. These men in the last war were brought to combat on your side; they served you with fidelity, as they fought with valour, and conquered for you in every corner of the world.' William Pitt (the Elder), Earl of Chatham, Speech 1766.*

29  *And the soldiers started to wear, not the full or great kilt or féileadh bhreacain – the twelve yards of tartan wrapped round the waist, positioned by a broad belt, with the residuum carried as a shoulder plaid – but the féileadh beag (wee kilt), which divided the garment into the modern buckled and pre-pleated version, with an optional, independent plaid over the shoulder. This form of kilt was invented by an Englishman – Thomas Rawlinson of Glengarry – who designed it for his workers in the iron smelting business he owned.*

30  *Rosebery was a Scot himself! Tsar Nicholas II used to say that, because of the queen's love of Scottish fresh air, Balmoral's bedrooms were colder than the Siberian steppes.*

31  *We are lucky, I guess; if Ivanhoe had been more popular I'd be wearing chain-mail to formal dinners.*

man of genius; his novels[32] became defining of our Scottish heritage, and for good or ill, Sir Walter brought the future King George IV to Edinburgh, where that portly prince became the first monarch since Charles I to wear the tartan.[33]

Where there is genius, there is usually some chancer on the make. So into our history come the Sobieski Stuart brothers. This pair of mountebanks claimed to be the grandsons of Bonnie Prince Charlie,[34] which had given them unique access to the ancient catalogue of tartan: the *Vestiarium Scoticum*, which defined patterns by family. Walter Scott scoffed, but almost everyone else bought in to the farce – no tourist poster would ever be the same again.[35]

---

[32]   *And more – Sir Walter's financial crises caused him to mine the vein of Scottish stories intensively.*

[33]   *It remains controversial – many Lowlanders felt aggrieved to be lumped in with the 'teuchters'. Many of taste felt nauseous (though fortunately the* soi disant *'Chief of Chiefs' chose to wear flesh-coloured stockings (or tights) to spruce up the leg department. Elizabeth Grant of Rothiemurcus reports a contemporary quip from Lady Saltoun: 'Some one objecting to this dress, particularly on so large a man, whose nudities were no longer attractive, "Nay," says she, "we should take it very kind of him; since his stay will be so short, the more we see of him the better."' Memoirs of a Highland Lady, Elizabeth Grant of Rothiemurchus, Vol. II, p.166.*

[34]   *By and large the harmless occupation of pretending to be a pretender comes around – like stock-market crashes – every generation after the last people to lose money have died and a new pool of gullibility is available. Only a few years ago the rather extraordinary Prince Michael of Albany was so ubiquitous.*

[35]   *Though there was some antagonism from traditionalists who objected to (a) the perceived dilution of the tradition of the Highland kilt and (b) its introduction into Edinburgh and the Lowlands: the* Scotsman *(28 July 1830) published this poem by 'Alister Macintrowsers':*
Oh never since when within me
Did feelings of poetry rise,
Till the highlanders of Bruntsfield
Filled my soul with surprise–
With shame and grief to think of
The tartans and the hose
The Gaelic tongue and bagpipes,
Turned into raree shows.

> The Plaid itself gives pleasure to the sight,
> To see how all the sets imbibe the light;
> Forming some way, which even to me lies hid,
> White, black, blue, yellow, purple, green, and red.
> Let Newton's royal club thro' prisms stare,
> To view celestial dyes with curious care,
> I'll please myself, nor shall my sight ask aid
> Of crystal gimcracks to survey the plaid.[36]

Two influences from England would focus all this multicoloured energy. Firstly, the Highland Society of London wrote to each of the chiefs asking him to describe his tartan, that it might be definitive within each clan; secondly (and more importantly), Queen Victoria came to Scotland and fell in love with our country and our people.[37]

In her life, Victoria rarely did things by halves. So she and Albert built the castle of Balmoral (which is still the summer holiday home of our Queen) and fell into the idealised Highland life that any romantic would die for. (Though the politicians in the cabinet found travelling there from London almost as big a shock as the tartan décor upon arrival.)

Out of this came the sentimentalised Victorian music hall approach, often thought of as the Harry Lauder genre, of outlandish tartans and comic book 'Jocks'. The railways allowed popular tourism for the first time and soon the tartan fashion was found throughout the country. Ladies with tartan shawls made in Manchester would listen to 'Fingal's Cave' or the 'Scottish Symphony' by Mendelssohn or spend the evenings reading Walter Scott or singing Burns's songs in arrangements by Haydn or Beethoven.

There was a reaction, and many Scots rebelled against the 'Tartan Tory' view, and cringed when the tartan in particular was over-used in cliché. But for many, the tartan and its heritage (albeit sanitised) was a strong and potent culture. Even today our Queen keeps close links to

---

36   'Tartana', Allen Ramsay.

37   *Not just with John Brown.*

this Scottish outlook:[38] she is woken in the morning by her personal bagpiper (playing at a discrete distance outside the bedroom!), while the royal gentlemen often wear kilts for public and private events. But how is this seen by our wider community?

## What about Today?

> To wear the kilt is my delight,
> It isn't wrong, I know it's right.
> The highlanders would get a fright
> If they saw me in my troosers.
>
> Let the wind blow high and the wind blow low
> Through the streets in my kilt I go
> All the lassies cry, 'Hello!
> Donald, where's your trousers?'[39]

This rather messy history has a great benefit: we all share in the tartan today. We observe the spirit of the tradition of wearing, rather than being shoehorned into a legal set of rules.[40] Drop into a Scottish town one Saturday and you are as likely to see some lads in kilts and rugger shirts wearing heavy boots to the match as a traditional full-dressed groom on his way to be married. In Edinburgh, one street corner has a piper in full fig, the next a stag party in a Saltire flag kilt,[41] and round the corner the doorman of one of the grand hotels, looking as if he's just stepped off the grouse moor.

---

[38]  *Her wedding too had several Scottish themes: her pages wore Royal Stuart tartan kilts; favours were posies of white Balmoral heather; and the hymn chosen – before the wedding, Dr William McKie, the organist of Westminster Abbey, had to have the Scottish setting of the 23rd Psalm (a much-loved tune called 'Crimond') sung to him as there was no copy of it in England.*

[39]  *Traditional, sung by Andy Stewart. A few of the verses of this popular (rightly so) traditional tune made famous by one of our greatest singers.*

[40]  *A bit like being regulated by the UK's FSA rather than the US's SEC!*

[41]  *And probably a 'Jimmy Hat'.*

The tartan has a life of its own, or reflects something in our cultural genes. A perfect summary is:

> Tartan survives: for once, postmodernism justifies history more than historians. Its critics are linked in combat with the faded world of Harry Lauder; those who today wear it or are conscious of its brand are truer to the complexities of its long history, intertwined for three hundred years with the political and cultural outlook of Scotland.[42]

Which means there's no excuse for you not to get dressed up! If you have a Scottish name then there will be a kilt in it[43] – either directly if you come from a great clan, or indirectly if you are from one of the smaller families[44] who sought protection with an alliance under the big guys.

It's all to do with allegiance – so if your granny's family or your godfather had a tartan, you can adhere to that loyalty. Or join in through the rapidly-growing number of speciality tartans. Towns, universities, football clubs, sex shops,[45] countries, counties and provinces have designed tartans to celebrate their heritage. The Scottish Parliament passed a Bill recently, The Scottish Register of Tartans Act 2008, to establish an official national register of tartans to preserve the 'agreed' patterns on a searchable database. In the meantime, a couple of independent private organisations have lists and charts to help.[46]

If that's all too much of a palaver, just wear one of the two 'universal tartans':

---

[42] Patriot Dress and Patriot Games: Tartan from the Jacobites to Queen Victoria, *Murray G.H. Pittock, 2007.*

[43] *Possibly in a variant spelling.*

[44] *Called 'septs'.*

[45] *OK, not quite yet...*

[46] *There are all sorts of extraordinary tartans being created every week: while writing this, the Elvis Tartan was launched to commemorate the 30th anniversary of the great man's passing (or is it most seemly to say 'death'?). A sett of black, baby blue and pink gold connects Graceland with Andrew Pressley, who left Aberdeenshire in 1713.*

- The Black Watch: The dark green and blue.
- The Royal Stuart:[47] A scarlet with yellow, white and green.

With a flexible interpretation of tradition, anyone can wear these two – in history one reflected service to the nation, while the other reflected loyalty to the Crown; now I think they have become the red and green definitions of Scotland.[48]

---

[47] *Or Stewart – Mary Queen of Scots left Scotland as Mary Stewart to marry in France, but the French don't use 'w' much, so she amended her spelling. Not that that did her much good, really.*

[48] *Mind you, the range of unusual tartans is growing at a rate. Here's the McGinn A to Z of odd: All Breeds Dairy Goats; Australian Donkey; Barbecue; Bristow Helicopters; Burberry (protecting copyright, I guess!); Catalan Barcelona Olympics; Correctional Service of Canada; City of Rome Pipe Band; Da Vinci Rosslyn Code; Diana Princess of Wales Memorial; Encyclopaedia Brittanica; European Union; Federation of Circles and Solitaries (Michigan); Franconian (Malt Whisky Society of Bavaria); the Gouranja; Highland Spring; Holiday Inn Crowne Plaza; Irn-Bru; Sultan of Johore's Regiment; Java St Andrew's Society; Keepers of the Quaich; Ordo Supremis Militarisis Templi Hierosolymitain); Lady Boys of Bangkok; Lands End; Makhtoum (Dubai); Manhattan Financial; Niagara Falls; Norwegian Centennial; the Open Championship; the Olympics; Polaris; Quaboos (Oman); RMS Queen Mary; Romantic Scotland (Madonna); Rotary; Round Table; Salvation Army; Shrek; Singh; Sikh; Sheriff's Office of Spotsylvania County, PA; Racing Stewart (Sir Jackie, of course!); the Rhythms of Evylen Glennie; Tommy (Hilfiger); Tokyo Bluebells; Une Energie Nouveau en France; Utah Centennial; Virgin; Wagga Wagga NSW; Wombles; Xavier; Youd (Korea); but not one single Z (for shame).*

## Daytime and Evenings[49]

> Nowhere beats the heart so kindly
> As beneath the tartan plaid[50]

So how should you wear your tartan? The kilt is only part of the equation.[51] We need to get you kitted out to look the part.[52]

Just before we start, let's get all of the schoolboy humour out of the way. It is *absolutely* true what people say.

It is, however, a great shame that this one question – what is under the kilt? – dominates discussion of our national dress. As my wife says, such a lot of fuss over such a little thing.

So now your drawers are back in your drawers, what else is needed to let you out in the braw afternoon?

- A white shirt with a plain-coloured tie[53] (or, informally, an open neck).

- A jacket which is a bit shorter than a blazer/sports coat (either black with metal buttons or tweedy green[54] with horn or leather buttons).[55]

- Knee-length socks: thick wool, of a solid colour – red,

---

[49]  *What you want to wear at nighttimes is beyond the scope of this book!*

[50]  *'Charles Edward at Versailles', W.E. Ayton, Lays of the Scottish Cavaliers, 1849.*

[51]  *Did I mention that you wear it with the pleats at the back and the flat bit at the front? Just checking, certainly Juice Couture on 5th Avenue in New York needed a lesson when they dressed their mannequins back to front!*

[52]  *There's nothing wrong with wearing a pair of tartan trousers (or trews) and a navy-blue blazer (in the day) or a DJ (in the evening). Strictly speaking, 'trews' are not synonymous with 'trousers' as the latter have an outside side seam that the former do not (though it would take sharp eyes on a dark night to spot that difference).*

[53]  *Purists frown on a tartan tie with the kilt. If you want to be totally tartan, then feel free, but it goes without saying: the tie should be the same sett as your kilt.*

[54]  *Often Lovat Green, which was designed by Lord Lovat for his ghillies and soldiers as camouflage, initially on the stag moors, then on the battlefield, now in the golf club bar.*

[55]  *A nice alternative is an Aran or Newfoundland knit or similar heavy white/cream woolly jumper.*

green or blue are standard, to match with the predominant colour of your kilt, though black is quite trendy at the minute. These are held up by garters[56] with little flags or flashes in a matching or contrasting colour. Matching tartan flashes are popular just now.[57]

- When it comes to choosing shoes, the baseline must be shiny brogues[58] in black or brown, but informally anything short of wellington boots is alright. Mind you, on a typically rainy day those wellies might be a good idea.

Full dress in the evening is much more elaborate – but you needn't splash out at first; there are hundreds of hire shops that can rent you the full McMonty – which is a great way to start. There is nothing quite as handsome!

The biggest difference is in the jacket; either:

- The 'Prince Charlie Jacket': A short, black,[59] single-breasted tuxedo and waistcoat with silver buttons on the front, cuffs, tail and shoulder (worn with a dress white shirt and black bow tie); or

- The 'Doublet':[60] A closed double breasted jacket with double rows of silver buttons on the front, a high collar with lace at the throat (the 'jabot') and cuffs.

The socks and shoes call for that bit extra too! Shoes will either be ghillie brogues – open-topped tongue-less black leather shoes with the classic punched pattern of a brogue, with laces two-foot long, tied twisted round the wearer's leg; or, if very formal, patent leather pumps with silver buckles. Socks again reflect the wearer's weltanschauung: the base case is creamy-white with tartan flashes, or more elaborately, you can wear socks woven in your tartan with contrasting flashes.

---

[56] *No fetish; these are under the top of the sock.*
[57] *Although quite expensive!*
[58] *Wingtips, in US terms.*
[59] *You will see occasionally blue, green or even scarlet jackets!*
[60] *Sometimes in velvet – the names vary between tailors – Montrose, Kenmore, etc.*

That's the clothing – but there are important elements of kit that round off the ensemble:

- The Sporran: If not one of the greatest of Scotland's inventions, certainly a highly practical one. This combination of pocket, handbag and athletic support sits in front of the kilt. In the daytime, it is traditionally of tooled leather (two tassels for lads, and three for men) while in the evening, animal fur (sometimes even whole animals) with silver decorations is the norm.[61]

- The Belt: Before dark, any heavy brown belt will do, while formally a black leather belt closed with a flat silver plate (often embossed or engraved with Celtic symbols) is worn.

- The Skean Dhu: The wee dagger in the right-hand sock.[62] Most people, I think, have one to use regardless of the time of day – mine is black with a cairngorm semi-precious stone set in the top of the handle.

- The Fly Plaid: On very formal occasions (and more often in North America) you wear a piece of matching tartan over your left shoulder, secured by a large, silver, circular brooch (which often has a big semi-precious stone in the middle).[63]

- The Kilt Pin: Neophytes look for extra safety by using this to pin the flap down at the front – NO! Take your chances like the rest of us (more importantly, the kilt won't hang right, or even worse it won't swing as you walk!). Wear it about a hand's breath up and three fingers in from the front

---

[61]  *Pipers wear a crazy pattern of sporran that looks like a giant's paintbrush (or the bum of a heiland coo) – you'll sometimes see that species employed after dark.*

[62]  *But these days, please be careful not to fall foul of the law. You can buy ones with a fake plastic blade so that you can travel with hand baggage on the plane. For the Tartan Day commemoration on the steps of the US Capitol, attendees are respectfully advised to leave the Black Knife at home.*

[63]  *The use of tartan also extends to other formal wear, and not just bowties and cummerbunds. I was at a Jewish wedding last week in London and the gentleman from Glasgow beside me bore a fine tartan yarmulke.*

bottom-right corner. If it's a simple pin shape, the head of the pin should be downwards.

I've just noticed that I might have alienated half my potential readership by solely talking about what the boys get up to.

In very formal traditional evenings, white dresses with tartan sashes[64] would be the height of good taste and custom. By and large, ladies should use the tartan as a design concept in their clothing. Whether Westwood and punk-like or Ralph Lauren and preppy, tartan exercises quite an influence on modern design, so the most straightforward thing to do, dear female readers, is go shop!

> Lowland lassie wilt thou go,
> Whare the hills are clad wi' snow:
> Whare beneath the icy steep,
> The hardy shepherd tends his sheep;
> Ill nor wae shall thee betide,
> When row'd within my Highland Plaid.          [wrapped]
>
> Lowland lads may dress mair fine,
> Woo in words mair saft than mine!
> Lowland lads hae mair o' art,
> A' my boast's an honest heart,
> Whilk shall ever be my pride!
> O row thee in my Highland Plaid.
>
> 'Bonny lad, ye've been sae leal,          [loyal]
> My heart would break at our fareweel,
> Lang your love has made me fain,
> Tak' me – tak' me for your ain!'
> Cross the firth, awa' they glide,
> Young Donald and his Lowland bride.[65]

---

[64]  *There are a bizarre set of rules on these. I researched them for the last book and I really can't face them again – please refer to p.46 of the UBSB! Wear your sash across the chest and over the right shoulder is a rule of thumb. Or maybe use a fringed pashmina shawl across both shoulders, in a solid colour to match your man's kilt.*

[65]  'O Row Thee in My Highland Plaid', Robert Tannahill.

# 7

# Hands across the Seas

Whereas 6 April has a special significance for all Americans, and especially those Americans of Scottish descent, because the Declaration of Arbroath, the Scottish Declaration of Independence, was signed on 6 April 1320 and the American Declaration of Independence was modelled on that inspirational document;

Whereas this resolution honors the major role that Scottish Americans played in the founding of this Nation, such as the fact that almost half of the signers of the Declaration of Independence were of Scottish descent, the Governors in 9 of the original 13 States were of Scottish ancestry, Scottish Americans successfully helped shape this country in its formative years and guide this Nation through its most troubled times;

Whereas this resolution recognizes the monumental achievements and invaluable contributions made by Scottish Americans that have led to America's preeminence in the fields of science, technology, medicine, government, politics, economics, architecture, literature, media, and visual and performing arts; Whereas this resolution commends the more than 200 organizations throughout the United States that honor Scottish heritage, tradition, and culture, representing the hundreds of thousands of Americans of Scottish descent, residing in every State, who already have made the observance of Tartan Day on 6 April a success;

Whereas these numerous individuals, clans, societies, clubs, and fraternal organizations do not let the great contributions of the Scottish people go unnoticed:

> Now, therefore, be it Resolved, That the Senate designates 6 April
> of each year as 'National Tartan Day'.
>
> *US Senate Resolution 155*[1]

BEYOND OUR CRAGGY SHORES, Scots men and women have emigrated
to all points of the compass and have lived lives in every country on this
planet. It's a widely recognised phenomenon. The English author, Sir Walter
Besant described it:

> Wherever the pilgrim turns his feet, he finds Scotsmen in the
> forefront of civilization and letters. They are the premiers in
> every colony, professors of every university, teachers, editors,
> lawyers, engineers and merchants – everything and always at
> the front.[2]

It's not surprising therefore that there are a couple of festivals which
exist abroad with no equivalent in the home country.

The biggest of these is Tartan Day. While originally founded in
Canada,[3] the event has really taken off since the US Senate adopted its
Resolution. While there are ceremonies in many states, and a speech on
the steps of the Capitol attended by men in kilts, New York city has taken
it to heart and is the epicentre of the festival. But of course the Big Apple[4]
has to have a tartan week, not a day (New Yorkers never do things by
halves), which is now being called Scotland Week by the Scottish Government, but is really known by the locals by its original tartan title.

During the week there are all sorts of debates, plays, book readings,
poetry sessions, concerts and hoolies,[5] often graced by the presence of

---

[1]  *Proposed and carried* nem diss *by Senator Trent Lott (Mississipi-R) on 20
     March 1998.*

[2]  *An English author, so must be unbiased.*

[3]  *Naturally our cousins in New Scotland – aka Nova Scotia – lead the way, on
     6 April 1987, with all of the provinces (save Quebec and Newfoundland)
     following over the years.*

[4]  *The Big Haggis might be its nickname for this festival – not bad, as it's a mix
     of all sorts of things and not to everyone's taste.*

[5]  *A 'hooley' is more than a 'swally' but not enough to cause a 'rammy'.*

members of the Scottish Executive. The programme changes each year and some years are more successful than others. It can be a lot of fun, particularly if the weather is fine and clear for the parade. Since 1998, the streets of New York (more precisely along 6th Avenue from 45th Street to 58th Street) have been carpeted by the stirring sounds of hundreds (nay, thousands) of pipers, interspersed with Scottish societies, clan groups and various guys just looking for a party.[6]

In the evenings, with the Empire State Building lit up in the blue and white of the Scottish Saltire, there are parties and programmes a-plenty. From 'Dressed to Kilt' – a tartan-themed fashion show (where it's often the personalities on show, rather than the clothes) – to the range of whisky tastings available, it's boisterous, a bit controversial and quite unlike anything you'll find at home. While that raises some sneers, a few hackles and a lot of debate, it's well meant, particularly in the US. Virtually every national group has its corner of Manhattan, but there's no Little Scotland, and our cultural contribution to the history of North America was understated to the point of oblivion for many, many decades, so this could just be what's needed to grab attention and finally remove the most dreaded question any Scot is likely to be asked in the USA:

'Say buddy, what part of Ireland are you from?'

---

6   *Which includes the Tartan Army of Scottish football fans – so long as there's not a match on at the time!*

## Kirking the Tartan

> Whose love is given over well,
>  Shall look on Helen's face in Hell.
> Whilst they whose love is thin and wise
>  May view John Knox in Paradise.[7]

On a similar theme, there's a lot of tosherie goes on at the other celebration in the US and Australia, Kirking the Tartan.

I remember a dewy-eyed American gentleman explaining when I first visited the USA in 1981, that he was sorry that I'd missed sharing in the Kirkin o' the Tartan in his city, as I wouldn't be at the ceremony in my home of Glasgow. I nearly told him the truth, that it didn't happen there as far as I knew, but asked him to tell me more.

He told me an old, old tale of how, in the aftermath of Culloden, the vengeful Sassenach[8] passed laws outlawing the tartan. As the cloth was collected for destruction, old women hid snippets in the thatch of their cottages, particularly those near holy samples the Prince had distributed from his own plaid. Once a year at divine service in the Highland kirks, these fragments of Scotland's true spirit would be brought out of hiding to be blessed by the minister until freedom came back to Scotland.

Amen.

Please replace your hankies, ladies and gentlemen, for it is a truly sweet, emotive and factually groundless tale.

There is a good story behind this ceremony though, and it bears a valuable lesson. The format does seem ancient and traditional when you see it – pipers and drummers leading a procession of tartan flags[9] or bolts

---

[7]  'Partial Comfort', Ogden Nash.

[8]  A word which strictly means 'southerner' so should encompass Lowland Scots as well as English, but typically it's now an insult against the Anglos.

[9]  I have heard that some kirks enjoin a strict precedence: clan flags first in alphabetical order, followed by the local state tartan, then all other state tartans in order of accession to the Union, followed by clubs and societies by date of foundation.

of cloth,[10] and bagpipes providing the anthems during the service, with a roll call of clans present,[11] of course, and the minister's blessing of the tartans (linking the heritage of the tartans with the heritage of the saints) and finally, prior to the recessional of pipes, drums and tartans, a Scottish blessing, which might sound a bit like this:

> May the blessing of light be on you – light without and light within. May the blessed sunlight shine on you like a great peat fire, so that stranger and friend may come and warm himself at it. And may light shine out of the two eyes of you, like a candle set in the window of a house, bidding the wanderer come in out of the storm. And may the blessing of the rain be on you, may it beat upon your Spirit and wash it fair and clean, and leave there a shining pool where the blue of Heaven shines, and sometimes a star.
>
> And may the blessing of the earth be on you, soft under your feet as you pass along the roads, soft under you as you lie out on it, tired at the end of day; and may it rest easy over you when, at last, you lie out under it. May it rest so lightly over you that your soul may be out from under it quickly; up and off and on its way to God.
>
> And now may the Lord bless you, and bless you kindly.
>
> Amen.[12]

But the ceremony was a total invention by a Scots-born minister in Washington DC.

The Rev. Peter Marshall had been born in Coatbridge, but his ministry took him to America. In the dark days of 1940/41, when the land of his birth and her dominions were the last bulwark against the Nazi terror, he worked ceaselessly to bring attention to the justice of the war against Hitler and to galvanise support behind F.D.R.'s appreciation of the danger that regime posed to the whole free world.

---

[10] *Though in some ways this looks like stocktaking day on Princes Street.*

[11] *The relevant clan members in the congregation rise and remain standing. This is sometimes ended with 'Clan Dia' or 'All God's Children' (aka 'Jock Tamson's Bairns') so that everyone in the church is upstanding.*

[12] *Quoted from the St Andrew's Society of the State of New York newsletter,* The Pibroch, *by kind permission of President Duncan Bruce.*

One of his sermons at New York Avenue Presbyterian, to illustrate the resilience of the British people under bombings and privations, was preached as a metaphor on 27 April 1941 and was called Kirking the Tartan, and so the tradition was born.[13]

So that's one reason why you won't find this celebration if you visit Home!

Caledonia! thou land of the mountain and rock,
Of the ocean, the mist, and the wind–
Thou land of the torrent, the pine, and the oak,
Of the roebuck, the hart, and the hind;
Though bare are thy cliffs, and though barren thy glens,
Though bleak thy dun islands appear,
Yet kind are the hearts, and undaunted the clans,
That roam on these mountains so drear!

A foe from abroad, or a tyrant at home,
Could never thy ardour restrain;
The marshall'd array of imperial Rome
Essay'd thy proud spirit in vain!
Firm seat of religion, of valour, of truth,
Of genius unshackled and free,
The muses have left all the vales of the south,
My loved Caledonia, for thee!

Sweet land of the bay and wild-winding deeps
Where loveliness slumbers at even,
While far in the depth of the blue water sleeps
A calm little motionless heaven!
Thou land of the valley, the moor, and the hill,
Of the storm and the proud rolling wave–
Yes, thou art the land of fair liberty still,
And the land of my forefathers' grave![14]

---

[13] *Rather like the Oscar-winning film* Mrs Miniver *captured the English predicament and raised awareness, so the Kirking reached out to the ordinary Americans in support of F.D.R.'s message, and as ever they responded with courage, determination and sacrifice. For that we give real thanks.*

[14] 'Caledonia', James Hogg.

# 8

# Blood on the Borders

Hoys, Yes! That's ae time!
Hoys, Yes! That's twae times!
Hoys, Yes! That's the third and last time!
This is tae gie notice!
That there's a muckle Fair to be hadden in the Muckle Toon o'
the Langholm, on the Fifteenth day of July, auld style, upon His
Grace the Duke O' Buccleuch's Merk Land, for the space o'
eight days and upwards; and a' land-loupers, and dub-scoupers,
and gae-by-the-gate swingers, that come here tae breed hurdums
or durdums, huliments or buliments, hagglements or bragglements, or tae molest this public fair, they shall be ta'en by order
o' the Bailie an' the Toon Cooncil, and their lugs shall be nailed
to the Tron wi' a twalpenny nail; and they shall sit doon on their
bare knees and pray seven times for the King, thrice for the
Muckle Laird o' Ralton, and pay a groat tae me, Jaimie Ferguson,
Bailie o' the aforesaid manor, an I'll away hame an' hae a barley banna' an' a saut herrin' tae ma denner by way o' auld style.
Huzza! Huzza! Huzza![1]

A BORDER IS AT one level a defining line, an ending (or a beginning) – a
line drawn in some sand or frozen in masonry – as the Great Wall of
China, or the famous scene with Steve McQueen on his motorcycle in *The
Great Escape*. Often, of course, they are made by features of the earth –
seas, rivers and mountains present unarguable divisions which allow a new
Mormon state in Utah or the preservation of the lost tribe of the Kukuana
in *King Solomon's Mines*. Perhaps a history of bravery gives an Alamo or
a Thermopylae, where the boundary remains marked in blood and
sacrifice. Sometimes sheer weariness is the cause – oftentimes friendly, as

---

[1]  *Traditional: Langholm Common Riding, Third Calling. More about this later,
but no hagglements or bragglements in the meantime or there will be trouble.*

across the 49 degrees of latitude separating Seattle and Vancouver,[2] but sometimes sinister, as the 38th parallel's DMZ arbitrarily divides South Korea and its industries from its poor siblings in the north.[3] However, in the world after Checkpoint Charlie, the closest most of us come to borders is the interminable queue at the airport,[4] hoping that the forms are filled in quickly and we can proceed to the baggage lottery to see if we have won this time, or if two weeks of dirty Scottish laundry has now embarked on its independent odyssey to some lost corner of the world.

But often borders aren't lines; for centuries they were battlefields, with an elastic frontier depending on might not cartography; lands like the Khyber Pass, where local families and tribes had actual control in the interstices between two engaged powers.

So was the history of the Borders between Scotland and England, from the abandonment of Hadrian's Wall by the Romans through to at least the 17th century (and there's a good argument for saying a good 80 years after that).

This area was known in those days as 'the Debateable Lands' because this was where the valour of Scotland and the might of England tussled, and in between those tussles, allowed a hardy breed of lawless men to grow – called the reivers – and to operate a life of blood feud, blackmail and banditry.

Even by the complex standards of the Scoto–Anglo interface, this is a hairy subject – but it would be wrong to think that it was a simple political battle. While the predominant thread – and the major battles – were 'official' proper international matches – Scotland vs. England – the gaps were filled by the Borderers on both sides. As can be imagined, families in the area would sometimes find the datum line shifted and they became English for a few years, or reverted to the Scots jurisdiction. So in time the north of England and south of Scotland saw communities

---

[2]   *Not always so peaceful – '54' 40' or Fight' was the slogan (a Gaelic word by the way) in the 1844 democratic campaign to push the US border in a straight line across the top of Oregon.*

[3]   *The divide in this case of course is so much greater – a mediaeval nuclear power is a terrifying thought.*

[4]   *A terminal disease.*

of the same surname: the Armstrongs of Liddesdale and Annandale were also in Cumberland; Bells and Halls were everywhere; the Elliots,[5] the Grahams/Graemes, the Kerrs/Carrs abounded.

What made the Debateable Lands hard work was the feuding between the families. This followed a very simple dance routine. Strong family A sends the lads round to weaker family B and pinches their cows.[6] Some days later Daddy A sends a message to Old Pa B that in return for payment – blackmail[7] – the cattle[8] would be returned, and in a special offer, for a like payment on a regular cycle, Family A would forbear from taking the herd again and turn this into a simple financial transaction (allowing the lads of A to turn their attentions to Family C along the road).[9]

Occasionally Family B would fancy its chances and either (i) resist the initial assault,[10] (ii) launch a retaliatory raid[11] or (iii) appeal to the Lords of the Marches – the cross-border police.[12]

The important thing to understand is that these raids were not exclusively international. There was a lot of S on S and E on E violence

---

[5]   *These chaps illustrate an allied issue: orthography. When you had an illiterate body and a hard name, the variant spellings multiplied. They say that across Scotland and England there are about 50 ways of spelling Elliot – I've never really found a wet day long enough to try, but feel free.*

[6]   *At this stage in the dance, burning thatched cottages, killing children and violating the womenfolk were optional.*

[7]   *Derived from 'meal' or 'mail' – the Scots word for 'rent' – 'black' denoting the underhand and illegal nature of the demand.*

[8]   *Or at least a substantial portion thereof, allowing for a 'service & handling' charge.*

[9]   *The McMob really – I wonder if the Kray twins had any Scottish blood in them? A new Dapper Don in Highland dress is a plot line even* The Sopranos *couldn't match.*

[10]  *A few broken heads might chase off the As, but by and large this would result in: burning thatched cottages, killing children or violating the womenfolk.*

[11]  *Allowing the Bs their fair chance to burn thatched cottages, kill children or violate the womenfolk.*

[12]  *Relatively pointless unless one king or other wanted to take the As down a peg or two by sending soldiers – yes, you've guessed it – to burn thatched cottages, kill children and almost certainly violate the womenfolk. By this stage the cows were sold, dead or eaten, but honour was saved.*

arising out of intertribal feud. So you'd find the English Armstrongs supporting the Scottish Armstrongs in a fight against the Fenwicks in Northumberland.[13]

The best tale of this hard and dark life was that of the twelve men of the Scotts who were overpowered deep in the English sector by their great rivals. When taken to the head of their enemy, bound but still defiant, the senior Scott was asked, 'Why did ye come so far to steal our sheep?' The reply, 'We came so far to steal your women, but when we saw what they looked like – we took your sheep', guaranteed a hanging.[14]

Hadrian had decreed the final boundary of his empire to run between Wallsend (Newcastle upon Tyne) and Bowness on the Solway Firth (now on the English side, south of Dumfries). Over the centuries the English couldn't pressure the west, with the natural protection of the Solway and its famously treacherous tides. So the border pivoted from about Gretna, as the fixed point in the west, up to a line on the Cheviots to Alnwick, finally pushing to bite out a quadrilateral, with Berwick-upon-Tweed as the furthest point of the north-eastern border.[15]

Now, this causes a few anomalies – like Koenigsburg or Strasbourg, Berwick is a town trapped in the borders of history, geography and law. It is the only English town with a football team that plays in the Scottish football league,[16] but it's not the southernmost – as Ayr United and its

---

[13]   *As time went on, more Borderers sought the peace of the king's justice, and the powerful noble families banded together in 1569 to request that the authorities help in the fight against 'all thieves of Liddesdale, Annandale, Ewesdale, Eskdale and especially to all Armstrongs, Elliots, Nixsons, Crosers, Lilles, Batesons, Thomsons, Irvines, Bells, Johnstones, Glendennings, Routledges, Hendersons, and Scotts of Ewesdale'.*

[14]   *But it's good to go out with a great line. My thanks to Bob Thian, who, in addition to being a great person to sit beside at a Burns Supper, told me this story of his family.*

[15]   *It is this angle that causes technical problems under the Law of the Sea for the independence claims to 'Scotland's Oil'.*

[16]   *Conversely, its rugger team is affiliated to both the RFU of England and the SRU of Scotland – a distinction shared with London Scottish Football Club (which is, of course, a rugby club).*

arch-rivals Killie and Stranraer, Gretna and Queen of the South[17] are all geographically closer to the Equator.[18] Its local regiment was the redoubtable Kings Own Scottish Borders (the KOSBies), whose museum still resides in the town, though the regiment itself has been absorbed into the Royal Regiment of Scotland.[19] On the other hand, it calls itself a 'borough' in the English spelling and has a mayor rather than a provost. Confused?

It is a beautiful town, and its history is encapsulated by the perfect fortification walls that still stand today, guarding the pretty Georgian buildings and the three impressive bridges across the Tweed. When captured by Henry VIII,[20] the peace treaty which allowed him to keep Berwick described it rather carefully as:

Berwick in England but not of England[21]

So the diplomats treaded very carefully and thereafter all deeds, treaties and laws were passed talking about 'Scotland, England, Wales, Ireland and Berwick-upon-Tweed'. It was only when explicit legislation was passed after a few centuries of careful circumlocution that Berwick was legally defined as English.[22]

---

[17]   *The soccer team of Dumfries, where the locals are known as 'Doonhamers'.*

[18]   *British geography is pretty unintuitive – did you know that Edinburgh on the east coast of Scotland is a few minutes further WEST than Bristol on the west coast of England?*

[19]   *Now the 1st Battalion RRS (or 1 SCOTS, in the rather prosaic nomenclature).*

[20]   *Who, on average, did more damage to the Borders than he did to his wives.*

[21]   *Treaty of Perpetual Peace 1502. This was just eleven years before the greatest Scottish defeat – not so perpetual after all. The document is a beautiful example of its genre and can be seen in the National Archives of Scotland, in Edinburgh – it is decorated on its borders by entwined thistles and roses, the first conjoined use of the two national flowers, to celebrate the betrothal of Henry VIII's sister (Margaret Tudor) to James IV of Scotland.*

[22]   *The Wales and Berwick Act 1746 (20 Geo II c. 42) defined that reference to 'England' would henceforth encompass Berwick. There was some doubt if that actually meant that Berwick was part of England, given the Treaty, but the dull prose of the Local Government Act 1972 and the Interpretation Act 1978 have (probably) resolved the question – except that these sort of questions never are resolved! At the time of writing, the Scottish Government has floated the idea of reabsorption.*

You can't talk about Berwick without answering the great question: is Berwick still at war with Russia?

The story goes that when the Crimean War was declared in 1853, it was in the name of 'Victoria, of the United Kingdom of Great Britain and Ireland, of Berwick-upon-Tweed and her other Dependencies across the Seas, Queen, Defender of the Faith'. But when we won, the Peace Treaty of Paris in 1856 omitted to mention Berwick in the recital of the treaty parties' styles and titles. Some form of logic suggested then that while all HM's other territories were at peace, Berwick was still on DEFCON 1.[23]

In 1966, it is said, an attaché from the Russian Embassy in London came north to call on the Mayor of Berwick and confirm that the USSR[24] wanted to resolve this issue once and for all. It is reported[25] that the mayor shook hands with the Russian, telling him that the war was over, and solemnly gave his benediction: 'the Russian people can now sleep peacefully in their beds again.'

Alas, although Queen Victoria was proudly enumerating Berwick as her possession as late as her coronation (1838),[26] she had stopped well before 1853. But it is a nice story. And I hope the Russian people are still peaceful in their beds, no longer awaiting the wrath of the 25,000 souls of Berwick-upon-Tweed.

## What I Have I Hold

Teribus ye Teri Odin,
Sons of Heroes Slain at Flodden,
Imitating Border Bowmen,
Aye Defend your Rights and Common.

Scotia felt thine ire O Odin,
On the Bloody Field of Flodden.
Where our Fathers fell with honour
Round the King and Country's Banner.

---

[23] *Equivalent to a Red Bikini.*

[24] *A nation which had a rather shorter existence than the Borough of Berwick!*

[25] *Mythically.*

[26] *Not that many from Berwick were probably invited.*

All was sunk in deep dejection,
None to flee to for protection,
When some youths who stayed from Flodden,
Rallied up by Teri Odin.

Armed with sword and bow and quiver
Shouting 'Vengance now or never!'
Off they marched in martial order
Down by Teviot's flowery Border.

Down they threw their bows and arrows,
Drew their swords like veteran heroes,
Charged their foes with native valour,
Routed them and took their colours.

Now with spoils and honours laden,
Well revenged for fateful Flodden.
Home they marched this flag displaying –
Teribus before them playing.

Annual since our flag's been carried,
Round the mair by men unmarried.
Emblem grand of those who won it,
Matrimonial hands would stain it.

Peace be thy portion, Hawick forever,
Thine arts, thy commerce flourish ever,
Down to the latest age they send it:
'Hawick was ever independent!!!!'[27]

What lesson can we garner from this element of our history? To fight
for our rights and our independence – an essential feature of the
Scottish psyche, which still can be seen in the great days of adventure,
proud defence of land and bravery on horseback performed in the Scots
Border towns every summer in the Common Ridings.

---

[27] 'Teribus': Hawick's Song, James Hogg, The Ettrick Shepherd (edited). The
opening line harks back to the Celts and Vikings as it is a corruption of 'tyr
i bas y tyr i Odin' or 'Land of death and Land of Odin'.

These annual celebrations of each Border town are truly community affairs. They are a very old tradition and celebrate the towns' independence and the integrity of their common lands – the patrimony of the towns-folk. Sometimes the tradition started like a 'beating of the bounds' after a court order confirmed the burgh's land rights but set it the ongoing duty of maintaining the boundary marks in good order. More often, it commemorates an act of gallantry in the long Border wars,[28] such as Fletcher of Selkirk returning alone from Flodden carrying the town flag safely home, or the young man of Hawick who captured an English flag in 1514, or the braw lads of Gala who slew the English raiders while they were stealing plums from an orchard.[29] A few towns' celebrations are more modern but seek to capture those same themes.

The big events are:

| Burgh[30] | Name | Date |
|---|---|---|
| Lauder | Common Riding | 1686 |
| Selkirk | Common Riding | 1540 |
| Hawick | Common Riding | 1703 |
| Langholm | Langholm Fair | 1759 |
| Galashields | Braw Lads' Gathering | 1939 |
| Jedburgh | Callants Festival | 1947 |
| Kelso | Civic Week | 1937 |
| Duns | Summer Festival | 1949 |
| Coldstream | Civic Week | 1952 |
| Peebles | Riding Out | *[31] |

---

[28]  *I told you all that would be relevant!*

[29]  *The town's motto is 'Soor Plooms' (Sour Plums), which is also a really sour green boiled sweetie.*

[30]  *If I have missed anyone, I apologise!*

[31]  *Peebles was traditionally held earlier at Beltane (q.v.) but revised this to the third week in June to coincide with the Ridings. Still they crown the Beltane Queen, even though the dates are a bit mixed up.*

Each Riding has its own principles, practices and procedures, which have evolved over the centuries and remain close-held traditions. In general, the common themes are:

- **A Principal Man:** One unmarried man[32] is elected by a traditional constituency within the town (the town council, or all the unmarried men of the town, or everyone resident). He becomes the embodiment of the burgh for the celebrations. Sometimes he is named after his duty in carrying the town flag: he is the Standard Bearer in Selkirk, and the Cornet[33] in Hawick. Sometimes he's named after the rough and tumble of the bad years – with a Braw Lad (a good fighter) in Gala, the Callant (a strong young man of Jedburgh) or the Reiver (a resourceful cattle thief) in Duns – while others take the name of the town – the Melrosian, the Kelso Laddie and the Coldstreamer need little explanation. Typically, the Principal is supported by his predecessors for the previous two years, to provide support and guidance, but also commemorating the bodyguard who would give their lives to save the Principal and allow him to fulfil his duty.[34]

- **A Horse:** The whole tradition is centred on the speed and efficiency of mounted attack in those bloody times. The Principal and his fellows need to be good horsemen!

- **A Flag:** The symbol of the burgh – in a crisis, the production of the burgh flag would be the rallying call for the men of the town to mount and ride. As with military flags, this standard[35] is the sacred essence of the town and lives must be lost rather than the flag be desecrated by falling into enemy hands.

---

[32]  *As described in 'Teribus' above, 'Matrimonial hands would stain it'.*

[33]  *An old military title for a junior officer of horse (c.f. 'ensign' in the army) – it's still in use in the Household Cavalry, where the equivalent of a 2nd lieutenant is called cornet today. Originally these young officers would have been the regiment's standard bearer in battle – as can still be seen at Trooping the Colour in London each summer.*

[34]  *A bit like the wingman in Top Gun – sort of 'take my broth away'.*

[35]  *Really a banner or guidon in shape with round swallow tails.*

Like all true folk traditions, every community follows a set of rituals that are organic and have weathered like the local stone – sometimes carved by man's hand, sometimes marked by moss or lichen, some corners with crumbles and others remaining right; over the centuries no two are identical.

Most begin with some form of Calling Out, where the provost or some other high heid yin[36] announces the Riding to the townsfolk and delivers the Flag into the charge of the Principal. Hawick's is the most flamboyant, and the town has its own set of songs – known by all – which punctuate the celebrations. Typically the townsfolk will gather to support, protect and honour the Principal; as they say in Selkirk, 'tae see him safe oot and safe in'.[37]

When the Flag is first on duty, the girls of the town show their love for it in the Bussing of the Flag. To buss is to kiss or reverence, and just as the ladies of old gave a knight their favour[38] by tying a handkerchief or ribbon on his lance, so the Principal's girlfriend and her chums decorate the flag with coloured ribbons. Sometimes these will be the town colours (the 'true blue and scarlett' of Selkirk), or they might be the Principal's lucky colour – for some reason Langholm uses the colours of the jockey who won that year's Derby!

The core purpose of all of this is Riding the Marches – the Principal and Supporters lead everyone on horseback around the traditional boundaries of the town. Sometimes formal challenges are shouted out to any enemy who might be prowling, sometimes toasts are given by local cottagers and farmers, sometimes the Flag itself is dipped into the rivers marking the limits – whatever the precise format, it is the power of the town[39] which must be exercised against military aggression or civil encroachment, preserving 'the Common Good' for the generations yet to come and commemorating those who have done such service for centuries before.

---

[36]  *As dignitaries are known in Scotland (not necessarily a compliment!).*

[37]  *So like Brian Hanrahan's famous news report: 'I've counted them all out and I've counted them all back', about the pilots in the Falklands in the 1982 war.*

[38]  *Metaphorical.*

[39]  *In legal terms, the civilians banding together to ward off evil was known in legal Latin as the* posse comitatus *– (the power of the county). The posse is a concept more familiar in cowboy movies.*

As a side bar, on days leading up to the Common Riding, there might be Ride Outs, which are subsidiary jaunts to outlying villages or farmsteads as part of the community celebration.

Amongst all the colour and tradition, there is usually one element that stands out in each festival – the unique 'party piece'.

Hawick has the exhilarating Chases. In these, the Cornet and the committee lead hundreds of riders in procession through the town to Niperknows Hill.[40] Then, with the Colour held high, and guarded unto Death by his Right Hand Man and Left Hand Man, the Cornet pelts up the hill at a full gallop, leading the unmarried men to the top to be rewarded with a traditional dish of curds and cream.[41]

In Selkirk, the underlying tale is sadder:

Frae every cleuch and clan
The best o' the braid Border
Rose like a single man
To meet the royal order.
Our Burgh toun itsel'
Sent its seventy doon the glen;
Ask Fletcher how they fell,
Bravely fechting, ane to ten!          [fighting]
O Flodden Field!

---

[40]   *The Chases were once run in Hawick itself, until a fatal accident in 1876 which resulted in the arrest of the Cornet!*

[41]   *Opinion is divided as to whether this represents the capture of the English Flag at the Battle of Hornshole or a re-enactment of the magistrates chasing off encroachers.*

Round about their gallant King,
For countrie and for croon,
Stude the dauntless Border ring
Till the last was hackit doon,[42]                    [hacked]
I blame na what has been –
They maun fa' that canna flee –
But oh! To see what I hae seen,
To see what now I see!
O Flodden Field![43]

So the highlight is the Casting of the Flags – commemorating the day that alone of all the men of Selkirk, Fletcher returned alive after Flodden against all odds, waving the captured flag of the English Macclesfield Regiment around his head and casting it to the ground, before collapsing exhausted. After the Riding, the Standard Bearer

---

[42]  *James was treated rather shabbily. His body was stripped naked and taken down to London to prove his death to Henry VIII (some brother-in-law!), but it was discovered that the Scottish king had been excommunicated and so couldn't be buried. His unentombed body was left in the Abbey of Sheen for about 50 years, and was looted in the destruction of the monastery by a merchant in Wood Street, London, who kept the body as a rather grisly sideshow. If anyone reading this has what they think might be the last mortal and unshriven remains of our late king in their loft or garden shed, please send a postcard to Holyrood Palace.*

[43]  'The Departure and Return', J.B. Fletcher. See more at www.selkirk.border-net.co.uk/history/battleofflodden.html. *These Border songs about Flodden follow a genre made famous by 'The Flowers o' the Forest', the great Scottish dirge with words by Jean Elliot, heard often on the pipes at funerals to this day:*
Dule and wae for the order sent our lads to the Border;
The English, for ance, by guile wan the day:
The Flowers of the Forest, that foucht aye the foremost,
The prime o' our land are cauld in the clay.
We'll hae nae mair lilting, at the yowe-milking,
Women and bairns are dowie and wae.
Sighing and moaning, on ilka green loaning,
The Flowers of the Forest are all wede away.

climbs on a stage in the Market Place and ceremoniously casts the town flag around him,[44] reliving the actions of brave Fletcher of Flodden Field.

In Kelso, the Laddie has to cross the Border into England to receive a Blue Bonnet,[45] while Gala's Braw Lad commemorates the marriage of James IV and Margaret Tudor with a wreath of red and white roses mixed with thistles. In Jedburgh, to the cry 'Jeddart's Here!' the final day starts with a cannon firing and a pell-mell horse race around the town.

As part of the festivities, the Riding will morph into a Highland games, or a fair or dance. Langholm combines its Riding with the ancient Langholm Fair and has the most famous examples of the Fair Callings – the stylised proclamations that are the chapter headings to the points of the ritual.

The First Calling reminds the burghers of the boundary marks and calls for their service in maintaining them today. A great procession forms behind the Cornet and his Flag, and prominent locals carry the four town symbols on high. They are an unusual selection: on the logical side is the Spade (a handy tool to have when marking the boundaries), but the others have deeper or odder symbolism: a huge Thistle and a Floral Crown are carried – the first to show how prickly the folk are in protecting their rights, the latter to show that independence of mind can go hand-in-hand with loyalty to the sovereign. The fourth is a Salt Herring and a Bannock, which are nailed to a wooden plate, itself nailed to a huge pole. No idea why.

After the boundaries are marched, the Crier makes the Second Calling:

---

[44]   *This is followed by the casting of flags representing the old trades and corporations of the burgh.*

[45]   *Commemorated by Sir Walter Scott in 'The Monastery' (1825):*
March, march Ettrick and Teviotdale,
Why the Deil dinna ye march forward in order?
March, march Eskdale and Liddesdale,
All the Blue Bonnets are bound for the Border

Now, Gentlemen, we hae gane roun' oor hill,
So now I think it's richt we had oor fill
O' guid strang punch[46] – twould mak us a' tae sing,
Because this day we have dune a guid thing;
For gangin' roun' oor hill we think nae shame,
Because frae it oor peats and flacks come hame;
So now I will conclude and sae nae mair,
And gin ye're a' pleased I'll cry the Langholm Fair.

And then to finish the proceedings and open the fair, the Third Calling (which is the epigraph to this chapter) begins the fun!

It's amazing in the speedy modern world to see a whole town's population turn out on the streets to celebrate a bond, defined in an historical event, but totally relevant to us today in terms of the civic spirit and neighbourliness. Who are the enemies now? Wrong question – it's the crystallisation of the pride of community, the belief that we are all in this town together; the border ridings are about 'us' not 'them'.

And that, dear friends, is a good place to finish recalling the long and formerly bloody traditions of the Borders.

This queer compromise between fairyland and battlefield which is the Border.[47]

---

[46]  *Punch was a very popular drink across Scotland in the early 1800s, as merchants and sailors came home from the first visits to India. Punch is a corruption of* 'painch', *'five' in Hindi, denoting the five ingredients of a traditional punch: hot water, lemons, strong spirit, sugar and spice.*

[47]  In Search of Scotland, H.V. Morton, 1929.

# 9

# Summer Games

I was out the whole day with Albert, in the forest in a perfectly tropical heat. Since we went to Allt-na-Giuthasach, our little bothy nearr Loch Muich on the 12th, the heart of the sun has been daily increasing, and has reached a pitch which makes it almost sickening to be out in it, though it is beautiful to behold. The sky these last two evenings has been like an Italian one, and for the last few days – at least the last four – without the slightest particle of cloud, and the sun blazing. With this, and not a breath of air. The mountains look quite crimson and lilac, and everything glows with the setting sun.[1]

WHEN THE SUMMER season dawns, tourists and town dwellers head for the coasts and the hills of Scotland to enjoy the traditional summer holiday as children for generations were chased out to play with the maternal injunction ringing in their ears: 'Out you go and play – it's no that wet.' For many years, when Scotland was home to more manufacturing and heavy industries, whole towns and cities would close on the same day for two weeks and the entire working population would decamp en masse.

The largest of these exoduses was the Glasgow Fair Fortnight. The Second City of the Empire closed its works and factories at 4pm on the same Thursday[2] in July every year – and in an attenuated fashion, many Glaswegians still follow the timetable, although Turkey, Morocco and Ibiza are more likely now than the old destinations of Ullapool, Ayr or Arran.

One particularly enjoyable feature remains to today's tourist: going 'doon the watter' – or sailing from Glasgow to one of the islands in the

---

[1] *Letter, Queen Victoria to Leopold I, King of the Belgians, from Balmoral Castle, 16 September 1851.*

[2] *Always the second Thursday after the first Tuesday in July.*

firth of Clyde. If you can, try and sail on the PS *Waverley* – the last ocean-going paddle steamer afloat.[3] With her characteristic painted funnel of red/white/black and the two big paddle wheels, she is a welcome and much-loved craft.[4]

I know the weather isn't all it might be, but everyone has a favourite local resort: Ayr with its long golden beaches, Largs in its former art deco glory, out to Millport to hire a bike or (far away on the other coast) Gullane or North Berwick to stride the dunes in the fresh air. Ice creams feature prominently, with the great Italian families, led by the high priests of Nardini or Zavaroni, serving cones, 99s, wafers nougats, double nougats or the fabulous oyster, maybe with a splash of raspberry goo on top.[5] On the way home a good fish supper – always haddock (or it was in those halcyon summers) – with good Scottish potatoes double cooked, heavily salty and tanging of malt vinegar, like the breath of the sea. Happy days!

## Spontaneous Exertion

Scotland is fortunate in having some of the most beautiful countryside in Europe,[6] with a mix of coastline, islands, lochs and glens, forests and heaths; but of all those things that capture the imagination, our mountains – the bens – must come top.

---

3   *She usually does a few trips from Tower Pier in London at the end of the season.*

4   *She was launched in 1947 to replace her predecessor, sunk at Dunkirk rescuing the British army in the dark days of June 1940. J.B. Priestly broadcast that day; was this about our wee Scottish boat?:*
    *'This little steamer, like all her brave and battered sisters, is immortal. She'll go sailing proudly down the years in the epic of Dunkirk. And our great-great grandchildren, when they learn how we began this war by snatching glory out of defeat, and then swept on to victory, may also learn how the little holiday steamers made an excursion to hell and came back glorious.' BBC broadcast, 5 June 1940.*

5   *If raspberry sauce at the ice-cream van ever saw a raspberry, I'd be surprised.*

6   *Compensation for the rain!*

I to the hills will lift mine eyes,
  From whence doth come my aid.
My safety cometh from the Lord,
  Who Heav'n and earth hath made.[7]

In the summer,[8] hillwallking is one of the most popular outdoor activities in our country. Uniquely, we have the odd concept of 'bagging the Munros', which has been invested with a certain formality and certainly warrants a toast upon achievement.

This takes a little explanation. In 1891, Sir Hugh Munro of the Scottish Mountaineering Club drew up a list ('Munro's Tables') identifying every mountain in Scotland of over 3,000ft in height. He defined a total of 236 independent mountains (with a further 255 'tops' or subsidiary peaks) – all in the Highlands – and in so doing, started a mania for climbers to ascend every single one! To this day, the separate mountains are called Munros in his honour, while the feat of an individual summit is called 'bagging' that particular mountain, and the SMC has maintained a list of everyone[9] who has scaled the lot.[10]

Modern science and the fascination of an interest group focussing on a relatively small question have led to a few promotions and demotions over the century and now the adjusted list stands at 283 Munros with 227 tops alongside.[11]

This list is ironically not cast in stone. There were 284 Munros until 2009 when Sgurr Nan Ceanniachean in Wester Ross was tested by new GPS

---

[7]   *Psalm cxxi, 1, Scottish Metrical Psalms, 1650.*

[8]   *And if you know what you are doing, are properly equipped and appropriately fit, in the winter, too.*

[9]   *Over 3,900 souls – and the number is rising rapidly.*

[10]  *Or as they quaintly describe it, 'completed' the list, thus becoming a certified 'compleatist' – handy Scrabble word, that one.*

[11]  *A refinement of the definition of a Munro being that it has to be 3,000ft or over and at least 500ft more prominent than any neighbouring peak. The joy of collecting extends to smaller hills too – the Corbetts (2,500–3,000ft) and the Grahams (2,000–2,500ft).*

methods and was found to be five foot short.[12] There is hope though that Beinn Derag in Torridon might breast the tape, being 2,999ft today.[13]

It would only take our top seven peaks to beat Everest. Or if you confine yourself to Europe, it's the rough equivalent of balancing Mont Blanc on top of the Matterhorn – or one-and-a-half Mount McKinleys in US dollar terms![14]

| E | 1 | Ben Nevis | 4,409ft |
| V | 2 | Ben Macdui | 4,295ft |
| E | 3 | Braeriach | 4,252ft |
| R | 4 | Cairn Toul | 4,236ft |
| E | 5 | Sgor an Lochain Uaine[15] | 4,127ft |
| S | 6 | Cairngorm | 4,081ft |
| T | 7 | Aonach Beag | 4,049ft |
| 29,035ft | | | 29,449ft |

## The Invisible Enemy

When you participate in Scotland's great outdoors, you face one of the great dangers and downsides of our fair land. Every year, Scots and Sassenachs, returning diaspora[16] members and travellers, tourists and day-trippers set out for our dramatic countryside and instead end up on the menu for The Midge.

It will have blood; they say[17]

---

[12]  *You win some, you lose some.*

[13]  *Building a cairn is cheating, regardless of what happens in Wales (or Hollywood).*

[14]  *For the classically trained, we could not only pile Pelion (6,490ft) upon Ossa (5,417ft), but do it twice!*

[15]  *The Angel's Peak.*

[16]  *A term now widely used, though it gives me some concern. Many rightly think of one particular Diaspora, a part of another national story.*

[17]  *Macbeth, W. Shakespeare, Act III, Scene IV.*

If a formal charge were being drawn up to prosecute this fiendish little biter, it would be in its Latinate name: *Culicoides impunctatus*. This 2 mm cousin of the mosquito is tiny little bug with very large jaws! My research tells me that boy midges[18] are rather innocuous little fellows, buzzing about, shooting the breeze, having a crack, but it is Mrs Midge[19] that's the menace. In one of biology's cheery jests, Mrs M. can only lay her eggs after having a nice feast of mammalian blood, so from June through to September we provide the needful to allow Mr & Mrs Midge to generate a happy family with 2.4 (thousand) little ones. What makes this particularly interesting is that the Midges live with their ten million cousins. When gorged with blood, Mrs M. emits phemerones which attract every other female midge to come and bite you. So by the end of the average day, you'll be godparent to about a million midges!

You will be safe in Princes Street Gardens, or even better in a Rose Street pub, so it's an avoidable problem, but wherever there are damp,[20] uncultivated fields, forests, woods, bogs or marshes[21] they will be a pest. The Highlands are awash with them and you'll find them throughout the lowland west coast. They are attracted by the $CO_2$ we exhale, so unless you are adept at holding your breath, they will find you – particularly in the cool of the morning or the evening; hot temperatures and windy days oppress them.

Every family has a unique (but inefficient) repellent they try and use: from wearing white clothes, to DEET[22] or citronella oil, or Avon's Skin-So-Soft (my favourite). The biting is bad enough – but it's the two-day-

---

[18] *Or sometimes people call them a 'midgie' – which I think is an incorrect backformation from the plural 'midgies'.*

[19] *A truly Kipling-esque species, the F of which is more D than the M.*

[20] *In Scotland – surely not!*

[21] *That's a pretty big percentage of the Scottish landmass.*

[22] *Or any form of UN-banned chemical weaponry.*

afterwards itch that is so infuriating. You will actually see wild red deer shift up to the tops of hills to escape the maddening little brutes. So you will need some aftercare – witch hazel or similar.[23]

What the heck: it's all part of the fun of being outdoors. Next you'll want your barbeque sausages cooked in the middle and not burned on the outside.

## The Gathering of the Clans

> When Death's dark stream I ferry o'er,
>  (A time that surely shall come,)
> In Heav'n itself I'll ask no more,
>  Than just a Highland welcome.[24]

If you have no head for heights, but are undeterred by the chomping *Culicoides*, you can spend most of the summer weekends touring the range of Highland games.[25]

The basis of these competitions is the tradition of the chief watching his men perform feats of strength and agility so that he could choose the mightiest warriors to fight beside him. Legend has it that the first formal games was a practical interview by King Malcolm Canmore,[26] where he had men race up Craig Coinnich (outside Braemar) to find the fastest messenger. This history is often challenged;[27] some hold the Ceres in Fife was the site of a games to choose the bowmen who fought with

---

[23] *Firstly, don't scratch – didn't your mother tell you that only makes it worse? Secondly, the rapid application of whisky (externally and internally turn and turn about) at least makes you feel a bit more at ease with the wider world.*

[24] *'Epigram on Parting with a Kind Host in the Highlands', Robert Burns.*

[25] *Actually this would be a tour of the world, as you will find games of over a century old throughout North America, Australia and New Zealand. But home's where the heart is!*

[26] *Canmore was a nickname given to the king meaning 'Big Head' – I think because of hat size rather than any ability at Sudoku.*

[27] *But never in Braemar.*

Bruce at Bannockburn, while others hold for whichever festival they themselves appear in.[28]

There's an old set of Homeric epithets[29] associated with many of the clans, the world at large ascribing a particular characteristic to the whole family:

| | | |
|---|---|---|
| The sturdy Armstrongs | The trusty Boyds | The crooked[30] Campbells |
| The clavering Clarks | The dirty Dalrymples[31] | The doughty Douglases |
| The lucky Duffs | The bauld[32] Frasers | The gallant Grahams[33] |
| The gay Gordons | The haughty Hamiltons | The handsome Hays |
| The gentle Johnstons | The jingling Jardines | The crabbed Kerrs |
| The lightsome Lindsays | The brave Macdonalds | The gabby McGinns |
| The fiery Macintoshes[34] | The luckless Mcleans[35] | The proud McNeills |
| The manly Morrisons | The fause Menteiths[36] | The windy Murrays |
| The bold Rutherfords | The lousy Turnbulls | The worthy Watsons |

---

[28] *Probably the oldest recorded competition is in the Lowlands, where 2008 saw the 500th running of the Red Hose Race, which started when James IV chartered the estate of Carnwath to Lord Somerville in 1508, giving him the express duty to organise a three-mile race within the estate to find the fastest messenger to bring news of any English invasion to Edinburgh. The winner's prize, a pair of red woolly stockings, was chosen so that the watchmen of Edinburgh could see him from a distance. The laird had to get royal permission for the only cancellation ever, during the recent foot-and-mouth crisis.*

[29] *sc. traditional insults.*

[30] *Some say the greedy Campbells, though as 'Cam' in Gaelic means physically crooked, the first and older epithet is a good pun.*

[31] *Sometimes Dunbars are held to be dirtier.*

[32] *That's 'bold' rather than follically-challenged.*

[33] *In the US, the Golden Grahams.*

[34] *The wet-weather Macintoshes is an alternative.*

[35] *The dental Macleans?*

[36] *From the Menteith who betrayed Sir William Wallace. Oddly, the only 'lake' in Scotland is the Lake of Menteith (with all others being lochs, of course).*

Of course, within the clan more subtle identification was used – in the old days, every adherent to the clan would wear an identifying flower or plant on his bonnet; these days each clan member has the right to wear a clan badge,[37] depicting the clan crest set inside a belt, sometimes with the clan motto or war cry[38] written on the belt's strap. Both the crest and the slogan have to be approved by Scotland's chief herald, the Lord Lyon.[39]

There are hundreds of clans and families (most now have websites) but here are the 20 most common:[40]

| Clan | Plant Badge | Motto | Crest |
|------|-------------|-------|-------|
| Bruce | Rosemary | *Fumius* (We Have Been) | Lion |
| Campbell | Bog myrtle | *Ne Obliviscaris* (Forget Not) | Boar's head |
| Cameron | Oak | *Aonaibh Re Chiele* (Unite) | Five arrows[41] |
| Douglas | Birch | *Jamais Arrier* (Never Behind) | Salamander in flames |
| Fraser | Yew | All My Hope is in God | Strawberries[42] |
| Farquharson | Scots fir | *Fide et Fortitudine* (Fidelity and Strength) | Top half of a lion bearing a sword |
| Gordon | Ivy | *Bydand* (Stedfast) | Buck's head over a coronet |

---

[37] *Not the chief's coat of arms – that is actually illegal under Scots Law (Lyon Act 1672 as amended).*

[38] *'Slogan' in Gaelic.*

[39] *More about this unusual judge later…*

[40] *Statistically, that is – no reflection on social standing.*

[41] *Strangely similar to that of the Rothschild banking dynasty.*

[42] *A pun on 'fraise', the French for strawberry.*

| Clan | Plant Badge | Motto | Crest |
|---|---|---|---|
| Grant | Pine | Stand Fast[43] | Rock in flames |
| Gregor and McGregor | Scots fir | *Is Rioghal Mo Dhream* (My Race is Royal) | Lion's head crowned |
| Kennedy | Oak | *Avise la Fin* (Take Thought about the End) | Dolphin |
| Macdonald[44] | Heather | *Per Mare Per Terras* (By Sea and by Land) | Fist in armour holding a cross |
| Mackenzie | Holly | *Luceo Nor Uro* (I Shine but do not Burn) | Stags' heads with antlers |
| Macintosh | Red whortleberries | Touch Not the Cat bot[45] a Glove | Rampant wild cat |
| Maclean | Crowberry | Virtue Mine Honour | Castle tower |
| Macpherson | White heather | Touch Not the Cat without a Glove | Seated wild cat |
| Menzies[46] | Rowan | *Vil God I Zal* (With God I Shall) | A savage's head |
| Robertson | Bracken | *Virtutis Gloria Merces* (Glory is the reward of courage) | A right hand holding a crown |
| Scott | Whortleberry[47] | *Je Suis Prest* (I Am Prepared) | Stag |

---

[43] *Still the trademark of the whisky company of the same name:*
Lord grant guid luck tae a' the Grants
Likewise eternal bliss,
For they should sit amang the Sa'nts
That maks a dram like this

[44] *Five branches.*

[45] *Bot = 'but with a'.*

[46] *Pron.* MING-eeze.

[47] *Now often marketed as a 'blaeberry'.*

| Clan | Plant Badge | Motto | Crest |
|------|-------------|-------|-------|
| Stewart/Stuart | Thistle | *Virescit Vulnere Virtus* (Courage Grows Strong at a Wound)[48] | Pelican feeding her young[49] |
| Wallace | Oak leaf | *Pro Libertate* (*For Freedom*) | Armoured arm bearing an unsheathed sword |

So get dressed in your team ki(l)t and follow me to the games!

## I'm Up For It

12 September 1850: We lunched early, and then went... to... the Gathering at the Castle of Braemar, as we did last year... There were the usual games of 'putting the stone', 'throwing the hammer' and 'caber' and racing up the hill... it looked very pretty to see them run off in their different coloured kilts, with their white shirts.[50]

A typical games (if there be such a thing) will be a gallimaufray[51] of the so-called heavy events, different track and field events and the cultural competitions in dance and piping.

Highland games – and please remember that some of the games will be held outside the Highland line – come in all shapes and sizes. The biggest by far is the Cowal Games in Dunoon, Argyllshire, partially because its piping competitions are one of the five top annual events in the bagpipers' season.

---

[48] *Of course the Royal Family holds the ancient symbols of kingship, the lion rampant and the unicorn, the motto 'Nemo Me Impune Lacessit' ('Annoy Me and Die'), the slogan 'In Defense' and the royal badge of the red lion, the crown and the sword.*

[49] *In her piety, as the heralds call it – a symbol of self sacrifice, as she pecks blood from her own breast to feed her young chicks – this is often a Christian symbol.*

[50] Leaves from the Journal of Our Life in the Highlands, *Queen Victoria, Folio Society, London, 1973, pp.50–2.*

[51] *A Scottish word which could be translated as 'pot pourri' had John Knox vowed that there would be none in Scotland.*

They will see over 3,500 competitors and three times as many spectators over the games' three days.[52]

The oldest games is (traditionally) Braemar; but documentary evidence points to Burntisland (1652)[53] and Aboyne (1703)[54] as the oldest pre-Victorian events. Perhaps the most picturesque is Lornach Games – founded in 1823 by Sir Charles Forbes and still commanded by his descendent, Sir Hamish Forbes.[55] Here the *pièce de résistance* is the opening March of the Clansmen, where the local men with their laird at their head, dressed in traditional clothing and armed with pikes and the fearsome Lochaber Axe, march around the district calling at the houses of the games patrons and asking for hospitality at each. This has become quite a media event – partly because of the glory of the sight, but helped by the great comic Billy Connolly, who moved here a few years ago; you'll see Highlanders and celebrities gazing at each other in wonderment.

The mother and father of all though is the last in the season – the Braemar Gathering and Highland Games. It is always under the chieftainship of the monarch, ever since Queen Victoria rebuilt her castle of Balmoral and adopted the Scottish people. This event marks the end of the Royal Family's summer break in Scotland (so you will see the Queen and Prince Phillip, along with Prince Charles, Camilla[56] and the Princes), at the end of the season of games on the first Saturday in September.

---

52   *The last Thursday, Friday and Saturday of August.*

53   *In mid-July.*

54   *On the first Saturday in August, every year since the Laird of Grant commanded his folk to meet him in the field carrying: 'Highland coates, trewes and short hose of tartane of red and greine sett broad springed, and also with gun, sword, pistoll and dirk.'*

55   *The seventh baronet.*

56   *The moment the Prince of Wales crosses the Scottish Border he and his wife are known by their Scottish titles: the Duke and Duchess of Rothesay. He also bags a few other Scottish honours: he is Earl of Carrick, Baron of Renfrew, Lord of the Isles, Prince and Great Steward of Scotland, Keeper of the Great Seal of Scotland and a Knight of the Thistle. The Prince is regularly seen in kilt, always with lead gunshot sewn into the hem to give a bit of extra weight and avoid a royal exposé.*

In between these huge days, towns, villages, islands and communities will get together in local events, which, though smaller, carry the authenticity and friendship that must have been felt in the old days (mind you, the competitive spirit isn't diminished! Village rivalry is worse that Montague vs. Capulet).

Whichever gathering you choose to visit, a lot of the elements will be traditional sports and games. The heavy events are feats of individual strength. These are the classic games we all think of, maybe from eating Scott's Porage Oats as a laddie; they are fiercely competitive and, what's more, you have to be able to do them in your kilt.[57]

Tossing the Caber: This is the joy of cartoonists and purveyors of the double entendre throughout the world. But you would laugh at the other side of your face if you had to try this at home!

No one really knows why men started to take a long (17–20ft) and very heavy (130–150lbs)[58] tree trunk, smooth its branches off and then challenge each other to throw it about; but for whatever reason, this might be the premier event in today's games. The aim is not sheer brute force – the winner is not the man who throws his the furthest. The knack is a cunning combination of strength and dexterity.

The thrower has to pick up the caber by the thinner end, balance it carefully and then imagine himself running up to an unseen clock face on the ground. When he touches 6 o'clock, he throws up the caber to turn it once, such that the thicker end lands in the centre of the clock and the thin end falls at the 12 o'clock position. It's the placement of the end that determines the winner, not the distance or the weight.[59]

As Fats Waller would confirm, 'it's not what you do, it's the way that you do it.'

Putting the Stone (or Shot): This is probably the oldest trial, and there are many references in Gaelic stories to young men asserting their

---

[57] *There's even drugs testing nowadays – I hope not for alcohol though!*

[58] *That's about 6m and 70kg. As the caber dries it becomes lighter, so usually the organisers will soak the caber in a nearby loch to saturate it and ensure it keeps its weight. (I am not sure who's strong enough to fish it out of the loch…)*

[59] *And I got to the end of that description without a single rude joke to offend my editor!*

manhood by lifting a huge stone (outside the chief's house or the kirk) called the *Clach Cuid Fir*.[60] A very famous example can be seen in Balquidder Kirk, near Loch Voil.[61] Here the purpose was raw strength – to raise the 100lb[62] or more weight for a certain number of seconds (or sometimes to place it on top of a wall).

A variant, adding dexterity to strength, was the *Clach Neart*, where a river stone of 20 or 30lbs was thrown or 'putted' from the shoulder. It is out of this tradition that the modern put comes.

This is more mainstream now. Once each games would have its own traditional stone that everyone would throw, but the range of sizes, shapes and weights made it impossible to compare feats across country. The modern 'stone' is in fact likely to be a standard iron ball of 16 or 22lbs[63] weight. The putter[64] can run up about 7ft and then throws the stone with one hand upwards from shoulder height. Distance is the criterion and the Scottish records stand at 53ft 4 in for the larger shot and 65ft 3 in for the smaller.[65]

Throwing the Hammer: This is really the industrial equivalent of the shot. In the days before PlayStations, many tradesmen, such as blacksmiths, paviours, foresters and draymen, worked with heavy hammers and mallets, and would while away the evening hours by playing catch – throwing their tools at each other – or seeing who could throw his hammer the furthest, or even who could catch another man's hammer.[66]

That sounds like a recipe for disaster (and a few lost teeth) and so a vestigial hammer has developed – though none the lighter. It is based

---

[60] *'The Manhood Stone'.*

[61] *The burial place of the famous – or infamous – Rob Roy MacGregor.*

[62] *45kg, perhaps.*

[63] *A mere 10kg.*

[64] *Male or female.*

[65] *You can work out the metric conversion yourself this time. Both were set in 1982, and held to this day (at least at the time of writing), by an Englishman: Geoff Capes, who was a popular athlete (the most capped male British athlete in his day) and a famous TV strongman of the period. He is now one of the world's most successful budgerigar breeders.*

[66] *That game didn't die out – just the participants.*

on a head the same weight as the stone/shot, but is fixed to a 4ft wooden shaft. In this test, the thrower whirls round and round at the 'trig' until the momentum is right for the release.

All that kinetic energy propels the weapon over twice as far as the putter can put. The records are 156ft 8½ in for the 16lbs[67] and 129ft 10½ in for the 22lbs.[68]

Given the ingenuity of mankind, there are many other heavy things that the public can watch being thrown – weights (typically very heavy) or discuses[69] and even bales of hay, to be forked over a high bar. But once you have the idea of the three games above, you can work out the nuances.

In between the heavy events there will be different types of field event. The clan needed stamina and speed as well as strength! There will be foot races (flat or uphill), track and cross country in all sorts of age groups (both male and female); you might even find bicycle races![70] Add in long jumps and high jumps and, to be honest, you have the sort of events that you'll see in any corner of the world at school sports day or the county show.

A huge[71] draw is usually the tug o' war – again, not a uniquely Scottish sport,[72] but it's a great sight to see two teams of burly men (between five and eight) grab opposite ends of a long rope and use all their collective strength[73] to pull their opponents more than 12ft straight back – there's no hand-over-hand pulling permitted. It's a best-of-three competition and a well-matched pair of teams can be at the strain for 20 or more minutes.[74]

The real theme of the games is SKILL more than STRENGTH[75] – so

---

[67]  *Bruce Aitken (Aboyne 2000).*

[68]  *Mat Sandford (Halkirk 1998).*

[69]  *What is the plural of discus? Discuss!*

[70]  *Albeit not in kilts.*

[71]  *In both senses of the word.*

[72]  *It featured in the Olympics between 1900 and 1920.*

[73]  *And a bit of guile.*

[74]  *Amongst the official rules are regulations on heel size, hands on the ground and use of 'foul language', where there is a strict three-strikes-and-you-are-out policy. Which does seem a bl\*\*dy shame if you let slip a couple of bl\*\*ding swearwords under the d\*mn excitement.*

[75]  *If in doubt, chuck it about.*

it will be no surprise that the cultural events are also keenly contested and lovingly watched over.

Piping: A pipe band in full dress and full throat, bagpipes booming and drums underscoring the warlike music, is another fine image, but there will be keenly-contested solo playing, too. The greatest test of a piper's mastery of his music and his instrument is often said to be the 20-minute Pibroch[76] – which is like a fugue or canon, where an ancient tune is taken as the theme. After playing it plain, the master piper weaves variations around it until, as the climax, the old simple tune comes back round to bring us home.

Once upon a time it was felt to be discourteous to appoint one piper a 'winner' over his fellows and so for many years the prize went to 'he who pleased the judges'. In these more competitive days, winning is entirely acceptable.

Highland Dancing: again, years of teaching and practice are needed to master the steps and rhythms of these classic dances. Please don't get confused with Scottish country dancing or ceilidh dancing – the competitive Highland dance is a different family.

There are four classic competition dances – and I bet everyone knows about the most famous:

- The Sword Dance (or *Gille Calum*) – legend says this was invented by old Malkie Canmore again when he danced over his own sword and that of his vanquished opponent. His troops henceforth danced before any battle; if the steps fell true, then victory was at hand. To this day it is danced over a pair of crossed swords on the floor.

- The Highland Fling is hardly less famous.[77] This is the one with the arms up in the air – the dancer dances on one spot

---

[76]   *More properly* Piobaireachd – *the Gaelic for 'the Music of the Pipes'.*

[77]   *It's a pretty good cocktail, too! Take 2 fl. oz of Scotch whisky, 1 fl. oz of dry vermouth, 8 dashes of orange bitters. Pour all ingredients into a mixing glass and add ice, stir, strain into a martini glass, garnish with a twist of orange. Drink, remix and repeat until you can say* 'Pibroch of Donuil Dhu' *in a perfect Gaelic accent.*

(originally it was on his shield)[78] and his arms rise above his shoulders and head, imitating the antlers of the stag, while his feet trace the intricate steps.

- The Reel of Tulloch is a very cute story, as it developed in the village of Tulloch, where the minister used to be late for church on Sunday. As he had the only key, his parishioners were stuck outside. In the cold winter months, they developed this dance (stamping feet and clapping hands) to keep warm!

- The Sean Truibhas[79] (or Old Trousers) remembers the dark days when it was illegal to wear the kilt and the men were constricted into much-hated trousers. It starts off slow, as the men couldn't move as freely, and then picks up pace as the hated bags are thrown off, to finish in the happy days of the restoration of the tartan![80]

One of the key things about the games (whether wet or dry) is that they are a huge, popular and family affair. You'll find eccentric events tucked away from the judges' eyes, things to bring a smile to even the biggest couch potato – from Hurling the Haggis (key rules – use a one-handed throw from the shoulder and it must not burst on impact[81]) to Throwing the Welly (which is the partner to the haggis as the hammer is to the stone)! Of course, in the pouring rain there is no more fun than to watch a pillow fight on a pole (preferably greasy) over a tank of ice-cold water (no rules at all and the best is when both protagonists end up in the drink!).[82]

---

[78] *The round Highland shield called a targe, sometimes with a spike in the centre – that aided concentration!*

[79] *Pronounced 'Shawn Trews'.*

[80] *For some odd reason, in 1986 it was agreed that two interloping dances – the Sailor's Hornpipe and the Irish Jig – could also be allowed. To this day many people just don't see the point of including the English naval dance or the national dance of Ireland, any more than a tango in a kilt. Quite a flash that would be.*

[81] *It should of course be cold and uncooked.*

[82] *It's fair to say that King Malcolm had nothing to do with inventing these – even the greatest heroes have limitations.*

And the end of the day? The massed pipes playing, the prizes (cups, medals, bouquets) awarded, three rousing cheers for the chieftain and home to bed (maybe via the pub) in the happy knowledge that this has been done hundreds of times before and, God willing, will be done again many hundreds more ahead.

There are two important variants of these enjoyable days held in the Lowland cities. Edinburgh holds the annual Royal Highland Show at Ingleston (near the airport) every July. The real heroes here are the beasts – prize-winning animals[83] and producers of fine farm food – interspersed with good things to eat and drink. At a time when our farmers have a hard life for a poor return, it's pleasing to see tens of thousands of visitors attend this celebration of the craft and achievement of one of our oldest industries.

Meanwhile in the west, Glasgow is host to the World Pipe Band Championships on Glasgow Green on the first Saturday of each August. Here pipe bands from all over the world compete – and it is all over, with 16 countries represented at the last count – the top prize has been lifted by a Northern Irish band[84] for three out of the last five years, while the most successful junior band is from Houston, TX![85]

They say that the bagpipe is the missing link between sound and music, but on the day I defy anyone not to be moved and inspired by this unique musical instrument.

Massed pipes and eardrums!

Farewell to the Highlands, farewell to the North,
The birth-place of Valour, the country of Worth;
Wherever I wander, wherever I rove,
The hills of the Highlands for ever I love.

---

[83] *And it gets whole columns in the local press: Whose Coos is News? This is the Crufts for big beasts!*

[84] *Field Marshal Montgomery. And a regular runner-up has been Simon Fraser University of Canada, who won the Championship in 2008.*

[85] *St Thomas' Episcopal School Pipe Band.*

[*Chorus*] My heart's in the Highlands, my heart is not here,
My heart's in the Highlands, a-chasing the deer;
Chasing the wild-deer, and following the roe,
My heart's in the Highlands, wherever I go.

Farewell to the mountains, high-cover'd with snow,
Farewell to the straths and green vallies below;
Farewell to the forests and wild-hanging woods,
Farewell to the torrents and loud-pouring floods.[86]

---

[86]   '*Song: Farewell To The Highlands*', *Robert Burns.*

## 10

# Kings, Courtiers and Comedians

EDINBURGH'S HISTORIC Royal Mile stretches from the castle to Holyrood.[1]

And it's along this mile that we see the confluence of history and politics and religion that flows through Scottish life today.

---

[1] *The Palace of Holyrood House, to give it its true name, is the spiritual home of the Stuart line of monarchs, which held the throne of Scotland, then England and finally this United Kingdom, for 324 years. Of all the royal houses of Europe, though, the bad luck suffered by the Stuarts was unsurpassed.*

*Robert II was the first Stuart king, the son of the Steward of Scotland (hence the name) and Marjorie, daughter of the greatest King of Scots, Robert the Bruce; so the dynasty started in 1390. After not much to report, he was succeeded by his son Robert III in 1406, who was a permanent invalid from being kicked by a horse and died of a broken heart after his eldest son was murdered and the younger was captured by the English. That son, James I, was himself murdered in Perth in 1437. His son, James II, inherited but died in 1460 besieging the English in Roxburghe Castle when one of his own cannons exploded. James III faced a rebellion by his own son and was murdered by a priest after losing the Battle of Sauchieburn to the rebel, who became James IV in 1488. Ironically, James IV died after the largest ever Scottish army was destroyed by the English at the Battle of Flodden in 1513. James V died of grief in 1542 following yet another English victory (this time at Solway Moss) in 1542. Looking at his only daughter, his last words were 'It cam wi' a lass, it will gang wi' a lass'.*

*Mary's story is too long even for this footnote; Queen of Scotland as an infant and briefly Queen of France by marriage, as Queen Dowager of France she returned to Scotland after the death of her first husband to land in the middle of the Reformation. She remarried Henry, Lord Darnley (her cousin – they shared a grandmother who was Henry VIII of England's favourite sister) then murdered him (or at least acquiesced in the deed) and married an adventurer (possibly after being raped by him), was beaten by rebels, deposed in favour of her and Darnley's tiny baby boy and, after an unsuccessful coup de main, fled to England to face almost two decades of imprisonment at the hands of her cousin Elizabeth I, where, in 1587 in a scarlet gown, she faced the axe in Fotheringhay Castle.*

Her son, James VI, became King of Scots in 1567 and, at the death of his cousin Elizabeth I, in 1603 he ascended the throne of England too (Darnley having been a poor father but a rather good insurance policy). Other than a rather brutal, effectively orphan childhood, the execution of his mum, the early death of his eldest son and a complicated sex life, James VI & I ('the wisest fool in Christendom') had a better run than anyone since his great-great-great-great-great-great-great-grandfather. He shuffled off in 1625 (remaining the fourth-longest-reigning UK monarch), handing over the crown and history to Charles I, who followed his father's philosophy of the Divine Right of Kings without his sagacity of politics, and so on a cold January morning lost his crown and his head after an illegal trial at the culmination of the Civil War, leaving the regicidal Oliver Cromwell as 'Lord Protector' – king in all but right and name. The Scots immediately proclaimed Charles King & Martyr's elder son Charles II as king (and he claimed the English throne too) but it took until 1664 for him to return to power and London in the Restoration, which was in retrospect a huge street party, led by 'the Merrie Monarch' as Master of Ceremonies (a master with many, many mistresses!). Despite a good number of bastards (many of the dukes today can claim their coronets due to horizontal service in the female line), he left no legitimate heir and so his brother James VII & II ascended the throne in 1685, offended everyone with his Roman Catholicism, and was deposed/abdicated/did a runner in the Glorious Revolution of 1688, which brought his Protestant daughter, Mary II, and her husband, William II & III, jointly to the throne. After Mary's death (1694), Dutch William ruled until his horse tripped over a molehill and he broke his neck in the fall (to the joy of the supporters and adherents of the deposed and recently-deceased James; they rallied under his son and grandson, James 'the Old Pretender' and Charles Edward, 'Bonnie Prince Charlie'). William and Mary died without issue and so the crown fell to her sister Anne in 1702, who watched many pregnancies fail and one by one all of her children die before her own death in 1714, which brought the Stuart line to its end – and proved James V right after all; the line lasted from Marjorie to Anne. But the succession also came wi' a lass – James VI & I's granddaughter had married the Elector of Hanover in Germany and her grandson, George I, came to London and created the Hanoverian Dynasty, which, with minor variations, sleeps in Buckingham Palace today – by dint of its Scottish lineage.

## Royal Scotland

At the top of this historic path stands Edinburgh Castle – the fortress of the city since mediaeval times but now the haunt of tourists rather than of a guardian garrison. You'll still hear one gun firing (to signal one o'clock daily[2]) but it's no longer a serving base. There remains a guard, though not for the fortress and city[3] but for the Crown Jewels of Scotland, known through history as 'the Honours of Scotland'.

Housed in extraordinary security, these are the oldest royal regalia in the UK, as all the major English crown jewels were destroyed[4] by Cromwell at the end of the Civil War. The Scots (rather complicatedly) had handed over Charles I to be executed by the new regime but then crowned Charles II as soon as they could. Cromwell couldn't understand this[5] and marched north to capture the Honours, which had been moved to Dunnottar Castle, north of the crowning place of Scone.[6] As the Roundheads besieged the castle on its rocky outcrop, the Honours were lowered out of a window overlooking the cliffs, to be secreted in a basket of seaweed collected by an old and shabby woman. She took them to the parish church, where they were buried beneath the floor until the Restoration, when they returned to Edinburgh Castle and for some unaccountable reason were locked in a trunk and mislaid until 1819,

---

[2] *At the same time on Carlton Hill, at the other end of Princes Street, a large white ball is dropped to confirm the time to the boats in Leith harbour. Gun fires, ball falls and canny Scot says to gullible tourists – 'he's a bloody good shot that gunner…' At the time of writing the mechanism has been broken for a year. A complete balls down.*

[3] *'Nisi Dominus Frustra' is the motto of the City of Edinburgh – a bit ironic as they have that big castle there too ('Except the* LORD *keep the city the watchman watcheth but in vain', Psalm cxxvii, 1.*

[4] *Actually broken up and sold – Cromwell wouldn't have wasted a penny.*

[5] *I must admit, nor do I really, save that both acts probably appeared like a good idea at the time.*

[6] *The coronation of Charles II on the historic Moot Hill was a highly provocative act and a direct repeat of his ancestor, Robert the Bruce, who was made king on the same spot, without having control of the kingdom either.*

when Walter Scott[7] performed a Howard Carter/Tutankhamen moment of archaeological theatre and at last restored them to public view.

The Honours of Scotland consist of three priceless artefacts:

- The Crown – the symbol of kingship – is one of the oldest in the world (after the Iron Crown of Lombardy in Milan and St Stephen's Crown in Hungary[8]). It was remodelled by James V in 1540 from a previous crown[9] and is of Scottish gold, decorated with 42 stones and 22 freshwater pearls. It is an 'imperial crown', which means it has both a circlet round the head and a superstructure of arches fashioned out of gold and enamelled oakleaves, surmounted by a starry blue orb, itself topped by a cross of gold with a square amethyst in its centre and more Scottish pearls hanging from its arms. Due to the oddities of history it has only crowned two monarchs since its magnificent refurb.[10] Or perhaps it is due to more practical reasons – the Imperial State Crown (used for the UK coronation) is said to be heavy and to need training to wear, and it comes in at 910 g whereas the Crown of Scotland is a mighty 1,644 g.[11]

- The Sceptre – the symbol of temporal power – was a gift to

---

[7]   Who else?

[8]   Both republics, of course.

[9]   Even monarchs can be fashion victims – everyone's wearing their tiaras low this season...

[10]   Mary Queen of Scots and James VI were both infants at their coronations, so Charles I and Charles II were the only kings to be crowned with the whole works. Later monarchs, from fat George IV to our own dear queen, have been presented with the crown upon their first visit to Edinburgh, when they have touched it and returned it to the care of the Hereditary Keeper, the Duke of Hamilton (a cousin, being descended from the daughter of James II – for centuries the Hamiltons were the 'insurance policy' and would have been heirs had the king's only child died, so maybe he carried the crown in order to keep a good eye on it!).

[11]   Truly, 'uneasy is the head that wears the Crown'.

James IV by Pope Alexander VI[12] in 1494 and is in the traditional shape of a silver gilt rod, topped prettily in this case by a crown of dolphins bearing a large rock quartz and a pearl. You can see St Andrew and his saltire (representing Scotland) accompanying the Virgin and Child and supported in his work by St James of Compostella (commemorating Borgia's Spanish birthplace).

- The Sword of State – the symbol of justice to the king's people and retribution to his enemies – also came from the Vatican. Pope Julius II took time off building the Sistine Chapel to send James V this work of art. Unfortunately bashed when escaping from Cromwell,[13] the 4 ft-long blade is finely engraved with SS Peter and Paul[14] and Julius's name, while the Papal arms feature prominently on the scarlet and gold swordbelt which carries the red royal velvet scabbard.[15]

In the years after Jamie the Sax cantered off to his new life in London, and before the Union of the Parliaments, the absent monarch was represented in the Scottish Parliament by the Honours sitting on a velvet throne; so the royal assent to an act was signified by the physical parchment being touched by the Sceptre. Its last use was when the Earl of Seafield signified the promulgation of the Act of Union with England, with the evocative phrase:

An there's the end of ane auld sang.

Not an end, though; merely a 292-year pause for breath, for at the

---

[12] *The bad old Borgia.*

[13] *Possibly deliberately snapped to hide it in the basket.*

[14] *Peter for the Vatican and Paul because his symbol is the sword, by which he was executed.*

[15] *Knights of the Thistle were 'dubbed' (the traditional knighting ceremony involving the monarch touching both shoulders gently with a sword blade) using this sword until 1987, the Order's tercentenary, when it was retired with honour.*

opening of the new, devolved Scottish Parliament, the Crown was at its place beside the Queen.[16]

Just before you leave Edinburgh Castle's Jewel House, you can see a block of red sandstone which is (at first) nothing exciting after the gold and diamonds, but is perhaps the essence of kingship. This block of stone, so legend tells us, started off as a pillow and ended up as a throne.

This is the Stone of Destiny (also called the Stone of Scone[17]). Traditionally, it had served as a rest for the prophet Jacob[18] at Beth-el in the Holy Land. In the confused traditional history of the foundation of Scotland, it made its way (probably carried by the daughter of a pharaoh) to Iona.[19] It was on this stone that every King of Scots was crowned from Kenneth Macalpine in 837 until the Stone was stolen by Edward of England[20] and sent to Westminster Abbey in 1296. There, encased in a 13th century carved throne, it was integral to every subsequent coronation up to today.

While no one agrees on the true history of the Stone, its significance has never been in doubt – particularly in 1950 when four students broke into the abbey on Christmas Eve and carried it off.[21] It was eventually returned,[22] and it rested once again in London until it was agreed that

---

[16]   *The Sword and Sceptre are considered too fragile to be removed from their home.*

[17]   *Pronounced 'Skoon' not 'Scawn' like the bun (which itself should not be pronounced 'Skone').*

[18]   *'Jacob left Beersheba, and went toward Haran. He came to the place and stayed there that night, because the sun had set. Taking one of the stones of the place, he put it under his head and lay down in that place to sleep. And he dreamed that there was a ladder set up on the earth, and the top of it reached to heaven; and behold, the angels of God were ascending and descending on it!', Genesis xxviii, 12.*

[19]   *Some theories say to Ireland, where a bit was left as the Blarney Stone, but I'd take a lot of persuading.*

[20]   *Who called himself 'the Hammer of the Scots'.*

[21]   *Dropping it and breaking it in the process.*

[22]   *Or was it? The Stone of Destiny has more conspiracy theories about it than the J. F. K. assassination (maybe they are linked – that would explain a lot!).*

it should be housed at Edinburgh Castle in between coronations. So in November 1996 a military convoy brought it home after a 700-year absence, to the resounding sound of 21-gun salutes.[23]

This is what happens at one end of the Royal Mile, but there's more to see and do!

Let's wander out through the castle gates, flanked by statues of Bruce and Wallace, across the Esplanade[24] down Castlehill to the Lawnmarket[25] and thence across Bank Street (we don't have time to pop into Deacon Brodie's pub even for a quick one today), past Parliament House[26] (and its wigged and gowned advocates) and St Giles[27] (and its ministers) on the right and the City Chambers on the left, then down the High Street, dodging the ghostly tour guides outside the old Tron church, and on beyond the Netherbow, the old city gate, into Canongate, with the statue of Robert Ferguson outside Canongate Kirk,[28] and carry on until we reach Holyrood.

Nowadays there's a bifurcated Holyrood: the Palace of Holyrood House (the Queen's official residence in Scotland) and the new Parliament Building, also now known as Holyrood.

The Palace stands on the site of a Royal Abbey, which was requisitioned by the Stuart monarchs as a place to escape from the bleak and draughty castle. It's gone through many periods of neglect and decay,

---

[23]   *The reverse process will occur at the next coronation.*

[24]   *A small bit of which is legally Nova Scotia – when the Scottish settlement was founded, the king needed cash, so he created a new honour: a 'Baronet of Nova Scotia'. The lucky honourees had to pay but got a grant of land too. As Scots Law insisted on taking physical possession of the land, part of the castle ground was included in the Canadian colony so new baronets could stand on Canadian territory to complete the bargain.*

[25]   *The linen market.*

[26]   *If you are a local, you will likely make a ceremonial spit for good luck on to the cobbled pattern of the Heart of Midlothian here – the site of the hated tollbooth prison.*

[27]   *Pop in and see if you can find the angel playing the bagpipes. Bagpipes in heaven? Probably as welcome as mobile phones on planes.*

[28]   *Where Adam Smith lies. Keynes was right in that respect: in the long run we are all dead – even economists.*

but you can still see MQS's bedroom, where her secretary David Rizzio was murdered in her presence, and – not as historically accurate – the Great Gallery's collection of 89 portraits of the Kings of Scotland.[29]

It's guarded by its own police force – the High Constables under the leadership of the Hereditary Keeper of the Palace[30] – and, while used regularly, the palace has two festal weeks – General Assembly (more of that later) and Holyrood Week at the end of June, when HM returns to her Northern Capital and carries out a range of Scottish state occasions, beginning with receiving the keys of the city and of the castle, then a host of receptions and investitures in the Great Gallery, finishing at the famous Garden Party.

Queen Victoria started giving garden parties at Buckingham Palace in the 1860s and the Holyrood party is very similar. A cross section of all of Scottish life is invited: about 8,000 guests from charities, the armed services, civil servants, local people and award winners, who are invited to come in morning dress and top hat (summer frocks and hats for ladies) to share tea, sandwiches[31] and a selection of buns.[32]

Just before kick-off, the distinctive green uniforms of the Royal Company of Archers (the Queen's Bodyguard for Scotland) parade to protect their sovereign,[33] then at the stroke of four o'clock the National Anthem is played as the Queen and other members of the Royal Family come out to circulate amongst the guests for the next couple of hours.

---

[29] *Unfortunately not very historical as they (and 12 others now missing) were all commissioned by Charles II from one painter, Jacob de Wit – Charles wanted a bit of back-to-tradition propaganda, so some of the kings didn't quite exist and Jacob just made up most of the faces!*

[30] *Our old friend the Duke of Hamilton again.*

[31] *With the crusts cut off.*

[32] *Including Battenburg cake, named after some German cousins.*

[33] *At Buckingham Palace this task is performed by the famous Beefeaters in their Tudor gold and scarlet uniforms. The RCA is quite unique as it was founded, not as an army regiment, but as an archery club in 1676, receiving Royal Patronage in 1704 and becoming the Royal Bodyguard at the walter-scottathon in 1822. They still practise toxipholy (safely and mainly in private) and must be the only practising force armed with longbows in the world. Their uniform is a green tailcoat and trousers with gold stripes and buttons.*

As the bands of the Scottish regiments play musical selections, the Royal Party splits up and walks down paths cleared by the equerries and, entirely at random, many guests are invited to step forward and talk with the Queen.[34] To be so chosen can be a terrifying fright; Prince Philip says that one in every five men curtsey to the Queen in their astonishment.[35]

Then, with the accustomed precision of every royal event, the drums roll loudly at 6pm, the National Anthem is sung once more and the Queen and her guests depart, leaving a lot of washing up for someone.[36]

There is a lot of history and politics around the mechanisms of court, law, parliament and pageantry. Amongst some of the royal office bearers you might glance and see are:

- The Lord Lyon: Our friend the Chief Herald of Scotland, who takes a dim view of people flying the royal flags. Dressed like the White Rabbit in *Alice*[37] and accompanied by the heralds and pursuivants.[38] His role in ancient time was as the *Ard Seanachaid* – the man who memorised the king's genealogy to prove his right to rule by descent from the mythic chieftains. He now runs Scotland's heraldic court[39]

---

[34]   *So be prepared to answer 'What do you do?' or 'Have you come far today?'*

[35]   *It's quite a catering feat; one royal observer estimated that around 27,000 cups of tea, 20,000 sandwiches and 20,000 slices of cake are consumed, thus confounding the Glasgow stereotype of Edinburgh being inhospitable at tea time.*

[36]   *The Third Valet of the Dishwasher, no doubt. Certainly not a task for the Duke of Hamilton!*

[37]   *But he conducts himself in a more measured pace.*

[38]   *Who assist him in researching genealogy and in creating new coats of arms for Scots and those who can prove Scots descent. Colin Powell of the US recently was awarded a full set!*

[39]   *The last active heraldic court in Europe – it recently sued Porsche, who use a coat of arms as their logo – as the arms were not licensed in Scotland it was illegal! Judicial pragmatism allowed the bonnets to retain the marque, but the garages had to take their signs down. The Lyon Court is in the New Town, beside the wonderful Café Royal Oyster Bar on West Register Street.*

and is responsible to both the Crown and the First Minister of Scotland for the correct performance of ceremonials, including proclamations (such as accession of the new monarch) from the Mercat Cross outside St Giles Cathedral.

- The Lord High Constable: He has no real duties[40] but gets a beautiful silver rod of office and is personally responsible for HM's safety – though he no longer has to sleep across her bedroom door to block the way![41]

- The Washer of the King's Hands: Some centuries ago, an old chap called Howieson worked as a hand on a farm beside the pretty Cramond Bridge at the edge of Edinburgh. One day he heard a fracas while working in the fields and came to the rescue of a common-looking traveller who was being mugged. He didn't know that this man was his king, James V, who often rode through the country incognito to hear what his people were saying. The disguised James thanked Howieson and asked what reward he would have – Old Howie replied modestly that all his worldly ambition was to own the land he toiled on, but it was the monarch's and so that could never happen. Not only did good John Howieson get his lands, but he was given them for a small rental – that when called for by the monarch, John should present himself in the presence with a silver bowl to wash the king's hands. The family is still on duty with an heirloom bowl made for fat old George IV in 1822.

- The Hereditary Bearer of the National Flag of Scotland and The Hereditary Bearer of the Royal Flag: Hereditary rights sometimes get mixed up if the direct male line dies out. A good example is the Scrymgeour family, which carried the Lion Rampant beside Wallace on his campaigns and for Bruce on the glorious day of independence at Bannockburn,

---

[40]  *Certainly, he doesn't give out parking tickets.*
[41]  *The royal corgies' bite being much more of a deterrent.*

and thereafter beside each king from then to 1668, when the Earl of Dundee (as he had been promoted for good service) died with some confusion as to his succession. The powerful Lauderdales effectively pinched the Scrymgeour's lands and associated rights and exercised them until the coronation of George V in 1910, when the Scrymgeours took the Maitlands of Lauderdale to the House of Lords over the stolen lands and were awarded back the right to carry the flag. In 1953, for our current queen's coronation, a great compromise was agreed: the Scrymgeours carry the Lion Rampant and the Maitlands carry the Saltire. Honours even.

- The Moderator of the General Assembly of the Church of Scotland: For centuries the Kirk was at the heart of Scottish life and politics. The combination of strict Calvinsim and an elective form of Presbyterian church governance is often held to be a key stand in the mental genetics of our race. The first sets a hard work ethic while the second opens all opportunities to everyone.

  There are no bishops in the Church of Scotland: each Minister serves a parish, supported by the elders, forming a committee called the Kirk Session,[42] in whose hands the management of the church, congregation and parish falls.

  In true Calvinist belief, the Church is ruled by God, not by any human. In the 1560s, to reflect that, they created a governing body called a General Assembly, with representatives from every Kirk Session in the land, who would congregate in Edinburgh annually and elect a temporary chairman of proceedings, called the Moderator, who would be allowed to hold office for a single year only. It is important to remember that, while the Church of England is the established religion under the laws in England, the Church of

---

[42] *There are intermediate bodies – the Presbytery (which represents all the Sessions in a county) and the Synod (a regional body) – but there are no recorded funny anecdotes about either, so we'll leave them sitting quietly in the warm sunshine for the moment.*

Scotland is our national church, but independent of parliament.[43]

From 1707, in the dust of the parliamentarians' horses galloping off to London, to the fireworks of devolution in 1999, the annual General Assembly was felt by many to be the effective parliament of Scotland, certainly the formal voice of the nation.

The Moderator has a formal 18th-century coat and breeches, with a dog collar and a lace ruffle, but will mainly be found in the university gown of the traditional Scots preacher. Like the Speaker of the House of Representatives, he (or she) is an executive chairman of the week-long session every spring in Edinburgh where the governance of the Kirk and the good of the country are debated. This session is

---

[43] *There are certain (increasingly controversial) constitutional oaths that a new monarch must undertake to preserve the teachings and government of the Kirk within Scotland, but through the General Assembly and the freedom to elect ministers and officers it retains independence of action. In addition to theological disputes (not uncommon in reformed churches) there have been politico-theological scraps too. The most famous was 'the Great Disruption' of 1843, when much of the Church seceded over the question of who was to appoint the minister in each parish: the Kirk had agreed that the local laird could, while the Free Church was founded on the one-man-one-vote principal. It was a near civil war – as the rhyme characterised the two sides:*
*The Free Kirk,*
*The Wee Kirk,*
*The Kirk without the steeple:*
*The Auld Kirk,*
*The cauld Kirk,*
*The Kirk without the people.*
*The churches finally were reconciled in 1929, but leaving a rump outside: the famous 'Wee Frees', who maintain their own particular 'hellfire and damnation' services to this day. Allegedly, at an early ecumenical meeting, there was a dispute on how to lead the prayers – a compromise was broached by the Wee Free minister who said to his Kirk rival: 'Let's do two prayers: you pray to the Lord your way first, then I'll follow and pray to Him His way.'*

opened with as much ceremony as the Opening of Parliament, with the Lord High Commissioner representing the Queen, and even residing in Holyrood House.[44]

As the Kirk is now in a minority, there will be changes here in the coming years, but when you see the people gathering from all four corners of Scotland, just for a minute you can feel the devotion and commitment of the early reformers, and looking outward, see the effect that they had on each of us today.

Many at home wonder what this is all about, and have a dismissive view of all this ancient 'mummery', but many of us see in this real archetypes of the bravery and ingenuity of our forbears – these men and women are 3D history!

> And here a while the Muse
> High hovering o'er the broad cerulean scene
> Sees Caledonia in romantic view.[45]

## Political Scotland

> Fareweel to a' our Scottish fame,
> Fareweel our ancient glory;
> Fareweel ev'n to the Scottish name,
> Sae fam'd in martial story.
> Now Sark rins over Solway sands,
> An' Tweed rins to the ocean,
> To mark where England's province stands–
> Such a parcel o' rogues in a nation!

---

44  *In fact the Lord High Commissioner flies the Queen's own Lion Rampant flag, is addressed as 'Your Grace' and ranks in precedence third after only the Queen and Prince Phillip. But only for that week; then it's back to jeans and T-shirts.*

45  *'The Seasons, Autumn', James Thompson. 'Caledonia' remains a romantic name for Scotland – one of the many, and no less inaccurate than the others.*

What force or guile could not subdue,
 Thro' many warlike ages,
Is wrought now by a coward few,
 For hireling traitor's wages.
The English stell we could disdain,          [net, trap]
 Secure in valour's station;
But English gold has been our bane–
 Such a parcel o' rogues in a nation!

O would, or I had seen the day
 That Treason thus could sell us,
My auld grey head had lien in clay,
 Wi' Bruce and loyal Wallace!
But pith and power, till my last hour,
 I'll mak this declaration;
We're bought and sold for English gold–
 Such a parcel of rogues in a nation![46]

The political Holyrood is also a work of unique architecture. The Scottish Parliament building was commissioned[47] from the noted Catalan architect Enric Miralles to house the devolved Scottish Parliament[48] – its design is striking[49] and its different textures and organic shapes seem to echo the surrounding landscape of the Salisbury Crags. There are regular tours but the exciting time to see the building is at the opening of a session of parliament. The formal part happens within the chamber as the Crown of Scotland is escorted from the castle by the Scots Guards and their pipes and drums, to be ready for the First Minister and Presiding

---

[46] 'Such a Parcel of Rogues in a Nation', Robert Burns.

[47] At not inconsiderable expense.

[48] Note for overseas: since 1999 Scotland has exercised devolved responsibility over certain political powers without reference on those areas to the UK Parliament at Westminster – this is a relationship within the UK constitution that has some tensions and certainly the rules are not always as clear as you'd think.

[49] And as controversial as the cost – which was a famous saga of budgetary woes.

Officer to welcome the Queen, who makes the formal opening of the working session.

Once that's done and all the various parties have had their moment of hot air, the Riding of the Parliament begins. This is a modern take on the old practice of the 'lords of parliament' riding in full finery to the first meeting to show the populace the majesty of their leaders. Now, though, it's a parade of over 1,200 people in their own majesty. You will see national and international stars of screen and sports field along with 'local heroes' who make a difference in their communities; schools from each of the regions carry banners and are interspersed with theatre groups, bands and performers,[50] with representatives from many nations and all the lord provosts of the Scottish cities and the commanders of the three armed services in Scotland, all led to the glorious sound of the pipe bands.

The parade meanders from the squalor of Market Street to the green gardens at the parliament building, past the Queen and her Scottish ministers, to end with the Picnic in the Park, a festival of music and arts for the rest of the day.

There is a powerful symbolism in this too. Many hold that kingship in Scotland was 'of the Scots' not 'of Scotland', with the implication that there was a constitutional contract between the monarch and his (or her) proud Scottish people. There's a lot of evidence, and in our Declaration of Arbroath it is stressed immediately before the brave words which exemplify our cultural independence:

> But from these countless evils we have been set free, by the help of Him Who though He afflicts yet heals and restores, by our most tireless Prince, King and Lord, the Lord Robert. He, that his people and his heritage might be delivered out of the hands of our enemies, met toil and fatigue, hunger and peril, like another Maccabaeus or Joshua and bore them cheerfully. Him, too, divine providence, his right of succession according to our laws and customs which we shall maintain to the death, and **the due consent and assent of us all have made our Prince and King.** To him, as to the man by whom salvation has been wrought unto

---

50  *Including our friends from Up Helly Aa – the Jarl's Squad.*

our people, we are bound both by law and by his merits that our freedom may be still maintained, and by him, come what may, we mean to stand.

Yet if he should give up what he has begun, and agree to make us or our kingdom subject to the King of England or the English, **we should exert ourselves at once to drive him out as our enemy and a subverter of his own rights and ours, and make some other man who was well able to defend us our King;** for, as long as but a hundred of us remain alive, never will we on any conditions be brought under English rule. It is in truth not for glory, nor riches, nor honours that we are fighting, but for freedom – for that alone, which no honest man gives up but with life itself.[51]

It's a political credo that resonates still, and could well be the wellspring of the great tradition of Scots politicians and parliamentarians – not just at home, but in the far-flung countries where Scots have made a political mark in establishing modern democracies.

It has been my lot to have found myself in many distant lands. I have never been in one without finding a Scotchman, and I never found a Scotchman who was not at the head of the poll.[52]

## From Politics to Play Acting[53]

A Company of Stage-players, who are acting plays within the Precincts, and have begun with acting one, which is filled with horrid Swearing, Obscenity and Expressions of a Double Meaning[54]

---

[51] *The Declaration of Arbroath, 1320; my emphasis.*

[52] *Benjamin Disraeli; quoted by Duncan Bruce in his groundbreaking volume* The Mark of the Scots.

[53] *Not that much of a jump.*

[54] *An exhortation of the Presbytery of Edinburgh against an early attempt to stage plays in the city. Quoted at p.103 of* Crowded With Genius, *James Buchan, Harper Collins, 2003. That review would sell a play out nowadays!*

When our politicos are off on summer holiday, our capital is transformed into a Capital of Culture, for Edinburgh is the mother of the festival scene. Of course, it's a total mistake to talk of THE Edinburgh Festival – there are many,[55] including:

| | | |
|---|---|---|
| **Edinburgh International Festival** | Arts and music | The oldest |
| **Edinburgh Fringe Festival** | Everything you can imagine[56] | The largest |
| **Edinburgh International Book Festival** | Writing | Local talent[57] and more |
| **Edinburgh Film Festival** | Big screen | Luvvies |
| **Edinburgh Television Festival** | Little screen[58] | More luvvies |
| **Edinburgh Military Tattoo** | Military arts and music | The most misunderstood |

At the grey end of World War II, some grey men sat in the grey light of a grey Edinburgh building. It was 1947 and the physical rebuilding of Europe was in swing. They sought something equally – or even more – important: its cultural rebirth. The New and Old Towns of Edinburgh had been spared the bombings that its port of Leith and most of all the Clyde had faced. These far-sighted men – councillors and artists – sought to bring international talent to Edinburgh to create 'The Edinburgh International Festival', marrying some of the greatest performances in Europe with some of the finest architecture. Its mission was simply expressed:

to provide a platform for the flowering of the human spirit

---

55   *Mostly in August.*

56   *And quite a lot more.*

57   *J.K. Rowling, Ian Rankin and Alexander McCall Smith all live in the same part of Edinburgh – known affectionately as 'Writers' Block'.*

58   *Although John Logie Baird was a west-coast man.*

And it certainly has over the last 60 years. Under the leadership of its first director Sir Rudolf Bing,[59] it quickly achieved a position as one of the premier cultural events firstly in Europe and now globally. It is viewed across the world as a first-ranking showcase for opera, classical music and theatre.

Naturally, the Festival being Scottish, August 1947 saw some dissent, as some thought there should be more home-grown talent in the opening programme. Eight theatre companies who hadn't been invited hired halls independently during the Festival period and went ahead anyway! Thus was born the younger twin, the Fringe.

My good friend John Cairney (who has performed gloriously at both) likened the old Festival days at Edinburgh to a demure old granny inviting you to come to tea with a few friends while sitting in her bow window, admiring the day. Now he says the size and noise make it more like a slatternly old bag, boozed on the sherry, offering her delights to all at once.

There is certainly a thought that the sheer success of the Fringe is causing it problems. One of the guiding principles of programming the Fringe is that there are no guiding principles. Book with the organisers, book a venue, turn up, switch on the lights and you are off!

The Fringe in 2007 sold a record 1,697,293 tickets – 11 per cent increase year-on-year – and had 31,000 performances of 2,050 shows in 250 venues.[60] An estimated 18,626 performers were on stage, according to the organisers' press release. So you're not really going to see it all any more; the Fringe isn't even an iceberg – where you have a chance of catching 10 per cent, with the rest below the water. It now defies proportion and the culture vultures among you will fail in *Titanic* proportions to do more than grab a few cubes of ice on the way through. Assuming these shows last 55 minutes each and forgetting the travel

---

[59] *Who fled the Nazis from Austria in 1934, helped found Glyndebourne (the picnic capital of the world) and after Edinburgh's success, became General Manager of the Metropolitan Opera in NY, moving it to its current, now rather ugly, home in Lincoln Center.*

[60] *As the population of Edinburgh is 450,000 you can see it gets a bit busy in August.*

time between venues (or the mundane necessities of life), it would take the man on the Princes Street Omnibus about 78 days, 7 hours and 10 minutes to see everything![61]

No wonder there's an Edinburgh saying, 'September is for sleeping'.

I am persuaded that this is good – open access allows everyone a chance.[62] The theatre content is staggering. At one level there are new plays of outrageous talent that will move quickly from the disused public toilet[63] to a West End theatre in London and then to the brilliant lights of Broadway. At the other end of the spectrum are the competing claims of school drama groups, struggling professionals and the mad one-man output of amateurs looking to get it out their system. (Which includes me – with an ambition to bring a one-man show on Burns – 'One Man's a Man For a' That'. The frightening risk is that the one-man aspect is the size of the audience!)

There are groups reinterpreting famous works (*The Importance of Being Earnest* set in the gay scene of the NY Village) or presenting works of huge scope in a 45-minute confine (the whole *Star Wars* trilogy, the Sherlock Holmes stories or *Finnegans Wake* in Urdu) but there can be odd coincidences and concentrations. Last year you could choose a few different *Macbeth*s:[64]

- *An American Macbeth*[65]
- *Macbeth*[66]
- *The Macbeth Conspiracy*[67]
- *Macbeth – Frantic Redhead's Walking Play*[68]

---

[61] *The Fringe lasts for four weeks!*

[62] *Break into 42nd Street dreams here: 'You pack your scanties/And I'll pack my panties/And we'll shuffle off to Edinbro'!' (roughly).*

[63] *There are some odd venues; while some of the big corporate groups now have stables of venues, there are still school gyms, church halls and upstairs bars a-plenty.*

[64] *That's a lot of potential actors' bad luck in this clan of 'the Scottish Play'.*

[65] Macbeth *as an example of* US *policy in Iraq.*

[66] *Rather oddly, with Shakespearean text uncut, in English and as you learned at school.*

[67] Macbeth *meets* All the President's Men.

[68] *Not in a theatre but on a walking tour of the Old Town at night.*

- *Macbeth Re-arisen*[69]
- *Macbeth – That Old Black Magic*[70]
- *Young Macbeth*[71]

None, alas, sponsored by Scottish Widows!

If you haven't the time or patience to read the nearly 300-page programme then wander up and down the Royal Mile, where you will be accosted by leafleteers and see snippets of many productions acted out on the little stages set along the pedestrian part of the High Street.

There's also music and children's shows in equal abundance, with your choice of dance, art and photography exhibitions and more. But the thing that gets the attention year on year is the comedy. And that's the big business in Edinburgh now.

It certainly has created some stellar careers. In 1981 the first comedy awards were created[72] and the first winners were the Cambridge Footlights group, whose line-up included Hugh Laurie, Stephen Fry, Tony Slattery and Emma Thompson. Subsequent years launched Steve Coogan (1992) and Lee Evans (1993). There is controversy about the commercialisation of the genre and the perceived weakening of quality[73] but for most of us we'll have a few good nights out, more laughs than not and will come out into the pale night sky of Auld Reekie thankful to be in this most beautiful of cities at this most exciting of times.

---

[69] *The hilarious 'rediscovered sequel'.*

[70] *With Sinatra songs.*

[71] *Three actors only.*

[72] *Ironically, given the quantum of alcohol, by Perrier. Recently they were renamed the Ifs.*

[73] *It is true that in the early days of stand-up you'd get three comics doing 15–20 minutes each, which it is quite achievable to keep very funny. Then the format slipped to a 15 minute warm-up for a 40 minute slot, and now often you'll get the full hour from a famous or not-so-famous comic. There are relatively few people in the world with the gift of being (intentionally) funny and spontaneous for 60 minutes every single night. I'm not sure that there is that much unintentional comedy in the world either!*

The other festivals, if they will forgive me for ranking them thus, are smaller but no less vibrant. The Book Festival was an important element in Edinburgh's appointment as UNESCO City of Literature, while the Television Festival – appropriate in the homeland of John Logie Baird and Lord Reith – brings the most important broadcasters under one roof. You'll see much of the Scottish political establishment at the nascent Festival of Politics,[74] and the International Film Festival (now held in June rather than August) – which was founded in 1947 – is almost as old as Cannes.[75]

I want to put in a word for the 'untrendy' festival: the Edinburgh Military Tattoo.

Since 1950 the Esplanade in front of Edinburgh Castle has become home to Eiffellian structures of seats so that every night[76] over 8,000 people can huddle under blankets to see displays from military groups from around the world.[77] Many pooh-pooh this, but with the castle as its backdrop, and the spine-tingling finale of the lone piper on the topmost tower playing the town to sleep (to be rudely awakened by the fireworks a few minutes later), this show sells out within days of opening every year and raises over £5million annually for charities. So put your prejudice aside

---

74  *There are so many political Scots that they are sometimes referred to as the Scotia Nostra. Not to be confused with the important Edinburgh fund managers, who are the Charlotte Square Mafia!*

75  *Though given the Scottish weather, people tend to wear warmer clothes.*

76  *Twice on Saturdays, never on the Sabbath.*

77  *One favourite, given the close links between the two countries, is the Hans Majestet Kongens Garde – the Norwegian Royal Guard – in their striking black and white uniform. They adopted a penguin at Edinburgh Zoo, Niels Olav, as their mascot in 1961 and he (and his descendents) have been formally promoted on each subsequent visit by the regiment, with the penguin undertaking a formal inspection of the troops. Last year saw the first penguin in history to become an honorary Colonel-in-Chief, while this year HM King Harald V added the honour of knighthood – what's next?*

and come and see a part of Scotland that in other hands would be a Harry Lauder cliché, but here is an insight into our nation's soul.[78]

Who indeed, that has once seen Edinburgh, with its couchant rag-lion, but must see it again in dreams, waking or sleeping? My dear Sir, do not think I blaspheme when I tell you that your great London, as compared to Dun-Edin, 'mine own romantic town', is as prose compared to poetry, or as a great rumbling, rambling, heavy epic compared to a lyric, brief, bright, clear, and vital as a flash of lightning. You have nothing like Scott's Monument, or if you had that, and all the glories of architecture assembled togeth-er, you have nothing like Arthur's Seat, and above all you have not the Scotch national character; and it is that grand character after all which gives the land its true charm, its true greatness.[79]

---

[78] *Of course, there are other magic festivals across the country: the Mod (offi-cially, Am Mòd Nàiseanta Rìoghail (the Royal National Mod) is the largest Gaelic celebration in the world. In October each year since 1892, Gaels from all over Scotland and abroad gather to participate in competitions of literature and poetry, music and dance in a cultural Olympics all in the ancient tongue of Scotland. Increasingly, communities are finding different reasons to hold cultural festivals through the year. Perhaps it's reaching back to the old days, when the markets and fairs in towns would everyone together for a few days, leavened with the various outsiders coming for the trade. So we find the presiding genius of Sir Peter Maxwell Davies in Orkney creating the St Magnus Festival, or the Pitlochry Festival of Theatre in Perthshire. It will come as no surprise that one of the most popular, varied and boisterous festivals happens every May in Ayrshire at the Burns An' A' That! Probably the best way to capture the feel of his poetry and the pace of his life is to visit the town of Mauchline, as the local Burns Club transforms the community into the Mauchline of 1786 – complete with costumes and horse-drawn carriages! Rabbie wrote one of his poems, 'The Holy Fair', here after a day's visit to what was then an open-air preaching mission (with a fair bit of sinning on the side):*

| | |
|---|---|
| There's some are fou o' love divine; | *Some are drunk on love divine,* |
| There's some are fou o' brandy; | *And some just drunk on brandy;* |
| An' mony jobs that day begin, | *And many starting work today,* |
| May end in houghmagandie. | *End up in bed quite randy.* |

[79] *Letter to W. Smith Williams, Charlotte Brontë, 1850.*

# 11

# The National Spirit

*Sometimes a wife or bairn would come with a message; to such messenger was always offered whisky ... a woman with a child in her arms, and another bit thing at her knee, came up among them; the horn cup was in due course handed to her, she took a 'gey guid drap' herself, and then gave a little to each of the babies. 'My goodness child' said my Mother to the wee thing that was trotting by its mother's side, 'doesn't it bite you?' 'Ay, but I like the bite,' replied the creature that could hardly speak.[1]*

WHO CAN TALK OF Scots without talking of Scotch?

One of the lost poignant tombstones in Scotland is that of a nice old drunk – found in the peace of a wee country kirk, it says:

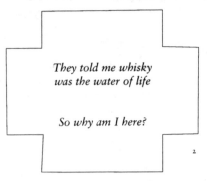

*They told me whisky was the water of life*

*So why am I here?*

[2]

Our usquebaugh is truly the water of life and of livelihood in Scotland. Across the world people boil various vegetable products, heat the liquid to boiling and capture the resulting rot gut. In a great stroke of fortune,

---

[1]    Memoirs of a Highland Lady, *Elizabeth Grant of Rothiemurchus, Vol I, p.272.*

[2]    *Dead drunk indeed.*

all of the elements meet in Scotland to produce the liquor par excellence – whisky.

We guard the tradition fiercely – the definition of what is a whisky is legally given under UK law and recognised by the EU and the WTO as a protected 'geographical indication', on a par with Parma Ham, matched by Melton Mowbray pies and branded like Burgundy. It is regularly enforced through the courts[3] (although there is an irony that the last government minister to sign the standards was most famous for feeding hamburgers to his daughter to alleviate fears about mad cow disease).

The inhabitants of Scotland have had their hand in this trade for a good while. I wouldn't be surprised that the old Iron Age chaps in Skara

---

[3]   *The Scotch Whisky Order 1990:*
      *Definition of Scotch whisky*
      3   *For the purpose of the Act 'Scotch whisky' means whisky—*
              *(a) which has been produced at a distillery in Scotland from water and malted barley (to which only whole grains of other cereals may be added) all of which have been—*
                  *(i) processed at that distillery into a mash;*
                  *(ii) converted to a fermentable substrate only by endogenous enzyme systems; and*
                  *(iii) fermented only by the addition of yeast;*
              *(b) which has been distilled at an alcoholic strength by volume of less than 94.8 per cent so that the distillate has an aroma and taste derived from the raw materials used in, and the method of, its production;*
              *(c) which has been matured in an excise warehouse in Scotland in oak casks of a capacity not exceeding 700 litres, the period of that maturation being not less than 3 years;*
              *(d) which retains the colour, aroma and taste derived from the raw materials used in, and the method of, its production and maturation; and*
              *(e) to which no substance other than water and spirit caramel has been added.*
      *Minimum alcoholic strength of Scotch whisky*
      4   *For the purposes of section 2(1)(b) of the Act there is hereby specified the alcoholic strength of 40 per cent by volume (being also the minimum alcoholic strength by volume prescribed in relation to whisky/whiskey by Article 3(1) of Council Regulation (EEC) No 1576/89 laying down general rules on the definition, description and presentation of spirit drinks).*

Brae had a wee still bubbling but the first documented reference to our national drink is, alas, in some early tax records.

> To Friar John Cor, by order of the King, to make aquavitae, VIII bols of malt[4]

From the king's order, we can surmise that the holy fathers weren't in the distilling business as a hobby: eight bols of malt (about 1,200 lbs) should convert into about 1,000 bottles of rather strong[5] booze.

To be fair to the old monks, they held a widely-thought belief that their dram was medicinally helpful[6] and prescribed it as a general elixir, with particular recuperative powers for stomach problems, chronic shakes and respiratory conditions.[7] In 1505, recognising the restorative properties of the drink, the king gave the Edinburgh Guild of Barber Surgeons[8] a patent to produce whisky, and for 60 years the monks and barbers went their merry way, until John Knox and the reformers literally destroyed monastic culture and cast the friars to the four winds.

Now, if a group of relatively educated men are forbidden their core competency, they will fall back on to whatever secular way they can find to make ends meet. Stills blossomed throughout the country as these former priests found a new way to minister to their flocks.[9] Everyone seemed quite happy (hic!) until King Charles I – the most prodigious tax raiser in history – had an excise act passed in 1644, setting duties to be paid 'on every pint of aquavit or strong waters sold in the country'.[10]

---

4   *Exchequer Rolls of James IV.*

5   *And possibly dangerous, given the lack of real understanding of the scientific process – but what a way to go in a period of low average life expectancy anyway.*

6   *Many of us still tak a wee yin tae keep out the cauld.*

7   *A quick swig if you had the pox was probably in order too.*

8   *In both Scotland and England the old trades union of hairdressers, by dint I suppose of having the sharpest blades, carried out surgery until the universities established medical faculties. Even today a traditional barber will have a red-and-white-striped pole outside his shop – denoting the 'blood and bandages' of his ancient profession.*

9   *Old habits die hard – nowadays the friars fry Mars Bars in batter!*

10  *Excise Act 1644 (Old Scots Parliament).*

The market fragmented into the licensed producers and the entrepreneurs with illicit stills behind the hills. For nearly 200 years the government sought to raise taxes while combating smuggling and moonshining with a growing body of excise officers[11] – it took them a long time to recognise that a Scot and his Scotch cannot be parted.

The Duke of Gordon, having seen how the Prince Regent enjoyed a large belt of illicit Glenlivit, used his influence in the House of Lords to reduce the hated taxes and make legal whisky affordable in 1823. On the one hand a philanthropist, on the other a shrewd investor, His Grace sponsored James Smith to take out the first new licence – the Glenlivit remains one of our favourite brands today.

That was the impetus the industry needed, the boom that made usquebaugh ubiquitous.

This autumn King George the 4th, then, I think, only Regent, visited Scotland. The whole country went mad... Lord Conyngham, the Chamberlain, was looking every where for pure Glenlivet whisky – the King drank nothing else – it was not to be had out of the highlands. My father sent word to me, I was the Cellerer, to empty my pet bin, where there was whisky long in the wood, long in uncorked bottles, mild as milk, and the true contraband goût in it. Much as I grudged this treasure, it made our fortunes afterwards, shewing on what trifles great events sometimes depend. The whisky and fifty brace of ptarmigan[12] all shot by one man in one day, went up to Holyrood House, and were graciously received and made much of, and a reminder of this attention at a proper moment by the gentlemanly Chamberlain ensured to my father the Indian Judgeship.[13]

From that point on, whisky became an industry, facing times of expansion and contraction, mergers and acquisitions, as the small family distiller

---

[11]  *Including, ironically, Robert Burns.*

[12]  *A small grouse – really more of a moan.*

[13]  Memoirs of a Highland Lady, *Elizabeth Grant of Rothiemurchus, Vol II, p.166. As W. S. Gilbert would say, 'It was managed by a job. And a good job too!'*

evolved into the international drinks conglomerate to supply not only our healthy domestic consumption, but increasingly global exports.[14]

> The Scotch do not drink... During the whole of two or three pleasant weeks spent lecturing in Scotland, I never on any occasions saw whisky made use of as a beverage. I have seen people take it, of course, as a medicine, or as a precaution, or as a wise offset against a rather treacherous climate; but as a beverage, never![15]

## Input

At last, across the weary faem,
Frae far, outlandish pairts I came.
On ilka side o' me I fand      [each]
Fresh tokens o' my native land.
Wi' whatna joy I hailed them a'–
The hilltaps standin' raw by raw,
The public house, the Hielan' birks,    [Highland birches]
And a' the bonny UP kirks!    [United Presbyterian = 'Wee Free']
But maistly thee, the bluid o' Scots,
Frae Maidenkirk to John o' Grots,
The king o' drinks, as I conceive it,
Talisker, Isla, or Glenlivet!
For after years wi' a pockmantie    [handkerchief]
Frae Zanzibar to Alicante,
In mony a fash and sair affliction    [worry]
I gie't as my sincere conviction–
Of a' their foreign tricks an' pliskies,    [pranks]
I maist abominate their whiskies.

---

[14] *The export market is more than £2bn annually and the industry is Scotland's second largest.*

[15] Collected Works, *Stephen Leacock, Professor of Economics, McGill University (founded by a Glasgow graduate).*

Nae doot, themsels, they ken it weel,
An' wi' a hash o' leemon peel,
And ice an' siccan filth, they ettle                    [such other, try]
The stawsome kind o' goo to settle;                         [sickening]
Sic wersh apothecary's broos wi'                    [bitter and nasty]
As Scotsmen scorn to fyle their moo's wi'[16]                   [foul]

Cognoscenti, connoisseurs and con artists all agree that each and every whisky[17] is born of two humble parents: fresh water and pure barley. The first stage in discussing what you are about to drink is to understand the inputs, which combine in a true mystery of creation.

First: the water. If there is a concept of 'terroir'[18] then it can be extended to Scotland's production of whisky, for the water of the locality is the first and prime concern of the distiller. There is some dispute about how many distinct regions there are, but the consensus is five (with a few 'outliers'):

- **Speyside:** The home of the whisky industry lies along the banks of the River Spey as it wends its hundred mile journey from the Highlands to the North Sea. Here over half of the active distilleries in Scotland are to be found – with many of the household names[19] known in the world at large.

*Classic labels include: Glenfiddich, Glenmorangie, The Macallan*

- **Highland:** The second-largest family covers by far the greatest area – the supreme natural beauty of the Highlands. Individual distilleries are found tucked away at the foot of purple-heathered mountains, many locked into tiny microclimates, which means that some of these drams are hard

---

[16] 'The Scotsman's Return from Abroad', A Child's Garden of Verses, Robert Louis Stevenson (though it seems an odd theme for a poem for children!).

[17] Did I remind you already that in Scotland there is no 'e' in 'whisky'? 'Whiskeys' are the produce of Ireland and North America.

[18] West Highland terroirs? The whisky domains – striking terroir into your hearts.

[19] At least in my household.

to fit into the recognisable family relationships the whiskies from the other regions share.[20]

*Classic labels include: Dalmore, Lochnagar*

- **Islay**: One of the southernmost of our islands, nestled off the coast of Argyll in its own peat-scented heaven, rained upon generously but none the worse for that – the high priests of strong flavour dwell in this island and produce (albeit nearly unpronounceable) whiskies redolent of seaweed, peat smoke and toilet cleaner.[21]

*Classic labels include: Laphroaig, Lagavulin, Bhunnabhain*

- **Campbletown**: This port on Kintyre[22] was for many years the industrial heartland of the whisky industry, with nearly three dozen independent distilleries cheek-by-jowl[23] producing over two million gallons of spirit a year for the Glasgow and Edinburgh blenders. No longer so, but the tradition of this outpost is maintained honourably by the last two producers:

*Springbank and Glen Scotia*

- **Lowland**: As in so many cultural areas, the Lowlander's contribution is often forgotten when set against the

---

[20] *Here are our famous outliers – I have great sympathy for those who adhere to a final terroir – the Islands: these are the non-Islay Highland islands, where there are usually more lighthouses than distilleries and more barrels than people! The roll of honour: Highland Park (Orkney), Tobermory (Mull), Jura (Jura) and the pale fire of Talisker (Skye).*

[21] *As many critics of NZ Sauvignon Blanc liken it to the question 'Which cat pee'd on my gooseberry bush?', so the weaklings and slackers decry the phenols of these oily malts. Don't knock it though – the peculiar smell of ammonia persuaded the US government to allow the importation of Laphroaig as a medicine all through the Prohibition years – I'll drink to that, Doctor!*

[22] *The Mull of Kintyre was of course the inspiration for Sir Paul McCartney – not to be confused with the island of Mull. I'll mull over those differences with a glass in my hand...*

[23] *Andy Stewart's second most famous song: 'Campbleton Loch, I Wish Ye Were Whisky'.*

grandeur of the Highlands. The fine soft waters south of the Highland Line can be used to craft a recognisable, if lighter, type of malt.

*Classic labels include: Achentoshan, Rosebank, Glenkinchie*

So that's us worked out the mother of our malts – let's have a look at daddy: the barley. You'll recall that barley is one of the legal 'musts' to create Scottish malt whisky.[24]

Barley grows well in Scotland, and there is evidence that our pre-historic ancestors cultivated it for sustenance; over the years their wiser progeny marked the 'bere' (to give it its Scots name) for shipment to the brewer and the distiller rather than the baker.

The golden grains are taken and soaked in the local water for a few days in the malting stage. The wet barley is then spread across the malting floor to allow the grains to germinate, releasing sugar from the grain's store of starch. Once sprouted (after about a week) the conversion will be complete and the  germination is closed off by heat. The green malt (as the wee sproutlings are called) is cast into a kiln, traditionally fired on peat,[25] though outside Islay other natural fuel will be used to limit the smell of the peat in the final output.

This malt is now ground into 'grist'[26] and this is thrown into the round mash tuns, where gallons of warm water are introduced. The heat and damp accelerate the production of soluble sugars. After this, the barley has become a sort of thin porridge, which the distiller calls the 'wort'. This is cooled and transferred into new containers or 'washbacks', where yeast is added to start the three days of fermentation, changing all that

---

[24]   *No rye, no wheat, no potatoes – all capable of making a good 'swally' but not licit here.*

[25]   *I am sure that everyone knows what peat is – a thick sod, not to be confused with Pete – who is a...*

[26]   *As in the proverb, 'more grist to your mill'.*

sugar into the first, weak alcohol, which is the 'wash'. This doesn't look much – it is really a weak beer; if we'd stopped at this point, Scottish history would have been radically duller!

Now the alchemy begins.

The wash is transferred into the first distilling tool: the wash still, and is boiled hard to reduce to a concentrate known as the low wines.[27] This is the raw material upon which the master distiller works his mystery.

He employs one of the most beautiful industrial machines: the still. Every whisky still is made of beaten copper in a shape like a dumpy onion. The exact shape of the still influences the quality of the spirit – as do other design features like the angle of the arm which leads to the condenser, and the height of the still above the fire.[28]

It would be wrong to think that the machine makes the malt. The chemistry is simple, that's for sure: the application of heat to the base of the still of wash causes the alcohol to evaporate (alcohol is more volatile than water, so the alcohol boils off first) and this rises, escaping through the swan's neck to be condensed by cooling, turning the precious alcohol back into liquid spirits.

You have to be careful though – the first trickle[29] is pretty rough, while there comes a point where the water evaporation slows so that the last portion of liquid is watery[30] and so is also sub-optimal. Only a master distiller can see the miracle – the 'Heart of the Run' – which is our first-born whisky running with 70 per cent ABV in its veins.[31]

---

27   *Sorry: no idea why, but we've increased out potency – alcohol by volume ('ABV') – from the wash's 8 per cent by three times to nearly 20 per cent – onwards and upwards!*

28   *Now usually industrially fired at this stage, rather than on an open flame of wood or peat. The taller stills will give a lighter whisky while the dumpy ones get a fuller, heavier spirit.*

29   *Called the Heads of the Distillery.*

30   *The Tails of the Distillery, naturally enough – both heads and tails, with good Calvinist thrift, will go back into the next wash to be distilled.*

31   *My American friends might be confused by ABV. For years the measurement of the alcoholic strength of a spirit was 'proof'. If the product were to be distilled such that the content was 100 per cent alcohol that would be defined as 200 proof (or effectively guaranteed death). So 'proof' is equal to 50 per cent ABV.*

I have to be careful, for of course this is not yet whisky. After production, there is a legally-defined maturation process too.

The first stage is to get the spirit into barrels, either at the full strength or reduced slightly with the local water to 60–63 per cent ABV. The barrel we imprison our liquid in is not any old keg. By law it must be of oak.[32] Those of us who dislike Australian Chardonnay know what a woody taste is transferred from the barrel to the contents – why doesn't that feature in Scotch?

The answer is, 'because of a happy act of parsimony'. While Scotland was exporting whisky, she was also importing sherry from Spain – and these casks that had held the Finos, Manzanillas, Olorosos and Amontillados of Andalusia were empty and cheap. So the distilleries started using sherry wood casks, which added a nuance of taste and colour to the whisky that was much appreciated. Then, in a moment of transatlantic symbiosis, a bright chap noticed that bourbon can only be matured in a brand-new oak barrel[33] – so we had a market in casks that were no use to the bourbon manufacturers. Nowadays, the great majority of our produce is aged in bourbon casks, but there is a trend searching for novelty and so some odd woods: port, Madeira or even cognac barrels are used.[34]

Not just the previous life, but the size of the vessel is an element of the creation of the final taste.

Casks have some wonderful and evocative names.[35]

---

[32]  *And not any old oak either – only the* Quercus alba *(aka white American oak) or the* Q. robur *(the European oak) are valid. It's nice to think that while the Royal Navy was being built out of English oak, the Scots oaks went to a different use!*

[33]  *The bourbon industry has to comply with some weird laws: for example, the great Jack Daniels Distillery is in a dry county of Lynchberg, TN and so cannot allow visitors to buy its famous whiskey!*

[34]  *Legend has it that fish barrels, from the herring industry, were scraped and boiled for use in Campbletown after the Great War – a fishy tale, perhaps?*

[35]  *Words that you'll rarely find in polite conversation.*

| Name | Former Contents | Capacity (Metric) | Capacity (Imperial) |
| --- | --- | --- | --- |
| Barrel | Mainly bourbon | 200 litres | 44 gallons[36] |
| Hogshead[37] | Wine | 250 litres | 55 gallons |
| Puncheon | Wine | 450 litres | 100 gallons |
| Butt | Sherry | 500 litres | 110 gallons |
| Pipe | Port | 500 litres | 110 gallons |
| Gorda[38] | Sherry | 600 litres | 130 gallons |

Now our spirit just has to sit and wait. The casks are locked in warehouses under the watchful eye of HM Customs. The 'fillings' as they are now called must lie and mature for a minimum of three years before they receive the final accolade of being a legal whisky.

Distillers are plagued by thieves, of course – the visible are the ones you can beat: the warehouses have heavy security, though not always what you'd expect. One in Dumbarton which had been plagued by burglars was managed by a classical scholar who remembered his Livy.[39] The historian of early Rome told how the sacred geese of the Capitol honked in wrath when the Gauls sneaked up in the night, thus alerting the defenders in the nick of time, and so for many peaceful years a web-footed constabulary protected the golden drams inside to great success.

The real thief is the evaporation – those lovely organic oak casks breathe, and as they do their breath smells of whisky. Every year, two and three percent of the precious liquor vanishes – this is known as the angels' share; it must help them jazz up their harp music on an afternoon!

While three years is the statutory minimum, a distillery will mature

---

36  *Imperial gallons, not US. Despite the American rhyme 'a pint's a pound the world round', the British pint is 20 fl. oz, not 16, so our gallons are bigger than yours. But then their gas is much, much cheaper.*

37  *There is also an Australian Wine Hogshead, which is a bit bigger – just showing off a bit.*

38  *From the Spanish: 'the big/fat one'.*

39  History of Rome, *Book V, 47: M. Manlius Capitolinus.*

casks for all sorts of ages – some dark corners host 50-year-old monsters of the deep, for so long as the fillings stay in the protection of the cask, they will grow in taste.[40]

## Output

> Fortune! if thou'll but gie me still
> Hale breeks, a scone, an' whisky gill,
> An' rowth o' rhyme to rave at will,          [abundance]
>  Tak a' the rest,
> An' deal't about as thy blind skill
> Directs thee best.[41]

The last phase – and the one which will release this drink of history to you, dear reader, is the bottling. It's not just a case[42] of filling a bottle and slapping on a label. This is the final process of taste creation, involving combining ages, possibly mixing types and almost certainly reducing strength.

Every label must have an age on it – the age of the youngest whisky that has been used. The master distiller will draw on his palette of different sized and aged kegs to create his perfect whisky.

If those whiskies are all from the one distillery then this bottle of whisky is called a single malt, while if it is from one particular cask then it's called a single cask malt. Sometimes, you'll find that the distiller marries single malts from a number of smaller distilleries; this relatively rare process nowadays creates a vatted malt, or he can sell his fillings to a blender who will mix it with what used to be thought of as the poor cousin of malts, grain whisky, to produce a blended whisky – the traditional Scotch of Johnny Walker or Dewers.[43]

---

[40]  *The moment it is bottled, its age and character is captured and will not grow. Mind you, it will stay in pretty good nick for a good long time until opened.*

[41]  *'Scotch Drink', Robert Burns.*

[42]  *Excuse the pun.*

[43]  *But these blends can be startling premium whiskies in their own right: Johnny Walker Blue or Chivas Regal retail for higher sums than many single malts, so it's not as easy (in fact just wrong) to sneer. It's all in your taste, and your budget!*

The last artistry is on strength: the bulk of production is reduced (using the same mother water) to the legal minimum of 40 per cent ABV, but 44–46 per cent is not unusual. Some bottles will come out at 'cask strength' – which equates to 50 or 60 per cent – there's power to your elbow! Chill filtering and colouring are among the additional processes which may also be applied in many modern whiskies.

Now bottled, the distiller pays his tax to the UK government[44] and a bewildering choice of 70 cl[45] bottles are made available for retail sale.

There's only one thing left to talk about – the moment we have all been waiting for – a dram.[46] Go on to any of the specialist websites and you'll learn of glass shapes and bottle angles and all sorts of complexity, for, as in everything, the higher the unit price the more 'etiquette' and 'ritual' people want to see to endorse their expense.[47]

For most of the whiskies you will have the honour and privilege of drinking, all you really need is a glass[48] and a bottle (and a friend). It is true that a little splash of flat Scottish mineral water[49] unlocks some of the secrets of the whisky[50] – but please, I beg you – no ice as it freezes the life out of the spirit and the spirit out of your life.

That dram was the highland prayer, it began, accompanied and ended all things.[51]

---

44  *In these iniquitous times about 73 per cent of the price you pay for a bottle of whisky goes to pay tax!*

45  *75 cl in the US, lucky devils – bigger bottles and lower taxes!*

46  *Or a snifter, wee nippy sweetie, a wee swally or if you are lucky – anither yin.*

47  *A wee Glasgow boy and his mammy (Mary McGlumpher of Possil Park) were looking in at a whisky tasting (they couldn't go in as you had to be over 21 – neither were) and saw a portly Edinburgh chap taste a whisky in a funny-shaped glass – then spit it out. He did the same again. Confused, the wee bauchle asked his hairy-Mary mither, 'What's that man daein?' 'Pacing himself son,' came his mother's wise reply.*

48  *Per person, please.*

49  *Most Scottish tap water is lovely, too, and refreshingly cheap.*

50  *So don't let any mad 'purists' put you off!*

51  Memoirs of a Highland Lady, *Elizabeth Grant of Rothiemurchus, Vol I, p.274. (She did write about more than booze!)*

## Slainte Mhath!⁵²

Hollo! Keep it up boys – and push around the glass,
Let each seize his bumper, and drink to his lass:
Away with dull thinking – 'tis madness to think –
And let those be sober who've nothing to drink.
Huzza boys! Let each take a bumper in hand,
And stand – if there's anyone able to stand.
How all things dance round me! – 'tis life, tho' my boys:
Of drinking and spewing how great are the joys?⁵³

So then, a toast: as we Scots have many whiskies, we have many toasts, too:

Lang may yer lum reek.⁵⁴

May the best ye've ever seen
Be the worst ye'll ever see;
May a moose neer leave yer girnal            [store chest]

Wi' a tear drap in its e'e.

Blythe tae meet,
Wae tae part,
Blythe to meet aince mair.⁵⁵

Or the great Caledonian Toast – which can only be proposed whilst standing on your chair with one foot on the table:

---

⁵² *The old traditional toast: 'good health' (slan–jay va).*
⁵³ *'Drinking Song: to the tune Lumps of Pudding', R. Fergusson, vv 1, 3.*
⁵⁴ *'May your chimney smoke forever' – still popular, albeit archaic given modern regulations.*
⁵⁵ *The Bon Accord Toast of Aberdeen.*

| | |
|---|---|
| *Suas i, suas i* | Up with it, up with it |
| *Seas i, seas i,* | Down wit it, down with it, |
| *A'nall i, a'nall i* | Over to you, over to you |
| *A'null i, a'null i.* | Over to me, over to me. |
| *Na h'uile la gu math diut, mo charaid.* | May all your days be happy, my friend. |
| *Sguab as i!* | Drink it up! |
| *Agus cha n'ol neach eile as a ghloine so gu brath!* | And let no man drink from this glass again![56] |

You have to have a certain amount of drink in you to perform this convincingly, but not so much that you over-balance on the swinging! Take care where you throw your glass, too – often the fireplace is a long way off if you haven't got good hand–eye coordination.

Often toasts are drunk out of quaiches – traditional metal[57] drinking vessels with flat metal handles. There the convention is not only to drink the whisky but to hold the inverted, empty quaich over your head to prove you have done honour to your host in draining every last drop.

It's fair to say that you can enjoy whisky, counter-intuitively, by having none at all! It's become one of the pillars of the Scottish tourist industry.

Following in the footsteps of the vineyards who gave tourists informal tastings at the winery, many of our distillers do a tour of the working distillery and then provide a wee snifter to encourage people to take home a bottle (or two[58]). They are among the most enjoyable days out[59] as you can experience at first-hand this ancient craft, and be impressed by the passion that still run through the veins of the employees.

The biggest concentration of potential visits lies along the Malt Whisky Trail[60] but if you can't get that far north, have a look at the Scotch

---

[56] *As you'll have guessed, you drink the whole glass and smash it!*
[57] *Mainly pewter now, but silver or silver gilt is handsome.*
[58] *Just to be polite – one can look a bit tight.*
[59] *Even for a teetotaller or the designated driver.*
[60] *www.maltwhiskytrail.com.*

Whisky Experience[61] just beneath the castle in Edinburgh, where you get a distillation of the whole experience.

You'll find more wine merchants (and supermarkets) nowadays taking time and care over the choice of their whiskies, so go in and have a look or check up their ideas – and cheap offers! But once you have your feet under the table and are ready to do PhD research, visit the website (or join in the events of) the Scotch Malt Whisky Society[62] – it's a long course (no one has yet finished it!).

Enjoy our gift wisely and not too well! (Or at least not too well, too often!) Come and join me in celebrating all the fine craftsmen and women in the distilleries across our country!

To the tune of 'When a Felon's not Engaged in his Employment' by Sir A. Sullivan:

> When a Scotsman's whisky glass is needing filling
> To his homeland in the Highlands he returns
> Seeking solace in the produce of pot stilling
> And the water that inspir'd Robert Burns
>
> We can sip our Cragganmore or Craigellachie
> And sniff a glass of Glenmorangie noo
> Wi Glenlivet and Glen Turret and Glenlossie
> Speyside gies us a dram that's always true
>
> *Chorus–*
> When the drinkin of a dram's to be done, to be done
> A Scotsman's lot is quite a happy one, happy one
>
> Not just Jura, Bunnabhain or Bruichladdie
> Fettercairn, Glenord, Glen Moray and TamDhu
> But Glentauchers or Glen Rothes or Glen Scotia
> Dalmore, Dalwhinnie, Deanston, Dufftown too!

---

[61] *www.whisky-heritage.co.uk.*

[62] *www.smws.com.*

Don't forget Ardbeg an' birks o' Aberfeldy
Tobermory, Tomatin and Tominoul
Ardmore, Aultmore an' Auchentoshan
Balblair, Balvenie, Ben Nevis and Cardhu
*Chorus*

The Macallan, Miltown Duff and now Glendronach,
Glenfiddich, Glenfarclas, Knockando,
The peaty breath of Laphroig or Caol Ila
Lagavulin and the isles creep up on you

From Orkney's Highland Park in the northlands
To Springbank in the loch of Campbeltown
The island tang of Talisker from out west
To Aberlour of Eastern renown
*Chorus*

Blair Athol and his brother Tullibardine
Bowmore, Inchgower, Macduff and Mannochmore
Mortlach or Linkwood or Loch Lomond
You'd drink until you fell upon the floor

The Bens abound: Riach, Rinnes and Romach
While Allt-na-bhainne flows down the hills in flood
Old Pultney, Scapa, Oban, Brackla, Speyburn
Glenburgie and Glencadam both taste good
*Chorus*

Lochnagar (which is a hill and not some water)
Bladnoch, Balmenach, Teanich and Tormore
Gen Garioch, Glenallachie, Glendullan
The Singleon, a Clyneish and some Longmore

Step down now from this jolly whisky platform
Stomp through the straths of Isla, Mill and more
The glens of Goyne and Kinchie and of Spey
And taste the spirit of our ancient Scottish lore

My head is reeling with the thought of whisky
So my song of praise is very nearly done
For in celebrating this my patrimony
I've tasted every single blessed one!
*Chorus, con brio*[63]

---

[63]   *And apologies for those (few I think) I have missed out.*

# 12

# Balls

Item it is decreed and the king forbids that any man play football under the pain of 4 [pence] to the lord of the land as often as he is convicted.[1]

Item it is ordained and decreet that wappenshaws be held... four times a year, and that football and golf be utterly cried down and not used,... And touching football and golf, we ordain that it be punished by the baron's unlaw; and if he does not take it, it is to be taken by the king's officers.[2]

Item, that football and golf be discontinued in the future[3]

And further, that football, golf or other similar unprofitable sports are not to be played anywhere in the realm, but for the common good and defence of the realm the practice of shooting bows and archery butts are therefore ordained in each parish, under the pain of 40 s[hillings].[4]

WHAT DO YOU THINK of when we turn to Scottish sport – is it watching Eric Liddell training on St Andrews' beach in *Chariots of Fire*? Or huddling over a polystyrene cup of Bovril to keep warm as you wait for the ball to land in the back of the Hampden net? Maybe it's belting out 'Flower of Scotland' before a defeat at Murrayfield, or hurling the bookies slip in the bin as that nag at Musselburgh was so slow it nearly came first in the race after.

Whatever it is, the Scots are passionate fans of whichever sport, to the extent that the old kings had to outlaw golf and football,[5] as they

---

[1]   Proceedings of the Scottish Parliament: James I: *26 May 1424* (*ref 1424/19*).

[2]   Proceedings of the Scottish Parliament: James II: *6 March 1458* (*ref 1458/3/7*).

[3]   Proceedings of the Scottish Parliament: James III: *6 May 1471* (*ref 1471/5/6*).

[4]   Proceedings of the Scottish Parliament: James IV: *18 May 1491* (*ref 1491/4/17*) – *the need for repetition at regular intervals seems to indicate a relative lack of success in enforcement!*

[5]   *For my American readers, soccer.*

felt that a good bit of archery practice would help in the wars against England. It's a testament to the stubborn nature of the Scots that they carried on playing over the regal prohibition, though history does show that better archers would have been a good idea.

## The Orkney Ba' Game

The competitive nature of men, especially Scotsmen, features in war, in commerce and, with even more gusto, on the sports field. This has been true since the dawn of time, and one of the oldest sporting events in Scotland takes place in Kirkwall, the county town of Orkney.

I know Orkney well; when I was a lad, I was captivated by the ancient remains: the beehive tomb of Maes Howe,[6] the standing stones of Stenness and, of course, the Stone-Age village of Skara Brae – enveloped in a jiffy bag of sand for about two millennia. At the other end of the timeline, there's a little Nissen hut near Scapa Flow which is the Chapel of St George – inside is a miracle of *tromp d'oeil*, as Italian prisoners in World War II painted this crinkly tin shed to become an Italianate chapel.

In terms of local affection, though, the Orcadians' favourite sight was always 'the Tree'. From the sleeping of Skara Brae to its awakening, the Orcadian archipelago was too bleak to encourage trees to grow. This solitary sycamore nestles between two shops on Main Street, and was a source of wonderment to the locals.[7]

---

[6]  *I was always told that there are only two examples of this architectural structure – the other is the Tomb of Agamemnon in Mykene. The tomb in Orkney is very eerie. On the winter solstice the rising sun shines straight down the entry passage and illuminates the burial chamber. There are more things in heaven and earth, my old Horatio.*

[7]  *And is now legally defined as one of 'the Heritage Trees of Scotland'; a list of 130 specimens of history including the Bicycle Tree of Brig O' Turk – which has eaten an anchor and a bike (don't ask) – through various 'doul trees' (or gallows trees) to the last surviving oak in Birnam Wood (which marched against Macbeth, as you'll recall) and the oldest living thing in Europe – the Fortinghall Yew, which has been in situ for over 5,000 years. Murray Pittock reminded me of the Clootie Trees, too, which anchor the fairy world and the human and have seen a resurgence in recent years, even spreading on to the Isle of Man.*

It's lucky to have survived the elements, but luckier perhaps not to have been trampled underfoot in the mad Orkney Ba' Game, which is played on Christmas Day and Ne'erday. The first written records are from 1850, but in common with many places in Europe,[8] early scrimmage football games between rival sections of a town, or between neighbouring villages, were often seen round about Easter time for many centuries before that.

Kirkwall divides its sons into Uppies from up-town and Doonies – you've worked this out already – from down-town.[9]

This is an old-style uninhibited mass 'football' game. Hundreds of men gather round the Mercat Cross in the shadow of St Magnus's Cathedral and at one o'clock, to a loud cry, the ball is thrown up and play begins in an almighty scrum, and there follows several hours of pushing and shoving as both teams try to force the ball through the narrow streets[10] of Kirkwall. Neither side stops until their respective goal is reached. The point is to score one goal – for that single point wins the game,[11] and the mass of seething players flows liquidly up and down the street, past the boarded-up shop windows, until an Uppie victory is cheered at the top of the town, or the Doonies claim the prize by immersing the ba' in the harbour waters. When victory is awarded – to the scorer, as much as to the team – the lucky man carries his prize, the ba' itself,[12] home to pass out a dram or two to his friends.[13]

---

[8] *Jedburgh in the Borders has a similar game, which has been played in the spring for at least 250 years – their event was inspired, legend has it, by a particularly sanguinary encounter with an English general's head.*

[9] *The lines are fuzzier now with new houses being built, so often family tradition plays a stronger role that postcode. Outsiders, or 'ferryloupers', were allocated depending on which way they entered Kirkwall!*

[10] *Using hands or feet or heads to move the ball (and/or opponents).*

[11] *Just as well, as even that can take a good few hours!*

[12] *Which he'll hang in his living-room window for the year in honour.*

[13] *There is also a boys' game – which starts in the mornings – and once, in the heady liberalism after WWII, there was a women's game in 1946.*

# Golf

> An ineffective attempt to put an elusive ball into an obscure hole, with implements ill-adapted to the purpose
>
> *President Woodrow Wilson*[14]

Of all the gifts Scotland has presented to the wider world, golf is the only rival to – or even victor over – whisky. In every continent men and women strive to perfect the techniques to shave another stroke off the score, to win the 18 holes and rest in the companionship of the 19th.

Golf developed naturally on the sandy dunes of the east coast in the early 15th century. The Dutch claim that it was their idea first, with a stick-and-ball game called kolven, but there were many such games about and it was our golf that established the three key elements: the club, the ball and the hole.

It really took off a couple of hundred years later when royalty, recognising that archery wasn't going to help win battles, embraced the game themselves. As you'd expect from a lass who liked her amusements, Mary Queen of Scots often played a round, while her son, in between anathematising smoking and witches, played a waiting game for his cousin Elizabeth's crown by whapping away with a mashie niblick. It was really James VI & I who introduced golf to the wider world, bringing a host of Scottish hangers-on and a bag of clubs to London. The Scots courtiers were strongly disliked by the English, but slowly the game caught the Sassenach attention and it has stayed there to this day.[15]

The home of the game was then Leith, the port of Edinburgh, and

---

[14]   *Of Scottish ancestry, he was an avid golfer, even developing black balls so he could play in the snow.*

[15]   *James's favourite palace was Greenwich, just outside London, where the heath nearby provided just the spot for a good round. The club there today, Royal Blackheath, dates its foundation to 1608 (traditionally, as the papers from before about 1800 are mislaid) and is the oldest golf club in England, but controversially claims to be the oldest in the world. On steadier evidence the club's Spring Medal, with winners stretching back in records to 1787, is the oldest golfing competition today.*

on a good day you could see Charles I enjoying a round more than a Roundhead, while his son James[16] famously played for Scotland in the first international match in 1682 – Scotland won.[17] The game grew in popularity and clubs began to form: the Royal Burgess Golfing Society (1735[18]) in Edinburgh and the Honourable Company of Edinburgh Golfers (1744); St Andrews was a later foundation (1754).

> Hard by, in the fields called the Leith Links, the citizens of Edinburgh divert themselves at a game called golf, in which they use a curious kind of bat, tipt with horn, and small elastic balls of leather, stuffed with feathers, rather less than tennis balls, but of a much harder consistence. This they strike with such force and dexterity from one hole to another, that they will fly to an incredible distance. Of this diversion the Scots are so fond, that when the weather will permit, you may see a multitude of all ranks, from the senator of justice to the lowest tradesman, mingled together in their shirts, and following the balls with the utmost eagerness.[19]

The thing that was lacking though was uniformity. At Leith the links consisted of five holes, while at St Andrews a massive 22 were in a round. Visitors to a club would be uncertain of what was permitted and what was not. So in 1744 in Leith, the Honourable Company of Edinburgh

---

[16] *James, then Duke of York and Duke of Albany (hence the names of the two great NY cities), was acting as commissioner (or governor) in Scotland, with Samuel Pepys the diarist as his secretary. There is no record of the duke playing golf in Pepys's diaries of that time, but 20 years before he saw him play pell mell (a stick-and-ball game): Tuesday, 2 April 1661, 'So I into St James's Park, where I saw the Duke of York playing at Pelemele, the first time that ever I saw the sport.'*

[17] *One of the few wins in that troubled man's career. He gave most of the winnings to his 'pro', a cobbler called Paterson, who bought a house on the prestigious Canongate in Edinburgh. He called it 'Golfer's Land' and had 'Far and Sure' as a motto over the door.*

[18] *Claimed by the club as 1735.*

[19] 'The Adventures of Humphrey Clinker, *Tobias Smollett, 1771. Still true!*

Golfers resolved to create a set of common rules. The first draft was 13 in number and they are pretty recognisable even today.

A hand instrumental in the drafting of the laws of golf was Scotland's senior judge, Duncan Forbes of Culloden, who was to do much to prevent the Hanoverian backlash after the Jacobite rebellion ended in his front garden two years later.[20]

The combination of political disturbance and the growth of Edinburgh caused the capital's clubs to flit between courses, while St Andrews stayed stuck to her home shoreline. When King William IV awarded his patronage to St Andrews the transformation into 'the Royal and Ancient' crowned it as the queen of golf, eventually the world over.[21]

Naturally, the oldest golfing competition was created in Scotland: the Open Championship, which remains one of the greatest sporting events and is the only one of the four major championships played outside the USA.

It was founded on the other side of Scotland – at Prestwick in Ayrshire in 1860, where contenders would play three rounds of the links course of 12 holes in a single day to win the Champion's Belt (and as time passed, cash too[22]). In 1870 young Tom Morris, the Tiger Woods of his day, won the belt for the third year running and was granted permanent ownership. Then Prestwick asked St Andrews and Edinburgh to join in the organisation and hosting (it finally devolved solely to the R&A in 1920). It took a year to organise and the Open resumed in 1872 with the new Claret Jug Trophy (commissioned for the huge sum of £30[23]).

Nowadays it revolves around a list of nine links courses – five in Scotland and a further four down south:

---

[20]  *He also had the licence to distil the popular Ferintosh whisky – a true Scotsman in his varied interests!*

[21]  *Now a distinct body to the club, the R&A governs the world save for the USA and Mexico, who operate under the USGA.*

[22]  *£6 in 1864. Last year, the winner netted £750,000.*

[23]  *It was promptly won by young Tom again – the only man to win four consecutive Opens.*

- St Andrews (The Old Course): The premier course in the world hosts the Open every five years.

- Carnoustie Golf Links (Championship Course): First held here in 1931, this is the course the players find hardest.

- Muirfield: The home of the Honourable Company of Edinburgh Golfers, it first hosted the year after it was purpose-built in 1892.[24]

- Turnberry (Ailsa Course): Now known as the Westin Turnberry Resort, this and Gleneagles were the two great golfing hotels and resorts built at the beginning of the 20th century. A relative newcomer, first staging the tournament in 1977.

- Royal Troon (Old Course): Also in Ayrshire and a host since 1923.

Alas, old mother Prestwick (after bearing two dozen children) was unceremoniously dropped by the organisers in 1925.

Golf is a very popular and, thanks to the very many municipal and local courses, very open sport in Scotland.


## Ra Fitba'

He's fitba' crazy, he's gane clean mad
The fitba's robbed him o' the wee bit sense he had,
It'd tak' a washerwoman his claes to rub and scrub,
Since oor Jock became a member o' that awfu' fitba' club.[25]

In terms, however, of weight of numbers, football is the national pastime or passion.

The history of football in Scotland mirrors much of its development in England, where various rule books were drawn together over time following the foundation of the Football Association in London in 1863.

---

[24] *When the club played at Musselburgh Links, the Open was held there.*

[25] *Traditional song.*

Nine years later, a group of Scots players challenged the FA to send a team to Glasgow on St Andrew's Day to play at Hamilton Crescent.[26] That was the first international football match and it played out to a nil:nil draw.

Thus started the grudge match known as SCOTLAND VS ENGLAND, which ran in a series of general ill-will and occasional riot out to 1984, when the fixture just fell apart in its own vitriol. There are the odd matches now in competitions when we will draw the 'auld enemy' to play in the holy stadium of Hampden. In the good old/bad old days this venue on the South Side of Glasgow would swell to 150,000 folk cheering, singing and eating pies. In today's world of relative comfort and the expectation of (a) safety and more importantly (b) hot and cold running toilets, the crowd capacity is about a third of its historic peak, but still pretty loud when in full throat!

> More football later, but first let's see the goals from the Scottish Cup final.
>
> *Des Lynam*

Emboldened by that first international game, Queen's Park in Glasgow (already a founder member of the FA in England) sent out a call to collaborate and in 1873 eight clubs agreed to form the Scottish Football Association and to establish a national championship. Of those initial eight, only Kilmarnock, Vale of Leven and Queen's Park[27] remain, while Clydesdale, Dumbreck, Eastern, Granville and 3rd Lanarkshire Rifle Volunteers[28] have hung up their boots.

These old names are evocative, and certainly we still like to have unusual names for our teams:

---

[26]    *The cricket pitch of the West of Scotland Cricket Club!*

[27]    *The only amateur side left playing in the leagues today, this historical club won eleven of the first 21 Scottish Cup finals, but they seem to have been put off their stride by the death of Queen Victoria.*

[28]    *A shame as I bet they were good at penalty shoot-outs.*

| Raith Rovers | play at | Kircaldy[29] |
|---|---|---|
| Queen of the South | | Dumfries |
| St Johnstone | | Perth |
| Heart of Midlothian | | Edinburgh |
| Caledonian Thistle[30] | | Inverness |
| Morton | | Greenock |
| St Mirren | | Paisley |
| Partick Thistle | | Glasgow |
| Hamilton Academicals | | Hamilton |

Team loyalty, as in all footballing countries, is strong, but the rivalry between the two large Glasgow teams, Rangers and Celtic, is the stuff of legend. These, 'the Old Firm',[31] fought heroic battles in the twin hearts of Glasgow Parkhead and Ibrox. The rivalry had for many years a dark core of sectarianism – the green Catholics vs. the blue Protestants – but times are changing, even if there are pockets of resistance.

In foreign cities wherever you go, you'll find a bunch of Scots supporters, whether part of the Tartan Army[32] network or not, all cheering for our lads whenever they play, and sometimes cheering a sensational victory.

---

[29]   *Famously, one English reporter commented on an historic win, saying that 'there would be celebrations on the streets of Raith tonight.'*

[30]   *The famous newspaper headline following their giant-killing match against mighty Celtic was a tour de force: 'Super Caley Go Ballistic Celtic Are Atrocious'.*

[31]   *A nickname of uncertain origin, generally believed to have been an insulting reference to the commerciality of the two clubs in the early days.*

[32]   *Including London and New York.*

# Rugby[33] – The Calcutta Cup

Football is a game for gentlemen played by hooligans while rugby is a game for hooligans played by gentlemen.[34]

Of course, there are two footballs. The Scottish Football Union[35] was also founded in 1873, in the wake of the first rugby international, where Scotland beat England by scoring a try and a goal compared to a solitary try.[36]

As with every sport, it is the clash with England that captures the heart and stirs the imagination. Initially the four national teams of the British Isles played in competition; they were joined in what became known as the Five Nations by France in 1910, and finally we have today Six Nations with Italy's accession in 2000. But only one match matters: the Calcutta Cup.

It is a beautiful trophy, although a bit fragile now,[37] with an imperial history.

At the peak of the Empire, some chaps thought that it would be a good idea to start a rugby club in Calcutta and it prospered in its own way until polo and tennis appeared (and seemed rather more practical games given the local climate). Recognising the inevitable, the club voted to wind up, but had a fair balance of cash to hand in the form of solid silver rupees. Some genius had the coins melted down to create a trophy for an annual match between Scotland and England. One glance at the three cobra handles or the fat elephant (resplendent with his howdah) balanced on top brings a hint of the exotic to the match and reminds us of those far-flung Scots of Empire – it is without doubt one of the handsomest pots you can win in sport.

---

[33] For my American readers: rugby or rugger is the game a bit like your football, with fewer men and without the body armour or the constant adverts.

[34] Traditional definition.

[35] Which only changed its name to the Scottish Rugby Union in 1924.

[36] Raeburn Place in March 1871 – this was the cricket ground of Edinburgh Academy. Pretty soon the cricketers were getting cheesed off – it's hard to keep the pitch perfect with the footballers of both traditions charging about!

[37] As the result of a number of incidents, including some of the Scotland team playing rugby with it down Princes Street in the late '80s!

Toughly fought and fairly partisanly supported, there is a great atmosphere at Murrayfield, on the outskirts of Edinburgh, on the alternate years that we play for the cup at home.[38] One of the best parts of the day for me and many others, though, is walking back with the crowds into Edinburgh, via the Roseburn Bar or Ryries at Haymarket or one of the many hostelries en route, all thronged with rugby fans.

There are many other sporting pastimes we share with our fellow European nations, notably horseracing – a very popular sport at home since the 17th century, and there is still a mix of all sorts of people at the great racecourses of Ayr (the Ayr Gold Cup and the Scottish Grand National). These, along with Hamilton, Musselburgh and Perth, guarantee a good day's racing. There are also a couple of unusual – virtually unique – activities. The first is shinty, which is an amalgam of field hockey, lacross and armed warfare – an exhilarating game to watch even if you haven't the faintest idea of what's going on at any moment. The other is curling – though who had the idea to create a version of bowls on ice with heavy granite stones instead of balls? It's a game of thought, strategy and funny little technical quirks beloved by many in Scotland and further afield.

## The National Anthem

Sport presents a slight constitutional problem for us. By a quirk of history, the four nations which make our United Kingdom (Scotland, England, Wales and Northern Ireland) are each permitted to field their own national teams in many international sporting competitions,[39] so you will see Scottish sportsmen and women competing against England and the other 'home' nations. So what anthem do we sing?

First things first. Let's look at the official national anthem of the United Kingdom.

Most people do not realise that the national anthem has no legal status or definition. Unlike the US, which rigorously guards 'The Star-

---

[38]   *The other years are at Twickenham, but are pretty much a whitewash of defeat, so a different outing altogether.*

[39]   *The major exception is the Olympics.*

Spangled Banner' under law, we rely on what the Royal Household calls 'a longstanding tradition'.

Now is the chance to nail one of the most irritating of pub fictions. The traditional and recognised national anthem consists of only *two* verses:

God save our gracious Queen![40]
Long live our noble Queen!
God save the Queen!
Send her victorious,
Happy and glorious,
Long to reign over us,
God save the Queen.

Thy choicest gifts in store
On her be pleased to pour,
Long may she reign.
May she defend our laws,
And ever give us cause,
To sing with heart and voice,
God save the Queen.

The popular misconception that the National Anthem has a political axe to grind is because the song and music were first sung in the aftermath of the '45 rebellion. It was common in those days for songwriters to add extra verses in to songs to be topical. In the case of the national anthem, such extra verses included these two unofficial offenders:

O Lord, our God, arise,
Scatter his enemies,
And make them fall.
Confound their politics,

Lord, grant that Marshal Wade,[41]
May by thy mighty aid,
Victory bring.
May he sedition hush and like a torrent rush,

---

[40]  *Substitute 'King' if appropriate!*

[41]  *An English general. He was responsible for making the first effective road system in Scotland (albeit to move loyal troops more quickly to extirpate the rebels). As immortalised by the verse: 'if you'd seen these roads before they were made,/ You'd lift up your hands and bless General Wade.'*

Frustrate their knavish tricks,
On Thee our hopes we fix,
God save us all.

Rebellious Scots to crush,

God save the King.

Despite the fact that these are not recognised words, they have allowed detractors to claim that this is at least an English or perhaps even an anti-Scottish anthem.

While this is tendentious, the practicality of wanting a specific rallying anthem for Scotland as a sporting entity (in addition perhaps to its United Kingdom anthem) is widely agreed.[42] At least, the *concept* is agreed – alas, we can't agree what to sing!

The purists would call for 'Scots Wa Hae' – the great battle hymn of our country[43] – the tune being the marching song of the brave lads under Bruce's command, with words captured by Burns. Like many mediaeval tunes, it lacks a bit of momentum at times,[44] but it has a stirring call to arms at the end:

Lay the proud Usurpers low!
Tyrants fall in every foe!
LIBERTY's in every blow!–
    Let us Do or Die!

The sentiment is wonderful, though it is tinged with the inevitability of a fair few of us falling en route (not always a cheerful thought). This, added to the difficult tempo, means it's not a natural choice in the 20th and 21st centuries, so a number of modern songs have filled the gap.

In athletics, the legendary Cliff Hanley's 'Scotland the Brave' is favoured:

---

[42]  *Though there are real dangers in singing foreign anthems before games: at England vs. Croatia in Wembley in 2007, the guest singer led the crowd in 'God Save the Queen', followed by the Croatian national song. Not being fluent in Croatian he could be excused for the mispronunciation which changed 'Mila kuda si planina' ('You know my dear how we love your mountains') into 'Mila kura si planina' ('You know my dear, my penis is a mountain').*

[43]  *It was famously sung on the morning of Waterloo by the Scottish regiments as they were sharpening bayonets for the day's work.*

[44]  *Although it does capture our grim determination.*

Hark when the night is falling
Hear! hear the pipes are calling,
Loudly and proudly calling,
Down thro' the glen.

*Chorus—*
Towering in gallant fame,
Scotland my mountain hame,
High may your proud
standard gloriously wave,
Land of my high endeavour,
Land of the shining rivers,
Land of my heart for ever,
    Scotland the brave.[45]

It has the benefit of a catchy tune and an iconic view of Scotland, if it is a bit sentimental, but I think its strength is that it sounds marvellous played by a pipe band. The downside is that most people think the words go something like 'Na na Na'na'na'naah, Ne ne Ne'ne'ne neehe'!

When you get to the world of rugby, we all remember the tremendous day in 1990 when the Corries' favourite, 'Flower of Scotland', was sung for the first time at Murrayfield, led by Princess Anne, before one of our greatest victories in the Calcutta Cup under the canny captaincy of David Sole.

O flower of Scotland
When will we see your like again
That fought and died for
Your wee bit hill and glen
And stood against him
Proud Edward's army
And sent him homeward
Tae think again[46]

---

[45]  *'Scotland the Brave'* © *Cliff Hanley.*
[46]  *'Flower of Scotland' by Roy Williamson.*

The footballers have joined in now to use it too, belting out at Hampden Park. It's a song that has tremendous popular appeal, partially tinged with a prickly anti-Englishness, but largely because the words and music fit so well and its folk basis makes it into a great 'belter' of a song in the inimitable style of the greatest Scottish folk duo ever.

There are occasional other candidates brought forward to try and break the deadlock. Sheena Wellington sang 'A Man's a Man' (again a Burns favourite) at the opening of the Scottish Parliament,[47] which of course captured the spirit of the occasion.[48] More recently, a group have acclaimed 'Highland Cathedral', a bagpipe hymn tune (from a German writer) associated with the Scottish regiments serving overseas. It's a hard choice!

In a 2006 poll[49] none of these five could muster a majority. 'Flower of Scotland' topped the list at 41 per cent, with 'Scotland the Brave' on 29 per cent; 'Highland Cathedral' (with 16 per cent) beat the two Burns songs into a tie at the bottom of 7 per cent each. No real answers there!

The one linking theme in this entire chapter is our ability to project an immense optimism. So we should use an anthem that projects that with pride. Let's see how this debate develops.

---

[47] *This wonderful singer's emotional rendition of this Burns classic must be one of the top three or four interpretations of a Burns song in history.*

[48] *Often described as the ultimate hymn to democracy (and significantly more relevant than, say, Schiller's 'An Die Freude', used for Europe), it captures the value of the ordinary individual and the capacity to reach out by recognising that our humanity is more defining than our outward social appearance.*
 *Then let us pray that come it may,*
  *(As come it will for a' that,)*
 *That Sense and Worth, o'er a' the earth,*
  *Shall bear the gree, an' a' that.*
 *For a' that, an' a' that,*
  *It's coming yet for a' that,*
 *That Man to Man, the world o'er,*
  *Shall brothers be for a' that.*

[49] *Arranged by the Royal Scottish National Orchestra and BBC Scotland. It had a weak turnout, with a mere 10,000-odd respondents.*

We're on the march wi' Ally's Army,
 We're going tae the Argentine,
And we'll really shake them up,
 When we win the World Cup,
'Cos Scotland is the greatest football team.[50]

---

[50] '*Ally's Army*' *by Andy Cameron, the theme tune for the 1978 World Cup in Argentina – it got to No. 6 in the* UK *charts, a rather better performance than the team. Not a suggestion for our anthem; I'm inclined to stick with the Queen.*

## 13[1]

# In Good Spirits: Hallowe'en

For many years, the Scottish nation has been remarkable for a credulous belief in witchcraft, and repeated examples were supplied by the annals of sanguinary executions on this sad occasion… The Earl of Mar, brother of James III of Scotland, fell under the King's suspicion for consulting with witches and sorcerers how to shorten the King's days. On such a charge, very inexplicitly stated, the unhappy Mar was bled to death in his own lodgings without trial or conviction; immediately after which catastrophe 12 women of obscure rank and three or four wizards, or warlocks, as they were termed, were burnt at Edinburgh, to give a colour to the earl's guilt.[2]

IF YOU HAVE EVER been in North America on the night of Hallowe'en, you will know that the whole continent goes mad – orange and brown décor appears like fungus and every householder buys in an industrial-sized sack of sweets and chocolate to fend off the inexorable queue of children coming to the door crying 'Trick or Treat!' All this looks like is National Obesity Day!

As the evening wears on, the eight million cable channels all show scary films and every underage drinker is well armed with a carton of eggs to hurl pointlessly at friends or foes or the particularly uptight neighbourhoods nearby.

The little kids are happy and the giant retailers even more so[3] but there is a general feeling that it's overblown.

---

[1] *Spookily enough…*

[2] Letters on Demonology and Witchcraft, *Letter IX*, '*Witchcraft in Scotland*', *Sir Walter Scott, 1830.*

[3] *The total spend is second only to Christmas – $5.07bn in 2007 across the US (NRF 2007 survey), which equates to the GDP of Macedonia or Georgia. The average family will spend $23.33 on costumes (including for pets) plus $19.84 on candy, $17.33 on decorations and a final $3.92 on cards.*

It is certainly unfair to blame the excesses on our American cousins, for all the elements of the American celebration have their roots in Scotland's ancient commemoration on this day – time and distance have allowed the event to mushroom, but the bases remain in the fairy-tale times of ancient Scottish prehistory.

Hallowe'en is our shorthand for the Feast of Hallow Mass Evening and falls on 31 October, when people in the Roman Catholic Church would prepare themselves for the holy day of All Saints on 1 November. In one of the many happy squattings that occured, the church's day fell on the ancient Celtic feast of Samhain.

Samhain, you'll remember, was the start of the New Year on 1 November. The old pagans believed that the souls of the dead would wander about on New Year's Eve,[4] which was a bit of a mixed blessing – so to keep your house free of the ghostly in-laws[5] you needed to light fires and keep lanterns burning.

It was obviously a strongly-held belief, because the first saints didn't try and break the tradition but enveloped it and recharacterised it as a Christian festival. And the traditional games, dressing and fires associated with Samhain continued undisturbed down to today.

This festival was very important in Scotland[6] and remains a big event,[7] so what are the key elements of Scotland's Hallowe'en? I'd suggest three:

## Turnip Lanterns

The massive American jack-o'-lanterns made out of pumpkins are the descendents of the rather more humble tumshie lantern of Scotland.

---

4    *We merely have the dead drunk wandering on ours.*

5    *Who are even more trouble than the physical ones…*

6    *So important that one of the original aims of the Burns Club of London, in addition to the celebration of Burns Night, was the celebration of Hallowe'en. The third aim was 'To encourage friendly intercourse between the members.' I have membership forms for anyone so minded.*

7    *The London Scottish Regiment still holds a full mess dinner to celebrate Hallowe'en in its London Barracks.*

The concept is the same; hollow out a vegetable, carve a ghostly face on one of the thin walls and light a candle inside – either as a static display at a door or window, or rather more excitingly, carried around all night with a string handle! As there aren't many pumpkins[8] in traditional Scots gardens, we've always made do with the turnip.[9]

The positive is that a nice-sized turnip looks like a skull (or a shrunken head), but the downside is the brute force needed to scoop out the rather woody flesh of the root vegetable when compared to the ease of eviscerating the squash. That being said, all that extra turnip can be well used in preparing a steaming bowl of clapshot to have with haggis or sausages as a fill-'em-up supper (and an antidote to all the sweeties!).

## Guising

Trick-or-treat is the spoiled grandchild of this ancient Scots tradition. I don't know where the 'trick' bit came in – it might be the influence of mischievous sprites in the German tradition – but the Scots traditional version is more benign.

Each child has to dress up – not necessarily in ghostly or ghastly attire – and to get a treat they have to go from door to door in bands, calling 'Gi'es Oor Hallowe'en', and perform a party piece or turn to entertain the folk of the house.

These early showings of theatrical talent can be as basic as a bad joke:

| | |
|---|---|
| KID | How much are they antlers, Mister? |
| SHOPKEEPER | A hunner pound. |
| KID | They're afwy deer. |

Or they could be a song, a dance or a magic trick. When each of the weans has performed his/her social obligation, then the householder will offer a reward – now a refreshing cascade of cheap sugar and E numbers, but in the good old days an apple or an orange or maybe some nuts would have been standard.

---

[8] *Pumpkins, like pomegranates, avocadoes, persimmons and lightly-cooked greens, are unknown in traditional Scots cuisine.*

[9] *Can you remember which veggie this is? (The orange one.)*

## Traditional Games

After the guising, when all are safe back home, after dinner, there are a bundle of silly, messy games of skill. The most famous is Dookin' for Apples.

Let's take the washing basin, place it in the middle of the room and fill it with water right up to the brim and then float apples in it. Each member of the company has to kneel down beside the basin and, with hands clasped behind the back, try and catch one of the bobbing apples using only their teeth.[10] Many a near death by drowning has cheered the festive scene but it's a risk worth taking, as great good fortune befalls any successful apple chomper.[11]

There is a more genteel version – or for little children – instead of kneeling on the floor, bring a chair over and sit it beside the basin with the back toward it.[12] The apple dooker kneels on the chair (hands again clasped behind) and an accomplice places a fork in their mouth – they have to drop the fork in the hope of skewering the apple.[13]

This bit of harmless fun is the last vestige of a druidic ritual. The ancient Celts felt much magic in trees[14] and they called the apple tree 'the Silver Bough'.[15] This could be used to access the invisible worlds, to meet the spirits of the dead and to foretell the future. To get to the Silver Bough, the postulant had to pass through an ordeal of water and one of fire. So the apples that we dook for are

---

[10] *An ironic concept given the history of Scottish dental hygiene – it is not permissible to take out false teeth or other dental prostheses to gain an advantage.*

[11] *Some families add some nuts to the water, either to make it more difficult or to introduce a choking hazard.*

[12] *Like a wee pulpit.*

[13] *Did I mention that china bowls aren't a good idea?*

[14] *Still many Scottish families will have a rowan tree (the mountain ash or Sorbus acuparia) planted at the gatepost or boundary of their house, as a witch cannot pass it. As I've never seen a witch in any of those houses, it seems to work pretty effectively.*

[15] *cf. the Golden Bough, or hazel, which represented wisdom (hence the nuts above) – or the Bronze Bough, or stripped pine, which represents DIY.*

talismans, while the water they float in could be thought of as the last vestige of the water ordeal.[16]

Best of all though (for those not cleaning up afterwards) is Treacle Scones.

A string is rigged across the room with newspaper underneath. Lots of newspaper, in fact. You then take half-a-dozen flat scones and smear them liberally with treacle, golden syrup or molasses. Each sticky cake is then tied to the main string to hang about head-high.[17] The contestants (with the obligatory hands behind back – or in pockets) have to jump and eat the scones. Particularly evil hosts blindfold the players as well – but that is hard. After ten minutes everyone should be a smiling and very sticky mess, with syrup on face, in hair, and probably on at least one wall too.

Maybe in a few years these conventions will have turned into a chapter of history as, even in Scotland, the American style is, like a brightly-coloured rhododendron bush, burgeoning into all points and corners to the exclusion of the native plants. Perhaps we can hold the tide – lang may the tumshies shine oot!

There is a sombre side to Hallowe'en though, as a lot of this came out of the relatively long-held belief that witchcraft was real. The Church focused on the biblical injunction 'Thou shall not suffer a witch to live'[18] and as part of the law of the land, about 4,000 so-called witches[19] were accused over the years, about 10 per cent of whom met a grisly end in the town square, being burned.[20] The last trial in Scotland was as late as 1722, although in a bizarre trial in 1944 a Scots spiritualist Mrs Helen Duncan – who seemed to know when British battleships had been sunk before

---

[16]   *There used to be a parallel, and in my mind quite daft, apple/fire dooking, where an apple was stuck on a long pole, with a lighted candle stuck on top of that – you had to eat the apple without getting burned. Should set your smoke alarm off!*

[17]   *In tenement life, where there would have been a kitchen pulley for drying the washing, that would have been used as the vehicle to hang the scones.*

[18]   *Exodus xxii, 18; see also Leviticus xxix, 26 and 31 or Deuteronomy xvii, 9–14.*

[19]   *Thanks to http://www.arts.ed.ac.uk/witches/introduction.html.*

[20]   *Normally after having been publicly strangled, though if the magistrates were feeling vengeful the witch would be burned alive.*

the Admiralty did – was found guilty under the Witchcraft Act 1753 and so entered Holloway Prison (and the history books) as the last convicted witch!

Leaving aside the witches, their cats and the ghostly noises, the liminal nature of the ancient Hallowe'en caused the barrier between this word and the next to thin – not only allowing the dead to walk, but also opening insights to the future. While the children guised and played, their older brothers and sisters would have the chance to divine the greatest question on young minds: who am I to marry?

All these customs have passed into obscurity[21] but are lovingly captured in Burns's long poem 'Hallowe'en', where he records how he, Jean Armour and their neighbours would frolic in the dark – ostensibly to use ancient mysteries to find a life partner, but actually relying on a quick squeeze and a kiss as a rather more reliable test.

As the coast of Ayrshire had a long tradition of being inhabited by fairies, witches and other infernal spirits, there would naturally be a great activity in the spirit world on the Hallowe'en night.

Firstly, the lads and lasses would go into the kailyard[22] together and, with eyes shut, each pull a cabbage stalk. If the root had earth stuck to it, that was a sign of good luck, while the shape of the stock prefigured the physique of the future spouse (so a small, thin, twisty one wasn't a great omen) while a taste of the plant stem would give an inkling of how sweet or sour tempered (s)he would be!

The girls had their own special augury in the barn. With no men present, they each drew three different stalks of oats. If the last was broken and had no grain on it then the girl would 'come to the marriage-bed anything but a maid'.[23]

Or they took two nuts, named them after themself and their partner and placed them right in the fire. If they burned quietly together, that meant long life and happiness, while if they sparked and jumped, it was time to call Relate.

---

[21] *Hardly surprising when more Scottish children are now born outwith wedlock than within.*

[22] *Cabbage patch.*

[23] *Pretty likely if Rab was about that night!*

Burns recalls many of the spells, which would be even more specific – typically the girl would slip out alone and either throw a ball of blue wool into the kiln, or take a handful of hemp seed[24] and score it into the earth with an incantation, or walk three times anticlockwise round the haystack, or even make the motions of winnowing the corn three times inside a barn with the doors taken off[25] – any of these would allow a glimpse of the intended.

The most powerful spell for a girl was to eat an apple in front of a mirror[26] while combing their hair by the light of a single candle – so they could see their future partner peering over their shoulder.[27]

A parlour game was to take three wooden dishes (or 'luggies') and place them on the hearth before the fire. One was filled with dirty water, one with fresh water and the third remained empty. The supplicant was blindfolded and had to put a left-hand finger into one bowl of choice. This was repeated three times – touching the clean water meant marrying a virgin, the washing up water fortold a marriage partner with 'a certain maturity of experience', while the empty bowl presaged a solitary life.

This was fun and games for the lads and lasses after a hard season in the harvest – play, games and a bit of love, under cover of ancient ritual. These games may have died but the point of Hallowe'en is still the fun. It's part of human nature to be fascinated by other worlds and to ascribe fantastic explanations to the things that seem to make little sense in ours. People now get too het up over Hallowe'en – Wiccans on the one hand and Evangelicals on the other – all endowing something that's just a folk memory with a meaningfulness it hasn't deserved for centuries.[28]

---

[24]  *Hallucinogens?*

[25]  *There were some strong lassies in those days.*

[26]  *A bit like in Keats's 'Eve of St Agnes'.*

[27]  *Mirrors are unlucky things, while the apple reminds us of the Fall, the hair combing of Mary Magdalene, and the candle of the light over the coffin – get the spell wrong and you might call up 'Auld Nick' himself! We all know that breaking a mirror causes seven years of bad luck, and I can remember houses in mourning where the mirrors were covered at the person's death and remained so until after the funeral.*

[28]  *If in fact it was ever deserved!*

Just look at Burns's poem and imagine yourself a couple of hundred years ago, with dark mornings and short winter days, and too few hours to get in the breaking-back work to keep the farm ticking over. A festival which focussed on frights to cause your girl to jump into your arms, or spells to allow a girl to name her boyfriend must have been a merry and a welcome time for the youngsters.

Just as Burns puts it in the last verse:

> Wi' merry sangs, an' friendly cracks,
>   I wat they did na weary;
> And unco tales, an' funnie jokes–
>   Their sports were cheap an' cheery:
> Till butter'd sowens, wi' fragrant lunt,                    [steam]
>   Set a' their gabs a-steerin;
> Syne, wi' a social glass o' strunt,                         [moonshine]
>   They parted aff careerin
> Fu' blythe that night.[29]

---

[29] 'Hallowe'en', Robert Burns. Sowans or sowens (pronounced 'soo-ans') were the traditional treat at Hallowe'en – they are made by fermenting the nutrient-rich inner husk of the oat over four or five days in lukewarm water. After discarding the husks, the starch residuum can be made into a porridge, enhanced with butter. Often a big bowl was prepared with a toy wedding ring in it; again, if it fell into your bowl, you would be the next to marry. This latter tradition was still found until quite recently, using mashed potatoes rather than sowans. In the final stages of the siege of Mafeking – F.M. McNeill reports in a footnote to The Scots Kitchen – when all else was eaten a resourceful Orkneyman of BP's staff made sowans out of the remaining horse feed. Be prepared with a vengeance! McNeill reports that sowans have 'a slightly sour taste which some find unpalatable at first, but which usually "grows on one"' (The Scots Kitchen, p.268).

# 14

# Town and Gown

The world continues to offer glittering prizes to those who have stout hearts and sharp swords

*F.E. Smith, Earl of Birkenhead, Rector of Glasgow*[1]

It is beginning to be hinted that we a nation of amateurs.

*Lord Rosebery, Rector of Glasgow*[2]

Scotland is renowned as the home of the most ambitious race in the world.

*F.E. Smith, Earl of Birkenhead, Rector of Aberdeen*[3]

You come from a race of men the very wind of whose name has swept to the ultimate seas.

*Sir J.M. Barrie, Rector of St Andrews*[4]

It's often said… that if you're lucky then eventually the university awards you a degree, but it's the university unions that give you the real education in life. On that basis 26 years ago I suppose you could say that I emerged well-educated.

*Charles Kennedy MP, Rector of Glasgow*[5]

EDUCATION HAS ALWAYS been revered in Scottish culture and for centuries the dream of many young men and women was to 'go up' to one of Scotland's universities. We were very proud that we had four[6] universities

---

[1]  *Rectorial Address, 7 November 1923.*

[2]  *Rectorial Address, 16 November 1900.*

[3]  *Rectorial Address, 16 November 1928.*

[4]  *Rectorial Address, 3 May 1922.*

[5]  *Rectorial Address, 10 April 2008. Charles is only the second person, after one of my other favourite politicians, Disraeli, to be twice elected Rector at Glasgow*

[6]  *Five if you count the two Aberdeen foundations individually.*

at the time of the Union of the Crowns, when England had but two.[7]
Scotland's belief and pride in education was specifically included in the
Treaties and Acts of Union with England as one of the main cultural
bulwarks to be preserved in the new United Kingdom:

> Her Majesty with Advice and Consent foresaid statutes and
> ordains that the Universities and Colledges [sic] of Saint Andrew's
> Glasgow Aberdeen and Edinburgh as now established by Law
> shall continue within this Kingdom for ever[8]

St Andrews, perched on the Fife coast, came first, with a Papal Bull creating it in 1413,[9] and it remains a very traditional seat of learning. St
Andrews' students were the last who had to wear the undergraduate
gown – a big, red, woolly thing formally called a toga – to classes every
day, and still do on special occasions.[10] There was a strict etiquette on how
to wear it – first years (called 'Bejants or Bejantines'[11]) had to wear it high

---

7   *Which you have to grudgingly admit have done quite well for themselves.*

8   *Act of Union with Scotland Act 1707, 5 Anne c. 11, at Article XXV, II. The
    idea of teaching from eternity and of fighting for traditional rights is echoed
    in the various founding charters – Glasgow's famously says* 'Nulli ergo
    omnino hominum liceat hanc paginam nostre ereccionis, constitucionis et
    ordinacionis, infringere, vel ei ausu temerario contrahire; si quis autem hoc
    attemptare presumpserit, indignationem omnipotentis Dei, et beatorum Petri et
    Pauli apostolorum ejus, se noverit incursurum.' ('*Let none therefore in any
    wise infringe this writing of our erection, constitution and appointment, or with
    foolhardy daring go in the contrary thereof; but if any one shall presume to
    attempt this, let him know that he shall incur the wrath of Almighty God,
    and of the blessed apostles Peter and Paul.*') Be afraid, be very afraid!

9   *Unfortunately the Pope in question was Benedict XIII, who is a universally-
    disavowed anti-Pope – there was some doubt about the validity of St
    Andrews' degrees until the passing of the Universities (Scotland) Act of 1858
    (but that's probably a scurrilous myth perpetrated by Glaswegians!).*

10  *With an odd quirk: each new student is given two mentors – an academic
    mother and academic father – and on 'Raisin Sunday' at the beginning of the
    year, they each tie a charm on to the fastenings of the gowns that the student
    carries throughout his/her academic life. The ancient gift given to the 'parents'
    of a pound of raisins has been commuted into the more acceptable bottle of
    wine. A formal Latin receipt is still granted!*

up on the shoulders, second year Semi-Bejants or Semis wore it on the shoulders but loosely, Tertians in the third year wore it off one shoulder, while Magistrands slouched along to their finals with it hanging off both shoulders.[12]

> Saint Andrews seems to be a place eminently adapted to study and education, being situated in a populous, yet a cheap country, and exposing the minds and manners of young men neither to the levity and dissoluteness of a capital city, nor to the gross luxury of a town of commerce, places naturally unpropitious to learning; in one the desire of knowledge easily gives way to the love of pleasure, and in the other, is in danger of yielding to the love of money[13]

Second comes Glasgow, with our Papal Bull of 1451, built on the model not of Paris and Oxford (as was St Andrews) but of Bologna. Glasgow's original Bull promised to create 'a fountain of knowledge where all might come to drink'[14] and we've been living up to that for over 500 years.[15]

> [My] first sight of a University was... Glasgow for the Bursary Examination. It was one of those flaming sunsets which in autumn sometimes illumine Gilmorehill, and its towers and pinnacles silhouetted against the western sky seemed to me like the battlements of a celestial city.[16]

---

11 *'Bec-jaune'* – *'yellow beak'* or *'tenderfoot'*.

12 *St Andrews can be pretty nippy, so maybe this was more practicality than abiding tradition.*

13 Journey to the Western Islands of Scotland, *Dr Samuel Johnson, Folio Society, 1994, p.6. I must admit that I tend to agree with Sam – St Andrews has an odd, bubble feeling, distanced from life. A nice enough bubble, mind you.*

14 *It's only in the last 20 years that the Glasgow student card stopped being issued in Latin (and a photo was added!). 'O mores O tempora' is all I can stutter out.*

15 *The* GU *union bar having been for many years the largest-selling outlet of the iconic Tennent's lager.*

16 Homilies and Recreations, *John Buchan, Hodder & Stoughton, 1939, p.288.*

Aberdeen is a marriage between Kings College (1495) and its mediaeval architecture and Marischal College (1593), which is a mighty granite wedding cake of pride. This noble institution, geographically distant from its sisters, remains independent-minded to this day, but maintains its tradition of teaching and research.

> Blythe Aberdeane, thow beriall of all tounis,    [beryl; jewel]
>  The lampe of bewtie bountie and blythnes,
> Unto the heaven ascendit thy renoun is
> Off virtue, wisdome and of worthines[17]

And the baby of the quartet, Edinburgh, was born in 1583 by fiat not from Rome – for the Reformation had changed all that – but from a resolution by the Town Council and a subsequent Royal Charter. Students here have the high honour of being awarded their degrees by being touched on the head by a 'bonnet' made of the fabric of John Knox's breeks![18] The pride of being independent of the ancient traditions is long-standing; the current principal likes to quote a passage from a Victorian encyclopaedia which, after detailing the academic dress of Oxford in a dozen columns, and Cambridge in as many, offers the laconic appraisal of Edinburgh's under-graduates:

> The students of Edinburgh live in their city and so do what they like when it comes to dress.[19]

Dundee occupies an anomalous position, having been a dependent college of St Andrews at the time of the Act, so sharing the constitution of the ancient universities, but becoming independent as recently as 1967.[20]

---

[17]  To Aberdein, *William Dunbar – although he's not so hot on spelling his home town...*

[18]  *Why the tattered bottom of his britches should morph into such an important symbol eludes me.*

[19]  *Quoted by Sir Timothy O'Shea – I stole the quote, but alas not the reference.*

[20]  *We are looking at historical traditions and festivals here, so no disrespect is intended to our younger sister institutions.*

As becomes ancient foundations, each carries a weight of tradition that can seem decidedly odd to outsiders,[21] odd enough to insiders and quite incomprehensible to most undergraduates.[22] Two of the oddest traditions, shared by all the ancient Scottish universities, are the way they award degrees and how they manage their powers.

Unusually in the English-speaking world, the Scottish universities have a four-year undergraduate arts course which results in a Master of Arts degree, not a Bachelors degree.[23] This is often an area of controversy.[24]

The other oddity is rather more interesting. Power in the universities is rather elegantly structured. Each is headed by the Chancellor, who is elected for life by all the graduates of the university. This officer chairs the congregational meetings of all graduates – the Graduate Council – and awards degrees, while the Principal – formerly appointed by the Crown, now by the university authorities – is the executive head and chairs the Senatus Academicus (or Senate), which is the board of professors and is responsible for academic standards.[25]

But the management body for the university (the Court) is chaired by a third official – the Rector. This ancient role is elected every three years by the body of students and so the Rector has always been seen as the protector of the rights of students.

It's an interesting early example of the division of powers that we

---

[21]  *Some oddities are historical links with the ancient Continental universities and some the belligerence of the Scots Kirk, but several are purely common-sense: half-term holidays were called 'Meal Mondays' as the lads would walk home to wherever and stock up with another sack of porridge oats to see them through the next five weeks.*

[22]  *The year names 'freshman', 'sophomore', 'junior' and 'senior' were taken over to the States by Witherspoon and the Scots and, while in desuetude in the mother colleges, flourish in every US college and high school. Similarly, before professors, teaching was managed by the regents. One regent would take a whole year class through all four years of teaching, then start again.*

[23]  *All our other faculties make do with BScs, etc.*

[24]  *Except in Oxford and Cambridge, where you are still able to buy your MA after a certain period of time in the outside world.*

[25]  *The Principal is usually appointed Vice Chancellor to deputise for the Chancellor for the specific purpose of awarding degrees only.*

see in the US constitution – of course, the Scots had a great hand in the foundation of the US, so it's hardly a surprise.[26]

In the 19th and 20th centuries, a rectorial election was a big event and a noisy contest. Perhaps it was because the senates were more strict and treated undergraduates like school children, perhaps because the voting age was 21 and so this was the one legitimate way to be politically active, but whatever the reason, in every third year the main political parties (and noted independents) would fight as hard as they did for a parliamentary seat.

In addition to the traditional speeches on the stump, hustings, posters, leaflets and beer, these days were famed for the riots that would inevitably break out. In the Glasgow archives are recipes for the best way to build a flour bomb.[27] Leading campaigners would be bombed, soaked, pelted with eggs or worse,[28] while burning leaflets, chalking slogans or simply kidnapping rivals were all in a day's work.[29]

Henry Kissinger once said 'Academic politics are so bitter, because the stakes are so low', but here we saw popular elections where the most important men of the day would put their reputations into the hands of some enthusiastic university kids and risk electoral defeat.[30]

---

[26] *See Duncan Bruce's pioneering work on this topic in his book* The Mark of the Scots.

[27] *Take a brown paper bag, add a dollop of yesterday's cold porridge and fill to bursting with plain flour (the expense of self-raising cannot be warranted), tie tightly, find opponent, aim and throw hard at head. Retreat to safety of multitude. Repeat until arrested.*

[28] *Dead cats were also a popular feature in the campus within towns.*

[29] *Makes Watergate quite tame… Probably the greatest was when 'King John' McCormack's supporters kidnapped his Unionist rival and kept him in a cage in George Square, encouraging the Glaswegians to feed him bananas.*

[30] *March 1899 saw the last recorded duel fought in Scotland. A Scottish Tory, R. H. Begg, supported Lord Kelvin for Rector and an Italian student called La Torre favoured Lord Rosebery. They fought with foils in the upstairs corridor of the old union (now the John Mac building). While Begg drew blood in the contest, avenging his candidate's honour, Rosebery won the election. Oddly enough, both candidates were subsequently elected Chancellor of the University. Poor old Begg died in action in the Great War and La Torre changed his name to Soprano and emigrated to New Jersey.*

In the 140 years leading to World War II, Glasgow had 13 UK[31] prime ministers serve as Rector.[32] The position was often held by academics and writers; Adam Smith, J. M. Barrie, Kipling, Andrew Carnegie, Marconi and John Stuart Mill all served at one time or another. Since the '60s, the trend has been to elect well-known comics, writers and celebrities, with the occasional political statement thrown in.[33]

Once the dust (or at least, flour) had settled and the votes were cast and counted[34] the Rector could look forward to the rectorial installation and the ensuing rectorial festivities. Often upon his arrival the undergraduates would unleash the carriage horses and pull the Rector-Elect themselves, a tradition still seen in St Andrews and remembered when Edinburgh 'chairs' her new rector by carrying him aloft on a Scottish *sede gestatoria*.[35] But the highlight of the day was the rectorial address – and so many famous political quotes came from those high personages addressing the intellectual hope of the country, as can be seen from the epigraphs above.

It is fair to say that the whole thing is much, much less important to today's students – but it is a signal remembrance that it is the students themselves who elect the chairman of the most powerful boards in

---

[31]  *And one French* PM.

[32]  *Lord Rosebery is the only man to have served as Rector at all four universities: Aberdeen 1878, Edinburgh 1880, Glasgow 1889 and St Andrews 1910. He was also Glasgow's Chancellor from 1910 unti his death. A hero of mine. He left Christ Church College, Oxford without a degree as he was made to choose between keeping his pack of foxhounds and continuing his studies. No question there. He left predicting that he would (a) be prime minister (he was, albeit a grief to him), (b) marry an heiress (N. M. Rothschild's only daughter, Hannah; a rather happier outcome) and (c) win the Derby (Ladas II in 1894, Sir Viso the following year and finally Cicero in 1905).*

[33]  *Chief Luthuli, Winnie Mandela and Mordechai Vanatu at Glasgow, for example.*

[34]  *Originally in four constituencies defined by birthplace ('nations') on the electoral college system, again like the US constitution.*

[35]  *Not because of the champagne celebration the night before – I am sure that the candidate can walk. (Though the late Reggie Bosanquet at Glasgow could have used the assistance!)*

academia. So any undergraduates reading this – get active and exercise your franchise.

Our friends in St Andrews[36] celebrate the ancient history of their foundation in the annual Kate Kennedy procession in March.

History records that their founder, Bishop Kennedy, had a beautiful niece, Kate, and the young students would parade in the springtime[37] in her honour. Many years after the demise of la belle Kennedy this undergraduate fest became more bacchanal than epithalamial[38] and the authorities agreed to suppress the tradition in Victorian times.

In 1926, inspired by the romantic address by Sir J.M. Barrie[39] which forms part of the epigraph to this chapter,[40] two undergraduates (one a direct descendent of the Kennedys, though one hopes not of the Bishop himself) petitioned the Principal to resurrect the procession to cement good relationships between Town and Gown and to raise funds for local charities.

And so it still happens today. The Kate Kennedy Club elects nine male freshers every year. One of these lads has the unsurpassed honour of playing Kate in the procession![41] 'She' is driven in an open carriage (a restored landaulet[42]) supported by heralds and shieldbearers, while the other club members appear in costume as Bishop Kennedy, as benefactors of the university

---

[36]  *Who oft have maintained a love of history of nearly Brideshead proportions.*

[37]  *When a young man's fancy turns to you-know-what.*

[38]  *More Courtney Love than courtly love.*

[39]  *Who, though from Kirriemuir, was not the author of the famous romantic ode 'The Ball of Kirriemuir'.*

[40]  *And you thought I just bunged them in to fill the white space.*

[41]  *There was a longstanding controversy here as, until quite recently, only men could take part, in both male and female roles – now Kate remains a man while some of the other women (and men) are women (if you see what I mean…).*

[42]  *For those of you not up to speed with carriage architecture, this is a small landau.*

like James VI, or as other famous men and women – Earl Haig and the poet Gavin Douglas – who have had walk-on parts in St Andrean history. In a reminder of the grisly parts of our Reformation, an empty carriage represents the coach of the last Catholic archbishop in Scotland, Archbishop Sharpe, who was murdered in the upheavals on the moor outside St Andrews.

Add pipers, the University Air Training Squadron overhead and 15,000 folk on the streets and you will see and share a unique look at Scotland's ancient educational system.

> As I was walkin' by the
> Blytheswood Cott,[43]
> I met the Clerk o' Senate,
> Says he to me 'Ye've nae degree',
> Says I 'an' well I ken it'. [44]

---

[43] *A famous, if not entirely salubrious Glasgow place of refreshment. Now, alas, derelict. I never thought a pub near a University could go bust. A true liquidity crisis.*

[44] *Traditional* GUU *Song (extremely polite version).*

# 15

# It's Good to Have Friends in High Places

Breathes there the man, with soul so dead,
Who never to himself hath said,
This is my own, my native land!
Whose heart hath ne'er within him burn'd,
As home his footsteps he hath turn'd
From wandering on a foreign strand!
If such there breathe, go, mark him well;
For him no Minstrel raptures swell;
High though his titles, proud his name,
Boundless his wealth as wish can claim;
Despite those titles, power, and pelf,                    [wealth]
The wretch, concentred all in self,
Living, shall forfeit fair renown,
And, doubly dying, shall go down
To the vile dust, from whence he sprung,
Unwept, unhonour'd, and unsung.[1]

## St Andrew: the History and the Legends

Ae day He wis traivlin aside the Loch o' Galilee, whan he saw twa brithers, Simon, caa'd Peter, an Andro his brither, castin a net intil the loch; for they war fishers tae tredd. 'Come efter me' qo he til them, 'an I s'mak ye men-fishers'; An strecht they quat their nets and fallowt him.[2]

---

[1]    'My Native Land', Sir Walter Scott.

[2]    St Matthew iv, 18–20 – from Professor Lorimer's wonderful Scots translation
of the New Testament. The Authorised Version is: '18 And Jesus, walking by
the sea of Galilee, saw two brethren, Simon called Peter, and Andrew his
brother, casting a net into the sea: for they were fishers. 19 And he saith unto
them, Follow me, and I will make you fishers of men. 20 And they straight-
way left their nets, and followed him.'

As our patron saint, I guess St Andrew must be in the running to be THE ultimate Scot. But who was he and why is he Scotland's national saint?

He is a busy man: being patron of Greece and Russia[3] while simultaneously protecting the interests of fishermen, sailors, spinsters, sufferers from gout and goitres. Why did he choose to look after a rather truculent people in a northern, rainy country that he never visited?

Andrew is a very important man in the story of Christianity. Having followed the teachings and career of St John the Baptist, Andrew was the first of the disciples to accept Jesus, and brought his elder (and now more famous) brother Peter to meet the Lord. As they toiled in the fishing boats of the Sea of Galilee, it gave Jesus the chance for one of his jokes: 'Come and I will make you fishers of men'.[4]

While Peter became the leader of the disciples,[5] his brother always remained personally close to his Master. It was Andrew who introduced the boy with the loaves and fishes to Jesus, and he brought the Greeks who visited Jerusalem to meet his Master, too; he was at the Passion and Crucifixion, and, to my mind significantly, at the Wedding at Cana – where Jesus's first miracle was to turn water into wine.[6]

At the birth of the Christian Church the 12 apostles spread across the world to give the great glad tidings. After the 'Acts of the Apostles', the Bible falls silent on the career and martyrdom of our saint, but well-founded tradition tells us that Andrew's mission was widespread: through Asia Minor to Scythia (as far as Kiev), and even founding the see of Constantinople. But, like each of the apostles, he fell foul of the

---

[3]   *Both rather more time-consuming than Scotland.*

[4]   *It's such an important story (or at least such a good joke) that it's also in St Mark i, 17.*

[5]   *And the first Pope. Not bad for two poor working-class brothers – the HQs of two religions are named after them – Roman Catholiscm and Golf.*

[6]   *Surely something that would appeal to the Scots. Mind you, Andrew was also involved in the Feeding of the Five Thousand and this miracle is still sometimes enacted at St Andrew's Night – I have seen a bowl of haggis passed round five hundred people to help themselves and there's always almost as much left over at the end!*

local Roman administration and at the age of 80 he was crucified on an x-shaped cross in Patras in Greece.[7]

Now the story gets complicated. He was buried in Patras and his shrine was venerated by the Church. When the Emperor Constantine the Great created the new capital of his reformed Christian empire, he pinched the saint's bones and enshrined them in the Church of the Apostles, which he built to rival St Peter's in Rome.

But trouble was ahead. In a dream, an ordinary monk called Regulus was commanded to break into the reliquary and take some of St Andrew's bones 'to the very end of the world'. The monk managed to snaffle a tooth, a kneecap, an arm bone and a few fingers and went down to the harbour to buy himself a boat. It's a long way to Tipperary, but it's a very long way from Istanbul to Scotland even as the saint flies. The actual itinerary is not recorded until (in what must have seemed like the end of the world indeed) poor old Regulus crashed the boat in what we now call St Andrews, to be rescued by the local minor king Angus and his men, who were so impressed by the holy man and his stories they soon became Christians and started a labour of love to built their own great cathedral to house the relics in piety and honour.

Poor old St Andrew's bones had a lot more moving to do. Constantinople was stabbed in the back by its Crusader allies in 1210 and the saint was a star part of the plunder, with his head going to the Vatican and most of the rest of him to Amalfi.[8] That treachery weakened the Eastern Empire, and many Gibbon fans[9] trace the inevitable decline and fall of that part of the Roman Empire from the shock of that perfidy. It took them some time, but at last the Turks destroyed Constantinople in 1452 and whatever relics were there were finally lost.

Closer to home, but continuing the tradition of destruction, the Scots reformers under John Knox tore down St Andrew's Cathedral in 1559 and cast his bones on to the dust heap.[10]

---

[7]  *Traditionally in the reign of Nero, on 30 November 60 AD, hence his feast day and his saltire cross symbol.*

[8]  *A rather sunnier coastline than Fife.*

[9]  *Funky historians.*

[10]  *One of the ruins still standing is the Tower of St Rule (as Regulus's name was translated into English).*

The remaining bones were allowed a few years of benign sleep in the Vatican vaults, until 1964, when, in a moving gesture of reconciliation between the Western Catholic and Eastern Orthodox churches, the Pope returned the head of the saint to Patras, where it rests today.[11]

So why does he look after us?[12]

## St Andrew's Cross[13]

An angel bearing the standard of our Lord's cross will go in front of you in the sight of many[14]

It takes more than bones to capture the warlike Scots' hearts.

True to form, King Angus[15] was facing a border war in 832 AD when the Angles of Northumbria invaded Lothian to capture Edinburgh from the Picts. King Aethelstan's Angles acutely surrounded the band of Scots and Picts, but obtusely waited to finish them off the next day after a good night's snooze. Engus remembered the promise that the monks of St Andrew had given – and prayed to the saint for aid. In his dreams, the king heard Andrew's personal promise to him: embrace the new religion, watch for my sign, and you shall triumph.

Next day, the pale blue sky was blazoned with the two white arms of St Andrew's cross, pointing towards the enemy. The Scots and Picts

---

[11] *There are two small relics in Edinburgh: a shoulder bone given in 1879 by the Bishop of Amalfi when it became legal to be a Catholic bishop in the UK (complicated story – really no time here for that one); and a small bone given by Pope Paul VI to the first Scottish cardinal created in 400 years, with the message 'Peter greets his brother Andrew'. Both rest in St Mary's RC Cathedral in Edinburgh.*

[12] *Let alone the Russians, the spinsters and the gouty. (I guess there's a fair amount of gout amongst Scottish drinkers, so I can understand that one!)*

[13] *Is he?*

[14] Scotichronichon, *Walter Bower* (ed. D.E.R. Watt), p.39. *This early (and rather unconventional) history of Scotland is on sale even today in Harrods, as it maintains that Scotland was named after Scotia, a daughter of Egypt's pharaoh.*

[15] *Or Hungas, Engas, Oengas or Ongas. He was a good king but a rotten speller.*

rose and fell on the Angles, cutting the head off their king and forcing them to flee south again.

Engus fixed his name as Angus and swore that his country's flag would forever be the colour of the blue sky and bear the white saltire cross of its confirmed patron: St Andrew.[16] The real miracle, of course, was that it wasn't a rainy day, or our flag would be on a pale grey background – there is still an argument over whether the Saltire's background should be a lighter blue or a darker.[17] However coloured, this is our Scottish national flag.[18]

Whatever the colour, the sentiment is the important part of the pride with which we see our flag displayed – one of the defining elements of the 'Scottish brand' – and not just on flagpoles! As the Heraldry Society of Scotland noted once:

> Irrespective of this flag code the irrepressible Scots will find ways of displaying their national fervour by wrapping themselves in or painting themselves with the Scottish National Flag.

---

[16] *The site is in a very pretty village and the Saltire Heritage Centre is well worth a visit. Many Scots claim that the Saltire is the oldest national flag still used, but I think that the Dannebrog of Denmark probably (just) beats us, both in age and in its heavenly origin – for it physically fell from the skies on the day of a battle.*

[17] *In quite a lot of circumstances, such as in the Union Jack or on our national football and rugby strips, the Scottish element is certainly a dark or navy blue. Recently, the Saltire's background has got lighter – global warming perhaps. The Lord Lyon has always said that the colour should be 'azure', the heraldic definition of blue, but to gain more specificity he agreed that the Scottish Parliament could decide. They chose Pantone 300 – sky blue, though this only has advisory not statutory authority.*

[18] *Of course, the United Kingdom also has its flag – commonly called the Union Jack (but more correctly, the Union Flag) – which is constructed on a base of the Saltire, with the crosses of St George and St Patrick added on top. The Lord Lyon confirms on his website that 'The Union Flag or the Scottish Saltire Flag may be freely flown by any Scot or Scottish Corporate body any-where in Scotland, to demonstrate their nationality and allegiance. No special permission is required, and either or both may correctly be flown.'*

> The code is designed to deal only with flying flags, the rest is left to personal consciousness and self dignity[19]

Following the election of the minority Scottish National Party administration in the Holyrood elections in 2007, the First Minister announced a more ubiquitous use of the Saltire as part of the policy of moving towards a more distant relationship with the United Kingdom.[20]

## At Home

> There was also an effort in certain classes to get up an observance of the day consecrated to the national saint, 30 November, 1662, a Sunday. Many of our nobles, barons, gentry and others of the Kingdom put on ane livery or favour of revenue thereof. This being a novelty I thought good to record it, because it was never of use heretofore since the Reformation.[21]

In the mediaeval church, the feast day of the national patron saint was a great event, known in Scots as Andermas. Of course, saints' days went out with so many other concepts after the Reformation. There was no popular celebration for a century, until a concurrence of national sentiment and a Sunday allowed a brief nodding of the Church's vigilance in the 1660s. From that point, through the Enlightenment to high Victoriana, the custom of a St Andrew's Night Dinner blossomed.

That's the good news. I'd recommend that those readers who felt unwell when discussing haggis should move swiftly on before I talk about the meal traditional for Andermas.

*Look Away Now*!!

While haggis was very popular, no St Andrew's Dinner was complete without a serving of a whole sheep's head.

---

[19]   'Draft Proposal for a Flag Code for the Manufacture of the Scottish National Flag', the Heraldry Society of Scotland, 2004.

[20]   But I'm not getting into politics here!

[21]   Domestic Annals of Scotland, Vol 2, From the Revolution to the Rebellion 1745, Robert Chalmers.

Again, we are faced with the ability of the Scot to make the most out of very little indeed. I think most culinary nations can cope with the concept of boiling up heads and bones and making a good broth or soup[22] but it takes nerves of steel to have the whole head there as your entrée.

The recipe – I just can't help but share this – is one easy to master:

First take a nice young fat head to the blacksmith's[23] and get him to burn off the wool – gently, of course, as you don't want to burn the skin.[24] The head and the four trotters will need to be soaked overnight in warm water.

In the morning the fun begins – you'll be pleased to learn that not everything in your pot is edible.[25] You'll have to take out the eyes, scrape off any burnt wool and then brush with a heavy vegetable brush until all's pale and clean. Then split the skull right down the middle and remove the brains[26] and any gristly parts, paying particular attention to cleaning the nostrils.[27] Halve the trotters lengthwise and remove the tendons with care. Give the whole lot another good wash, and into the pot it goes, with a gallon of cold salty water.

Now bring this to a rolling boil[28] after about one and a half hours, then the eight half-trotters need adding for a further good hour on a nice slow boil, when you can add the vegetables: a selection of sliced carrots, small (swede) turnips, and finally onions and shredded parsley after 20 minutes.

---

[22] *I am quite partial to a plate of 'powsoudie' or 'sheep's heid broth' myself.*

[23] *I'm setting quite a big excuse for you to leave this aside. Granny McGinn used to take hers up to the big stamping works that made nails, where the kind man would singe the head in the open furnace doors.*

[24] *If your head was a bit old and not very tender, the blacksmith and his lads used to have a quick game of football with it to tenderise it for you – you don't get service like that nowadays, even in Whole Foods.*

[25] *Phew!*

[26] *You probably don't want to know that we need these to make the sauce.*

[27] *Bless you.*

[28] *You'll have to keep an eye on this as I'd like you to skim off the scum that floats to the surface regularly.*

When you reach this point, put the lid on[30] and leave to simmer for one last hour. Traditionally, this would have been at the fireside rather than on the range.

To serve: take a huge serving plate[31] and sprinkle torn parsley over it. Lay the two half-heads flat and surround with the trotters and the tongue, cut into thin slices.[32] Then decorate the circumference of the plate with the vegetables and a liberal helping of boiled egg yolks.[33] Accompany the whole dish with servings of both parsley sauce and brain sauce.[34]

And that, piped in with due pomp and ceremony,[35] was the pride of every St Andrew's Dinner!

> O LORD, when hunger pinches sore,
> Do thou stand us in good stead
> And send us from Thy bounteous store
> A tup or weather head[36]

## And Abroad

> Beautiful glorious Scotland has spoiled me for every other country.[37]

The real impetus and celebration of St Andrew's came in the wide spread of emigrant and expatriate Scots communities. Whether by exile

---

[30] *Odds are you'll never want to look at this again!*

[31] *Or 'ashet' in Scots – from 'assiette' in French.*

[32] *You didn't see that one coming!*

[33] *Sometimes Scotch eggs (hard-boiled eggs wrapped in forcemeat, then dipped in breadcrumbs and fried).*

[34] *I know that you will never attempt this, so I'll skip the details.*

[35] *The principal toast of the evening, given without a speech, is traditionally 'the Pious Memory' (of St Andrew).*

[36] *'Grace before Meat', Robert Burns (perhaps it should have been a grace instead of meat?). Tups and wethers are different ages of sheep. Don't know which tastes better (or less worse).*

[37] *Letter, Mary Todd Lincoln, 21 August 1869.*

(after unsuccessful rebellion), by eviction (as landlords found sheep more profitable than renting out to subsistence farmers), by war (the Scots regiments to the fore as usual), or latterly by mind (the engineers, lawyers, doctors and lads o' pairts[38] who went out to build, manage and work the British Empire), St Andrew was a practical patron to the Scottish diaspora.

The critical juncture was fellowship – not initially in convivial terms, but in the cool-headed Scots practicality of looking after each other. As outsiders, the Scots men and women banded together into mutual societies that would look after their countrymen when sick or out of work, bury them and take care of their widows, and speak up to the local authorities to protect the rights of this new, yet hardworking, community.

The Royal Scottish Corporation in London (for centuries known as the Scots Box,[39] but now Scots Care) was the first of these charitable societies in 1603. Mind you, with the new King James I of England being the old King James VI of Scotland, there were a lot of 'Jocks' in the English capital.[40]

Of course, we'd hardly count London as foreign parts now,[41] but the spirit of St Andrew's Night flourished in the colonies and states. Starting, of course, in North America, but spreading globally, the Saltire closely following the Union Jack. While 'the pink bits are British' on the map, scratch the colour and you will find it's on an undercoat of tartan.

The oldest charitable institution in North America is The Scots' Charity of Boston, which was founded in 1657 (along the lines of the London Scots Box) to look after former Scots POWs who had been transported to New England as indentured servants by Oliver Cromwell. Following that example, from 1729 (starting with Charleston SC) St Andrew's Societies would spring up – but spontaneously, as there has never been a central headquarters. Today, throughout the US, you'll

---

[38]  A peculiarly Scottish concept – related to a 'Renaissance man' but not a 'know-it-all'.

[39]  After the strongbox to safeguard the charity's money – you can still see it in the HQ in Covent Garden, where this important work continues today.

[40]  Quite often resented as the king's favourites.

[41]  Strange in some ways, but hardly foreign.

often find that a State's oldest existing charitable body is the St Andrew's Society.[42]

And as communities met to look after their charitable plans, naturally an element of social congress grew around the meetings, with the greatest party being on their name day: 30 November.

Membership varies today, with the older societies still only admitting people with a proven Scottish ancestry. There used to be a feeling that St Andrew's Societies tended to be male-only and Caledonian Societies were mixed, but that's changing. Increasingly societies are welcoming all kinds and manners of folk, so long as they share an interest in the history and culture of Scotland, and a desire to roll their sleeves up and make some money for the good charitable causes.

All over the world the feast of St Andrew is celebrated.[43] The evening will often start with the flags of Scotland,[44] the UK and the host country being paraded into the hall (often with all the national anthems sung too!) and we'll see the same sort of mix between food, songs, music and speeches as you'd find in a Burns Supper.

As the sheep's head is nowadays still on the sheep's torso, the haggis is usually addressed instead, and the main toast will often be in a pair: one to Scotland and one to the home country.

After an evening of fine food and fellowship – with usually some fundraising too – the night's events are brought to a close with a rousing 'Auld Lang Syne'.

Sometimes these evenings can seem 'more Scottish than the Scots' but it is a tremendous testament to our culture and our widespread gene pool that many are sell-out occasions every single year.

Long may they continue!

---

[42] *In the interests of fair disclosure, I should say that the New York St David's Society plucked its first daffodil in 1801, and the St George's Society has carved its roast beef of Old England annually since 1770.*

[43] *In the US, because of Thanksgiving, the dinners are usually in mid-November.*

[44] *Very often both the Royal and National flags – luckily the Lord Lyon doesn't get out to many dinners!*

## Posh Balls and Village Halls

> [A]fter the more stately reels of the opening of the dance were over, when the servants and labourers and neighbours of that degree came in turns to the parlour... We were accustomed to dance with all the company, just as if they had been our equals; it was always done and without injury to either party. There was no fear of undue assumption on one side, or low familiarity on the other; a vein of thorough good breeding ran through all ranks... About midnight the carriage would be ordered to bring our happy party home. It was late enough before the remainder separated.[45]

Scotland has a great tradition of communal dancing.[46] Throughout the year you'll be able to find a chance to dance! There are two slightly different approaches.

- Scottish Country Dancing: The Royal Scottish Country Dance Society ('dedicated to dancing and teaching Scottish Country Dancing'[47]) has over 21,000 enthusiastic members (under the patronage of HM Queen Elizabeth II[48]) and deserves a song of praise from everyone for preserving the tradition of the Scottish Dance. After the loss of so many men in the Great War, the dance was in danger of dying out until two redoubtable ladies (Miss Stewart of Fasnacloich and Miss Milligan of Jordanhill) published an instruction book and created the Society in 1923.

  The old dance book I have on my shelves at home has a preface by Miss Milligan herself, where she, in rather old-fashioned words, expresses her view of this dance tradition:

---

[45] Memoirs of a Highland Lady, *Elizabeth Grant of Rothiemurchus, Vol. I, p.262.*

[46] *There is, of course, also the show dancing called 'Highland Dance', but we talked about that up in Chapter 9.*

[47] *Its website, www.rscds.org, does what is says on the tin.*

[48] *Who is known to be a good dancer Herself.*

Never forget that the chief object of these dances is social. Happy gay movement, jollity without licence, and cordial helpfulness all go into the making of a really good Scottish Country Dance.[49]

> All around the world, under the aegis of the RSCDS, in church halls, school gymnasia and village rooms, groups meet regularly to keep alive our traditional dances. In a spirit of good-humour, but with attention to detail and finesse, participants learn and perfect the steps and techniques of a programme of dances selected each year. There are even residential courses[50] to get you up to speed on the differences between reels and jigs and strathspeys![51]
>
> There are hundreds and hundreds of dances and variations (and as I am writing this, I bet a new one is being devised!).

- Ceilidh[52] Dancing: This is the informal end of the spectrum. Up and down the country people add a bit of dancing to a party and the ceilidh is born.

  Traditionally this would be the weekly social gathering of the village: food and drink[53] and entertainment all provided by the locals in the hall, giving a chance to meet and gossip and dance. When I was a Scout and spent most summers trekking across occasionally sunny hills, we'd camp on friendly farmers' lands and often get an invite to the local village ceilidh. The universal rule was that you had to dance with a different partner for every dance – the ideal being that everyone would have danced with everyone else

---

[49]  101 Scottish Country Dances, *Miss J.C. Milligan, Collins, 1956.*

[50]  *Including the Spring Fling, for under-35s. Why not give it a whirl?*

[51]  *Roughly speaking.*

[52]  *Probably the hardest word to spell in Scotland – say 'CAY-lee'.*

[53]  *Tea more often than not, and a table of food brought in by the neighbours for a pot-luck supper.*

by the end of the evening – kid, youngster, middle aged or octogenarian.[54]

It is an evening of enthusiasm rather than exactitude where the steps are involved. Some of the famous dances are hardly-concealed attempts to lift pretty girls off the floor in a whirl, while others become fairground attractions – faster and faster, higher and higher, longer and longer, until someone calls the truce.

## By Royal Command

At the opposite end of the social spectrum from the ceilidh, by far the poshest dance involving Scottish dancing is the Royal Caledonian Ball, largely because of the Queen's regular attendance. It has been held in the Grosvenor House Hotel for over 70 years, but its origins were in 1840, when the Duke and Duchess of Atholl held a ball for all their Scottish friends at their London mansion.

After a few years its popularity was such that the then duchess decided to turn it into a charity ball, selling tickets to raise donations for Scottish charities[55] supporting schools, homelessness in Scotland and in London, disabled ex-servicemen and cancer sufferers.

For most of its life, this event has had a strong theme of Atholl, although as the current duke lives in South Africa[56] the chairmanship is delegated to others. The opening of the ball still sees the last private army in Britain – the Atholl Highlanders – on parade and piping the guests who are to dance the formal opening set reel. The Highlanders then

---

[54] *I am indebted to Richard Saville, who coined Saville's Law, 'Start with the Plain and Finish with the Pretty', as a rule on how to approach your partners to maximise the fun of the evening.*

[55] *Which makes it possibly the oldest charity ball in the country – so maybe we Jocks aren't that mean after all.*

[56] *Not all dukes are upper-crust Anglos.*

show their forte by dancing the Eightsome Reel (which they claim as an Athollman invention[57]). The floor is then taken by the throng of guests, who dance away until the wee sma' oors of 3.30am. Included in the ticket price is a fine Scots breakfast and as much whisky and water as is needed.

It is quite a glamorous evening – and although there is a dress code of Byzantine complexity for those who wish to dance the opening reel,[58] the organisers say that all are welcome after that, so long as ladies wear long dresses or skirts and no Sassenach dinner jackets are worn by the men!

## Getting Stuck In

As with so many things Scottish, the secret is to get stuck in and try! Everyone should know the three classic dances: the Gay Gordons, the Dashing White Sergeant and the Strip the Willow.[59] The good news is

---

[57] *In one of my favourite collections of short stories,* The General Danced at Dawn *by George Macdonald Fraser, a mad McCrimmon general engineers a 128-some reel in the desert – that's class, even, as they say, 'for a Campbell'.*

[58] *And here it is!*
*(A) For Ladies (i) Essential: Ladies wear long evening dresses or, for those entitled to wear it, mess dress with a full-length skirt. (ii) Encouraged: Tiaras, Orders and decorations and clan tartan sashes [You'll find out how to wear these in UBSB!]. (iii) The wearing of white dresses is optional.*
*(B) For Gentlemen: (i) Essential to wear one of the following: (α) Highland evening dress – kilt and sporran; evening jacket (generally black broadcloth or coloured velvet); white evening shirt and black bow tie, or lace jabot, or (β) Full evening dress – evening tail coat; stiff white evening shirt and wing collar, white bow tie and white waistcoat, or (γ) Mess dress – to be worn according to current regulations. Where these allow for a more formal variation, such as a stiff shirt and wing collar with a black bow tie, this should be worn. (ii) Encouraged: Orders and decorations, Royal Company of Archers mess dress, Atholl Highlanders mess dress or Hunt livery. (iii) The wearing of red lapels on civilian evening tail coats is optional.*

[59] *This is the dance beloved of young farmers and aficionados of the heavy events, who often ensure that the lady's feet rarely touch the ground! There is an Orcadian version, where it's in one long, long line and Couple 2 will start the cycle once Couple 1 is five couples down, Couple 3 five after that, and so on.*

that there will be lots of people who know what's going on, so if you haven't a clue, try and find a partner who can point you in the right direction. Often if there are a lot of ingénues, the leader of the band or some kind-hearted soul will 'call' the steps.[60]

Dancing may not be uniquely Scottish, but it does strike a deep chord with us – whether an evening of dancing or a few sets after your Burns Supper – get up and cut the tartan rug!

> Our dancing was none of the... insipid formal movements... we flew at them like midgies sporting in the motting sun, or craws prognosticating a storm in a hairst day.[61]

---

[60]    *In return for a few free pints!*
[61]    *Letter, Robert Burns to James Smith, 30 June 1787. Hairst = harvest.*

# 16

# The Christmas Warm-up

Yule's come and Yule's gone,
And we hae feasted weel;
Sae Jock maun to his flail again,
And Jenny to her wheel.[1]

AS WE DISCUSSED in the early chapters, a combination of influences kept Christmas (or Yule) as a secondary feast when compared to Hogmanay, so the vivid description by Scott that heads this chapter would have been a historical fancy to many people. Such an ordinary day was 25 December that as Scott was writing the poem above, the courts still sat in judgement. The infamous body snatchers (or 'resurrection men' as the euphemism went) Burke and Hare were tried on Christmas Eve 1828 and sentenced on Christmas Day itself![2]

As the modern world has penetrated most of the corners of Scottish

---

[1]   'The Book of Days', Robert Chambers.

[2]   *Hare turned King's Evidence and peached on his quondam partner to save his scrawny neck, and so it was only Burke who got the unwelcome Christmas present: the Lord Justice-Clerk, in a black cap rather than a paper party crown from a cracker, passed these unfestive comments prior to pronouncing the death sentence:*

*'In regards to your case, the only doubt that has come across my mind, is, whether, in order to mark the sense that the Court entertains of your offence, and which the violated laws of the country entertain respecting it, your body should not be exhibited in chains, in order to deter others from the like crimes in time coming. But in taking into consideration that the public eye would be offended with so dismal an exhibition, I am disposed to agree that your sentence shall be put in execution in the usual way, but accompanied with the statutory attendant of the crime of murder, viz. – that your body be publically dissected and anatomised. And I trust that if it is ever customary to preserve skeletons, yours will be preserved, in order that posterity may keep in remembrance your atrocious crimes.'*

*Burke took the drop a month later on the Lawnmarket, with a jeering*

life, Christmas is the same combination of the Christian and the commercial as across the rest of the globe.[3]

In the old days, though, the turn of the year from what we call Christmas Eve through to the Monday after New Year was known as 'the Daft Days' – where a certain licence was given to all classes. I think of Christmas and Hansel Monday as being the supporters, or handmaidens, of the mighty Hogmanay!

Christmas Eve was marked in Aberdeenshire and the North East as 'Sowans Nicht' – we came across this particularly unpleasant dish at Hallowe'en[4] but the wise Doric speakers knew how to make the dish work – a generous helping of the local whisky turned it into an oatmeal cocktail, mixed in a big punchbowl and sat on the table with friends and family gathered round to talk and play and bring in the day of Christmas.

Not that there was much to bring in. In common with England, there were some druidic remnants that were once part of the traditional – kissing under the mistletoe and the Yule log being the two most obvious. But the Reformation saw to that – fun yes, but not on a holy day. Christmas was a time of reflection, not of joyous celebration of the birth of Baby Jesus.

One area that the Kirk couldn't control was the cookery book! It wasn't a great feast, but still the old favourite dishes would be made.

An early shortbread called gude-bread was prepared through the Daft Days, either to take as gifts or to have standing on the sideboard for guests.

On the day itself: more sowans sounds pretty inevitable,[5] while joint of beef, a goose or a goose pie would be common,

---

audience of over 25,000, and while his body lay waiting to be cut up at the anatomy theatre, one person a minute flocked by to have a prurient look. Thanks to the Lord JC's bright idea, you can still see the felon's bones in Edinburgh University, with a rather grisly set of lecture notes bound into a leather cover with the gold-stamped title 'Burke's Skin 1829'.

[3] But we keep up Hogmanay – having your Christmas cake AND eating it!

[4] I'm still trying to get the taste out my mouth.

[5] As popular as the Brussels sprout at Christmas today!

and the necessary stodge would be provided by a plum porridge. Not a plumb pudding as in England, but a beef stock, thickened with rough breadcrumbs and flavoured with pieces of veal, and abundant raisins and stoned prunes spiced with peppers, mace and grated nutmeg. Over time, the plum pudding won![6]

Wine and beer and whisky were all in use, but in moderation,[7] with a special concoction – Yule Ale – beer sweetened with honey – as a traditional toasting medium. A good day all round but not crucial to the life-cycle of the country.

There was no Boxing Day as we know it on 26 December, although many towns with a heavy Freemasonic history would see the lodge or lodges process on St John's day – 27 December. I think one of the most impressive processions still takes place by torchlight in Melrose in the Borders.

But as we know, everything is dependent on a good bringing-in of the year – so let's leave Christmas and move into the second half of the Daft Days – as evocatively captured by the unjustly neglected poet Robert Fergusson.[8]

> Auld Reikie! thou'rt the canty hole,          [merry]
> A bield for mony caldrife soul,          [shelter, dejected]
> Wha snugly at thine ingle loll,
> Baith warm and couth;          [congenial]
> While round they gar the bicker roll          [beaker]
> To weet their mouth.

---

[6] 'There the huge sirloin reeked: hard by
Plum-porridge stood, and Christmas pie;
Nor failed old Scotland to produce,
At such high time, her savory goose.'
Marmion again. Very Dickens-y!

[7] Don't peak too soon!

[8] Poor old Fergusson had real talent but died young in Edinburgh's madhouse (where the Bedlam Theatre stands now). Burns, who referred to him as 'my elder brother in the muse', paid for a headstone on his neglected grave in the Canongate Kirk.

When merry Yule-day comes, I trow                    [bet]
You'll scantlins find a hungry mou;          [rarely, mouth]
Sma' are our cares, our stamacks fou
O' gusty gear,                                  [tasty stuff]
And kickshaws, strangers to our view,            [canapés]
Sin Fairn-year.                                  [last year]

Then, tho' at odds wi' a' the warl',               [world]
Amang oursells we'll never quarrel;
Tho' Discord gie a canker'd snarl
To spoil our glee,
As lang's there's pith into the barrel
We'll drink and 'gree.

For nought can cheer the heart sae weil
As can a canty Highland reel,
It even vivifies the heel
To skip and dance:
Lifeless is he what canna feel
Its influence.

Let mirth abound, let social cheer
Invest the dawning of the year;
Let blithesome innocence appear
To crown our joy,
Nor envy wi' sarcastic sneer
Our bliss destroy.[9]

---

[9]   *From 'The Daft Days', Robert Ferguson.*

# Last thoughts:
# Here's Tae Us – Wha's Like Us

Currant-loaf is now popular eating in all house-holds. For weeks before the great morning, confectioners display stacks of Scotch bun – a dense, black substance, inimical to life – and full moons of shortbread adorned with mottoes of peel or sugar-plum, in honour of the season and the family affections. 'Frae Auld Reekie,' 'A Guid New Year To Ye A',' 'For the Auld Folk at Hame,' are among the most favoured of these devices. Can you not see the carrier, after half-a-day's journey on pinching hill-roads, draw up before a cottage in Teviotdale, or perhaps in Manor Glen among the rowans, and the old people receiving the parcel with moist eyes and a prayer for Jock or Jean in the city?[1]

IN CONSIDERING WHAT it is to be Scottish, and having spent a year looking at our peculiar festivals and customs, our history and beliefs, our dress and our diet, our bread and our circuses, we are here again about to prepare for Hogmanay. So sitting by the roaring fire, with a glass in my hand – what is it that makes the Scots unique?

There are many nations in the world – some older, some richer, many bigger, many larger in population – but this clan of men and women are recognised by accent, dress, gifts and above all attitude wherever they go.

Our country, Scotland, is a small land but one rich in its people, whether they live within its boundaries or are its children found in all the corners of the world. One of the things that makes us (and marks us) is the history of the people of Scotland – and I hope that through this book, and our journey together, you now know the Ultimate Secret to being Scottish – and why we have so many good reasons to celebrate!

---

[1]   Picturesque Notes, (*Ch. IX again*), *Robert Louis Stevenson*.

As my hero, Robert Burns, would say:

Here's a bottle and an honest friend,
 What was ye wish for mair, man?
Wha kens, before his life may end
 What his share may be o' care, man?
Then catch the moments as they fly,
 And use them as ye ought man!
Believe me, happiness is shy,
And comes not ay when sought man![2]

Slainte Mhath one and all! I hope that our time together has given you an idea about what makes the Scots tick and, most of all, made you want to join in – for that is the Ultimate Guide to Being Scottish: If you see a Scottish party – come and join in!

There is no special lovliness in that grey country, with its rainy, sea-belt archipelago; its fields of dark mountains; its unsightly places, black with coal; its treeless, sour, unfriendly-looking cornlands; its quaint, grey castled city, where the bells clash of a Sunday, and the wind squalls, and the salt showers fly and beat. I do not know if I desire to live there; but let me here, in some far land, a kindred voice cry out, 'O why left I my hame?' and it seems as once as if no beauty under the kind heavens, and no society of the wise and good, can repay me for my absence from my country. And though I think I would rather die elsewhere, yet in my heart of hearts I long to be buried among good Scots clods. I will say it fairly, it grows on me with every year: there are no stars as lovely as Edinburgh streetlamps.[3]

2    'A Bottle and an Honest Friend', Robert Burns.
3    The Silverado Squatters, Robert Louis Stevenson.

# Epigraph

From scenes like these, old Scotia's grandeur springs
  That makes her lov'd at home, rever'd abroad:
Princes and lords are but the breath of kings,
  'An honest man's the noblest work of God':
  An certes, in fair Virtue's heavenly road,
The cottage leaves the palace far behind:
  What is a lordling's pomp? A cumbrous load,
Disguising oft the wretch of human kind,
Studies in arts of Hell. In wickedness refin'd!

O Scotia! My dear, my native soil!
  From whom my warmest wish to Heaven is sent!
Long may thy hardy sons of rustic toil
  Be blest with health, and peace, and sweet content!!
  And O! May Heaven their simple lives prevent
From Luxury's contagion, weak and vile!
  Then howe'er crowns and coronets be rent,
A virtuous populace may rise the while,
And stand a wall of fire around their much-loved isle.

O Thou! Who poured the patriotic tide,
  That stream't through Wallace's undaunted heart,
Who dar'd to, nobly, stem tyrannic pride,
  Or nobly die, the second glorious part:
  The patriot's God, peculiarly Thou art,
His friend, inspirer, guardian and reward!
  O never, never Scotia's realm desert;
But still the patriot, and the patriot-bard
In bright succession raise, her ornament and guard![1]

### *Finis*[2]

---

[1]  *'The Cottar's Saturday Night', Robert Burns, final three stanzas.*
[2]  *The last word.*

# Appendix[1]

## The Battle Betwixt
## Glasgow and Edinburgh
## Being the Poetical Evaluation of
## Scotland's Two Great Cities
## By the Hand of
## An Impatial *Genius* and *Observer*
## William Topaz McGonagall
## The Poet and Tragedian
## Of Dundee

### Glasgow

Beautiful city of Glasgow, with your
    streets so neat and clean,
Your stately mansions, and beautiful
    Green!
Likewise your beautiful bridges across
    the river Clyde,
And on your bonnie banks I would
    like to reside.

### Edinburgh

Beautiful city of Edinburgh!
Where the tourist can drown his
    sorrow
By viewing your monuments and
    statues fine
During the lovely summer-time.
I'm sure it will his spirits cheer
As Sir Walter Scott's monument he
    draws near,
That stands in East Prince's Street
Amongst flowery gardens, fine and
    neat.

---

[1]   *Dedicated to my fellow members of the Winers' Club at Glasgow, who maintain the Immortal Memory of this mighty figure: the Neglected Genius of
Scottish Poesy.*

## Glasgow

(Chorus)
*Then away to the West – to the
beautiful West!*
*To the fair city of Glasgow that I like
the best,*
*Where the river Clyde rolls on to
the sea,*
*And the lark and the blackbird whistle
with glee.*

'Tis beautiful to see ships passing to
and fro,
Laden with goods for the high and
the low,
So let the beautiful city of Glasgow
flourish,
And may the inhabitants always find
food their bodies to nourish.
*Chorus*

The statue of the prince of Orange is
very grand,
Looking terror to the foe, with a
truncheon in his hand,
And well mounted on a noble steed,
which stands in Trongate,
And holding up its foreleg, I'm sure it
looks first-rate.
*Chorus*

Then there's the Duke of Wellington's
statue in Royal Exchange Square –
It is a beautiful statue I without fear
declare,
Besides inspiring and most magnificent
to view,
Because he made the French fly at the
battle of Waterloo.
*Chorus*

## Edinburgh

And Edinburgh Castle is magnifi-
cent to be seen
With its beautiful walks and trees
so green,
Which seems like a fairy dell;
And near by its rocky basement is
St Margaret's Well,
Where the tourist can drink at
when he feels dry,
And view the castle from beneath
so very high,
Which seems almost towering
to the sky.

Then as for Nelson's monument
that stands on Calton Hill,
As the tourist gazes thereon,
with wonder his heart does fill
As he thinks on Admiral Nelson
who did the Frenchmen kill,
Then, as for Salisbury Crags,
they are most beautiful to be seen,
Especially in the month of June,
when the grass is green;
There numerous mole-hills can
be seen,
And the busy little creatures
howking away,
Searching for worms among
the clay;
And as the tourist's eye does
wander to and fro
From the south side of Salisbury
Crags below,
His bosom with admiration
feels all aglow
As he views the beautiful
scenery in the valley below;

### Glasgow

And as for the statue of Sir Walter
  Scott that stands in George Square,
It is a handsome statue – few can with
  it compare,
And most elegant to be seen,
And close beside it stands the statue of
  Her Majesty the Queen.
*Chorus*

Then there's the statue of Robert
  Burns in George Square,
And the treatment he received when
  iving was very unfair;
Now when he's dead, Scotland's sons
  for him do mourn,
But, alas! unto them he can never
  return.
*Chorus*

Then as for Kelvin Grove, it is most
  lovely to be seen,
With its beautiful flowers and trees
  so green,
And a magnificent water-fountain
  spouting up very high,
Where the people can quench their
  thirst when they feel dry. *Chorus*

Beautiful city of Glasgow, I now
  conclude my muse,
And to write in praise of thee my pen
  does not refuse;
And, without fear of contradiction,
  I will venture to say
**You are the second grandest city in
  Scotland at the present day!**
*Chorus*

### Edinburgh

And if, with an observant eye,
  the little loch beneath he scans,
He can see the wild ducks about
  and beautiful white swans.
Then, as for Arthur's Seat,
  I'm sure it is a treat
Most worthy to be seen, with its
  rugged rocks and pastures green,

And the sheep browsing
  on its sides
To and fro, with slow-paced
  strides,
And the little lambkins at play
During the livelong summer
  day,
Beautiful city of Edinburgh!
  the truth to express,

Your beauties are matchless
  I must confess,
And which no one dare gainsay,

**But that you are the grandest city
in Scotland at the present day!**

**So that's that then – Edinburgh wins…**

# Some other books published by **LUATH** PRESS

### The Ultimate Burns Supper Book
Clark McGinn
ISBN 978 1906817 50 3 PBK £7.99

Everything you need to enjoy or arrange a Burns Supper – just add food, drink and friends.

Clark McGinn, one of the world's foremost Burns Supper speakers, presents all the information you need to enjoy a Supper. Whether host, speaker or guest, this book is full of advice, anecdotes, poetry and wit.

Includes:

- A complete run through of what to expect on the night, with a list of courses and speeches
- Advice on what to wear
- A section on how to prepare and present speeches
- A list of common Burns Supper questions (and their answers!)
- A selection of Burns' greatest poems,
- Answers your concerns about eating haggis and the pleasures of drinking whisky

*A lively, interesting and useful guide.*
THE HERALD

### Out of Pocket: How collective amnesia lost the world its wealth, again
Clark McGinn
ISBN 978 1906307 82 0 PBK £12.99

Written by a senior banker with many years' experience, this book takes the long view. It shows how simple the basics of banking are and tells the stories of how we lost money in similar ways over the centuries. Read it and you might just lose less money next time!

If only the world's finance ministers, bank CEOs, non execs, customers, borrowers, little old ladies, all of us, had read this book three years ago, or 30 years ago, we wouldn't be in the mess we're in. But we are. So read this book and weep. And take solace in the fact that financial calamities have happened many many times before, and will happen again.

*I started writing this book three years ago to amuse my fellow bankers. Little did we all know what was about to happen. But we should have. Sorry.*
CLARK McGINN

## Poems, Chiefly in the Scottish Dialect: The Luath Kilmarnock Edition

Robert Burns
With contributions from John Cairney and Clarke McGinn, illustrated by Bob Dewar
ISBN 978 1906307 67 7 HBK £15

*Poems, Chiefly in the Scottish Dialect*, was the first collection of poetry produced by Robert Burns. Published in Kilmarnock in July 1786, it contains some of his best known poems including 'The Cotter's Saturday Night', 'To a Mouse', 'The Twa Dogs' and 'To a Mountain Daisy'. *The Luath Kilmarnock Edition* brings this classic of Scottish literature back into print.

New material includes an introduction by the 'Man Who Played Burns' – author, actor and Burns expert John Cairney – exploring Burns' life and work, especially the origins of the *Kilmarnock Edition*. Looking to the future of Burns in Scotland and the rest of the world, Clark McGinn, world-renowned Burns Supper speaker, provides an afterword that speaks to Burns' continuing legacy.

## The Merry Muses of Caledonia

Robert Burns
Edited by James Burke and Sydney Goodsir Smith, with contributions from J DeLancey Ferguson and Valentina Bold, illustrated by Bob Dewar
ISBN 978 1906307 68 4 HBK £15

Lusty in language and subject matter, this is Burns unabashed. Labelled in the 19th century as 'not for maids, ministers or striplings', *The Merry Muses* still has the power to shock and titillate the modern reader.

This new edition, produced for the 250th anniversary of Burns' birth, includes specially commissioned illustrations from top political satirist Bob Dewar and an introduction by Burns scholar Valentina Bold. In addition, *The Merry Muses* was always intended to be accompanied by music, and for the first time the book is completed with notes to the tunes, created with reference to unpublished papers by James Burke, which he originally compiled for a 1959 edition of the book.

## Haud ma Chips, Ah've Drapped the Wean! Glesca Grannies' Sayings, Patter and Advice

Allan Morrison, illustrated by Bob Dewar
ISBN 978 1 908373 47 2 PBK £7.99

In yer face, cheeky, kindly, gallus, astute; that's a Glesca granny for you. Glesca grannies' communication is direct, warm, expressive, rich and often hilarious.

'Dinnae cross yer eyes. Ye'll end up like that squinty bridge.'

'Oor doctor couldnae cure a plouk oan a coo's erse.'

'This is me since yesterday.'

'That wan wid breastfeed her weans through the school railings.'

'Yer hair looks like straw hingin' oot a midden.'

'Ah'm jist twenty-wan an' ah wis born in nineteen-canteen.'

'The secret o' life is an aspirin a day, a wee dram, an' nae sex oan Sundays.'

Glesca grannies shoot from the mouth and get right to the point with their sayings, patter and advice. This book is your guide to the infallible wisdom of the Glesca granny.

## Scots We Ken

Julie Davidson
ISBN 978 1 906307 00 4 HBK £9.99

Natives know them. Visitors soon get to know them. Some, like the Golf Club Captain, the Last Publican and the Nippy Sweetie, are endangered species; others, like the Whisky Bore and the Munrobagger, are enduring figures on the Scottish landscape. Every generation produces its own variations on the Scottish character and it doesn't take long for the newcomers to become familiar social types like the MSP, the Yooni Yah, the Rural Commuter and the Celebrity Chieftain. Most Scots, if they're honest, will recognise a little bit of themselves in one or other of thes mischievous and frighteningly accurate portraits. Julie Davidson's wickedly observed profiles are complemented by Bob Dewar's witty drawings in this roguish gallery of *Scots We Ken*.

*The Scots Julie Davidson kens is a triumph of canny Scots-watching. Here for the first time is the famous Davidson wry take on the foibles and pretensions of the sub-species Scotus Domesticus won from years of anthropological field work and now distilled into sharp witty draughts complemented by Bob Dewar's incisively drawn portraits.*
MURRAY GRIGOR, Film-maker

## Great Scottish Speeches

Introduced and Edited by David Torrance
Foreword by Alex Salmond
ISBN 978 1 908373 27 4 PBK £9.99

 Some Great Scottish Speeches were the result of years of contemplation. Some flourished in heat of the moment. Whatever the background of the ideas expressed, the speeches not only provide a snapshot of their time, but express views that still resonate in Scotland today, whether you agree with the sentiments or not.

Encompassing speeches made by Scots or in Scotland, this carefully selected collection reveals the character of a nation. Themes of religion, independence and socialism cross paths with sporting encouragement, Irish Home Rule and Miss Jean Brodie.

Ranging from the legendary speech of the Caledonian chief Calgagus in 83AD right up to Alex Salmond's election victory in 2007, these are the speeches that created modern Scotland.

*...what has not faded is the power of the written and spoken word – as this first-rate collection of Scottish speeches demonstrates.*
PRESS AND JOURNAL

## Reportage Scotland: History in the Making

Louise Yeoman
Foreword by Professor David Stevenson
ISBN 978 1 842820 51 3 PBK £7.99

 Events – both major and minor – as seen and recorded by Scots throughout history.
Which king was murdered in a sewer?
What was Dr Fian's love magic?

Who was the half-roasted abbot?
Which cardinal was salted and put in a barrel?
Why did Lord Kitchener's niece try to blow up Burns's cottage?

The answers can all be found in the eclectic mix covering nearly 2,000 years of Scottish history. Historian Louise Yeoman's rummage through the manuscript, book and newspapers archives of the National Library of Scotland has yielded an astonishing amount of material. Ranging from a letter to the King of the Picts to Mary Queen of Scots' own account of the murder of David Riccio; from the execution of William Wallace to accounts of anti-poll tax actions and the opening of the new Scottish Parliament. The book takes pieces from the original French, Latin, Gaelic and Scots and makes them accessible to the general reader, often for the first time.

*Louise Yeoman makes a much-needed contribution to the canons of Scottish historiography, providing eyewitness, or as near as possible, to events which have shaped the country over two millennia.*
THE HERALD

## The Whisky Muse: Scotch whisky in poem & song

Robin Laing
ISBN 978 1 906307 44 8 PBK £9.99

Whisky – the water of life, perhaps Scotland's best known contribution to humanity Muse – goddess of creative endeavour. The Whisky Muse – the spark of inspiration to many of Scotland's great poets and songwriters.

This book is a collection of the best poems and songs, both old and new, on the subject of that great Scottish love, whisky.

*I first met Robin Laing and Bob Dewar within the hallowed halls of the Scotch Malt Whisky Society in Leith, where Robin and I sit on the Nosing Panel which selects casks of malt whisky for bottling, while Bob executes the famous cartoons which illustrate our findings and embellish the Society's Newsletter. The panel's onerous job is made lighter by Robin's ability not only to sniff out elusive scents, but to describe them wittily and accurately, and in this unique collection of ninety-five songs and poems about Scotch whisky he has exercised precisely the same skill of sniffing out treasures. As a highly accomplished singer-songwriter, he also describes them authoritatively, while Bob's illustrations add wit and humour. This splendid book is necessary reading for anyone interested in whisky and song. It encapsulates Scottish folk culture and the very spirit of Scotland.*
CHARLES MacLEAN, Editor at Large, *Whisky Magazine*.

## The Whisky River: Distilleries of Speyside

Robin Laing
ISBN 978 1 906817 95 4 PBK £12.99

Which river has half the distilleries in Scotland found along its length and in its surrounding glens?
Were monks at the forefront of developing whisky?
Which Speyside distillery produced chilli-flavoured whisky?
How did Glenrothes distillery expel its ghost?

Robin Laing set out to visit every distillery in the Speyside area, from Benromach to Tomintoul. There are descriptions of over 50 distilleries on Speyside, including The Macallan, The Glenlivet, Cardhu, Aberlour, Glenfiddich and Glengrant.

Each entry is part history, part travelogue and part commentary on the changes in the whisky industry.

Includes personal musings by the author, stories associated with the distillery and snippets of poetry and song.

Laing's 'spirit' guide in his journey is Alfred Barnard, author of 1887's *The Whisky Distilleries of the United Kingdom*. Barnard visited many of the same distilleries that Laing visits now and similarly left his impressions of the state of the facilities and the beauty of the surroundings. Much of this present book compares what Barnard found with what exists now, and the differences – and similarities – are often fascinating.

Details of these and other books published by Luath Press can be found at:

**www.luath.co.uk**

## **Luath** Press Limited

*committed to publishing well written books worth reading*

LUATH PRESS takes its name from Robert Burns, whose little collie Luath (*Gael.*, swift or nimble) tripped up Jean Armour at a wedding and gave him the chance to speak to the woman who was to be his wife and the abiding love of his life. Burns called one of 'The Twa Dogs' Luath after Cuchullin's hunting dog in Ossian's *Fingal*. Luath Press was established in 1981 in the heart of Burns country, and now resides a few steps up the road from Burns' first lodgings on Edinburgh's Royal Mile.
Luath offers you distinctive writing with a hint of unexpected pleasures.

Most bookshops in the UK, the US, Canada, Australia, New Zealand and parts of Europe either carry our books in stock or can order them for you. To order direct from us, please send a £sterling cheque, postal order, international money order or your credit card details (number, address of cardholder and expiry date) to us at the address below. Please add post and packing as follows: UK – £1.00 per delivery address; overseas surface mail – £2.50 per delivery address; overseas airmail – £3.50 for the first book to each delivery address, plus £1.00 for each additional book by airmail to the same address. If your order is a gift, we will happily enclose your card or message at no extra charge.

**Luath** Press Limited
543/2 Castlehill
The Royal Mile
Edinburgh EH1 2ND
Scotland
Telephone: 0131 225 4326 (24 hours)
Fax: 0131 225 4324
email: sales@luath.co.uk
Website: www.luath.co.uk